DIRTY ROTTEN SCOUNDREL

DIRTY ROTTEN SCOUNDREL

GREG MARTIN

BLAKE

Published by Blake Publishing Ltd,
3 Bramber Court, 2 Bramber Road,
London W14 9PB, England

First published in 2000

ISBN 1 85782 324 9

British Library Cataloguing–in–Publication Data:

A catalogue record for this book is
available from the British Library.

Typeset by t2

Printed in Great Britain by
Creative Print and Design (Wales),
Ebbw Vale, Gwent.

1 3 5 7 9 10 8 6 4 2

For Vittoria, who changed this leopard's spots

CONTENTS

CONFESSIONS OF A SERIAL PHILANDERER

'What is a promiscuous person? It's usually someone who's getting more
sex than you are.'
Victor Lownes *Playboy*
'Hell, if I'd jumped on all the dames I'm supposed to have jumped on,
I'd have had no time to go fishing.'
Clark Gable

OK. So I confess. I'm what they call a bit of a womaniser. Always
have been. And until the day finally comes when I meet that
ultra-special femme fatale who flips my switch, rocks my boat,
and rings my chimes big-time, chances are I always will be. I love
women, you see. Hell, I adore the little darlings! I was raised by

the female gender. So the smell of them is in my blood. I worship a beautiful woman's scent, her laughter, her smile, the shape of her legs, the way the expression in her eyes shifts when you catch her glance as you walk down the street.

To me the fairer sex have always been nothing less than glorious enigmas; exotic, fantastical creatures from another world designed to entrance, spellbind and captivate men's minds, hearts and bodies. Oh yes, let there be no doubt about it! I believe, sure as Taffy was a Welshman, that the female gender were specifically and magnificently created by the Good Lord himself to send all of us sorry male drones into raging throes of stratospheric ecstasy every time we lock eyes with them across a crowded room and that mysterious, thermonuclear furnace of sexual passion starts to assault our synapses, flooding our bloodstreams with raging, sensual desire, and bombarding our brains with all those wild fantasies of phenomenal lust!

So imagine for a moment what it would be like to find yourself, a normal, albeit very red-blooded bachelor — the kind of bloke who enjoys downing a simple pint in his local watching the likes of Owen, Beckham, Shearer, and Scholes trying in vain to recapture those magnificent glory days of '66 — caught up in the kind of bizarre sexual Salem witch-hunt/moral blitzkrieg I was subjected to during the six-week period beginning August 10, 1999. Imagine if it were you being slagged off, pilloried, as if you were some kind of depraved sexual vampire, when all your life you'd by and large treated women like veritable goddesses, and the most you could seriously be accused of is the odd tumble in the hay with, admittedly, a large number and variety of the lovelies. How would you feel? What's more, how would you feel if the vast majority of those women you'd had so much fun in the sack with had remained your very good friends?

You see the irony is this 'bounder' truly does adore the fairer sex. In fact, believe it or not, most of my pals are gals. But on that

Monday morning, like it or not, I was given a public image, and my life was changed forever. This book is a comic attempt to make some sense of that time. It's a romp, a caper, a jolly jaunt through a life packed with what has been more than a typical man's fair share of sexual encounters. It's also a tongue-in-cheek stab at *An Englishman's Guide To Women*, and *An Englishwoman's Guide To Men* at the millennium. Because, God knows, if things have gotten this bad for me, then we really all do need a helping hand!

Yet the last six months of 1999 were hardly a bowl of cherries for this dastardly serial philanderer. It was actually one of the most bizarre, and at times truly depressing periods of my life. As a close mate commented: 'O.K. So you've had a lot of women in your life. But this is ridiculous! Most of the ones that I know still adore the hell out of you. The way this has been framed anyone would think you'd been a serial axe-murderer!'

The timing of it was disastrous. For months I had been quietly, patiently working away, building up several potentially lucrative business projects. Two of them were just at that crucial, fragile stage when everything was set to come together. The primary business was to have netted me a very large sum of money right off the bat by the end of August. Then I fell for Tara, all the shit hit the fan, and I suddenly found myself embroiled in a nightmare scenario where old bugger-lugs — your everyday, basic bloke with a healthy, albeit unusually large, strong libido — was overnight being cast in the title role of a surreal Leslie Phillips sex farce called: 'Serial Philandering Scumbag Arch-Villain Of The Millennium Meets Seedy Rip-Off Merchant Par Excellence!' There were seriously damaging, insanely fabricated financial slurs and allegations on top of the weird barrage of lewd personal character smears, and my investors were panicking left, right and centre. A major, very conservative partner in one of the ventures I was involved in refused point blank to move forward unless I agreed to remove my name from the project entirely — a project which I had initiated, and in which, up until that point, I had taken all the risk.

Admittedly it was August when all this erupted, the traditional 'silly season' for the press. Holiday time, that period when news is at a typically all-time low ebb. And, in retrospect, if I had to give anyone a piece of simple advice, it would surely be: 'Whatever you do, don't have a scandal at the end of the summer!' But still, the frenzy and relentless brutality of the assault didn't add up. It was painful. Very painful. Painful for Tara, painful for me, and distressing for both our families. At one point I was receiving nightly frantic phone calls from Ms. T-P-T informing me this or that other trust-fund baby 'friend' had concocted yet another weird, sordid fable about the mythical depraved past of yours truly. And all this came on the heels of assorted members of her family fielding a veritable barrage of messages from all sorts of mysterious quarters confirming the nasty, wicked, ever-growing assortment of chinese whispers about this ol' Casanova reincarnated!

So why did it happen? Simple. A trio of dastardly villains, each apparently with both an intense dislike of Ms. Palmer-Tomkinson, and a majorly big axe to grind in my direction — decided to club together to do a very effective and thorough bang-up job. Lord Byron wrote in his epic poem 'Don Juan': 'Sweet is revenge — especially for women.' Know what I say to that? No shit! Sometimes revenge ain't just sweet for women. You've heard of the phrase, 'Hell hath no fury'? Well in the past three months I've lived through hell myself. And in a way I'm more than willing to wager very few other men have probably ever quite experienced it!

Having said all that, the ultimate decision to write this book came after one of my conversations with my beautiful little son, Connor Mackenzie, during those dark August days. Connor lives with his mother in the States, a fine woman with whom I have managed to maintain a fundamentally close, understanding relationship founded on our common bond: the shared desire for our little boy's happiness. A group of English journalists apparently had the taste and sensitivity to stake out her house in a tiny New England village three hours outside of Boston. Connor asked me, 'Daddy, who are all those weird men with cameras outside our house? What have you done?' Tara never had the joy of meeting Connor. And that's a shame. I've seen her up close with kids. She's a natural. If she manages to get her act together one day she'll more than probably make some man a very lovely wife, and her children a wonderful mother.

It's been truly bananas. Welcome to the monkey house!

CHAPTER ONE

'BOUNDER, CAD, SEDUCER'

'I've found the best way to keep my youth is to chain him to the bed.'
Tara Schwartz
'Girls are like pianos. When they're not upright, they're grand.'
Benny Hill

August 8, 1999

'Greg, it's Gretchen! I've just had some English journalist on the line offering me any amount of money I want if I tell him some kind of slanderous story about you! Are you O.K.? What's going on?' The voice is that of one of my dearest and oldest friends, feminist Broadway playwright Gretchen Cryer (and yes, I did sleep with her! Over twenty years ago!) The call is from New

York. I'm sitting in the Virgin Club Lounge at Heathrow, checking my messages while waiting for a night flight to Hong Kong with Tara Palmer-Tomkinson, a girl I've met barely two weeks before at Mick Jagger's fifty-sixth birthday bash at Cap D'Antibes in the South of France. The call goes on. 'They also faxed Robin last night. [Robin Cryer is Gretchen's daughter, a talented, budding singer-songwriter.] They offered to promote the hell out of her CD worldwide if she'd make up some horrible bullshit about you!'

The next message is from some very close pals of mine in Hawaii. 'Greg, it's Steve and Joanna. We're worried sick about you! Joanna's gotten over half a dozen calls since last night from a pair of Brit journalists trying to dig up some major kinda crap from your past! Please watch yourself, buddy. And call us! Take it from me, this is serious! I've been through this kinda shit myself! Some asshole out there is out to smear you big time!'

I turn to Tara. 'Jesus Christ! This is nuts! What the hell's up with the press in this bloody country?! I've got some newspaper calling people I know all over the world, trying to dig up a fabricated crock of malicious slander on me!' Tara turns to me and just smiles that beguiling, winsome, little puppy-dog smile. 'I'm so sorry, darling. I'm afraid it's my fault. Don't worry. It's just rumouritis. You've caught it from me. We've all been through it. Charles, Camilla, Mummy — all of us. They want dirt on you. That's all. If they don't find it, they'll just make it up. Ignore them.'

And, like a fool, that's just what I did.

January 21, 1957 1.33 a.m.

'Ooh, 'es bin 'ere before!' the buxom young cockney midwife remarked, as she swept me up in her arms, nestling me in close to her ample bosom. I stared up, goggle-eyed, at the wench. No doubt about it. She was a knock out. Sensual. Strapping. A full-blown earth mother.

'Ooh! Cheeky devil!' She let out a shrill giggle, as she handed me down to my mum. 'I swear the little sweetheart winked at me!'

I blinked at my mum. Then winked again. This time straight into the eyes of the lovely woman who had brought me into the world. And suddenly it all came flooding back. The midwife was right. I *had* been here before. *Many times*!

Casanova was reincarnated! Alive and kicking once again!

September 1, 1999

Headline: '*Oh, Greg, you're such a bounder! Tara's scumbag serial-philanderer left a trail of broken hearts and empty purses behind him across the length and breadth of America.*'

This article is little different from the others, except that it names my ex-wife and son, calling Natasha a 'wealthy New York socialite'. I ponder over my coffee how she and her family would react to that one. They're poor as church mice, and live way out in the boonies of wildest New Hampshire.

Later I pick up the phone and call her. I'm missing Connor like crazy. At times like these the angelic little voice of your child is like the healing, silver-tongued emissary of the Good Lord himself. Connor picks up the phone. 'Hi, Dad,' he says, sleepily. I ask him how he's doing. And have those silly men with the cameras finally gone away? 'Oh, sure,' he tells me, yawning. 'They were stupid, Dad. Really weird!'

Natasha comes on the line and asks me how I'm coping. I tell her the truth. I've known better days. She laughs, then tells me how the press went all over the town trying to dig up dirt on the now notorious scumbag, serial philanderer of the century. Unable to find a trace, they finally spoke to the innkeeper who gleefully told them he had something on me. Something real bad:

'Yeah! Sure! The last time he stayed here, Mr. Martin trashed the room!'

New Hampshire isn't called 'The Granite State' for nothing. Those people are nothing if not loyal. Natasha immediately drove over to the innkeeper's house.

'What's all this garbage about Greg trashing his hotel room?' she yelled at the guy. 'He's not Liam Gallagher!'

'Well,' said the innkeeper, 'he smoked in the bathroom!'

September 2, 1999

I've always been saved by my wacky, decidedly off-the-wall sense of humour. And the range of bizarre and comical self-images that have swept through my grey matter over the past few weeks have done a lot to keep me sane. One moment I'm some weird combo of Claus Von Bulow, Mohammed Al Fayed, and Bill Clinton, the next I'm a modern Mr. Rochester from *Jane Eyre*, dealing with what now very sadly appears to be an increasingly alarming, and borderline-insane young lady in my attic.

Tara's clearly slowly being driven mad by all the rumours. And while she now apparently hates me, she categorically refuses to leave me alone. One minute she's calling my mobile in a furious, gobsmacking rage, telling me: 'I'm going to see you dead! I want you out of this country! And I'm going to fucking nail you!' The next she's calling to apologise, telling me this or that blue-blood nobody has apparently told her I have yet *another* ex-wife, this time in sinisterly close proximity to Area 51 near Roswell, New Mexico, plus a herd of illegitimate alien-hybrid children spread across Asia from the foothills of the Tibetan Plateau to the darkest reaches of the Russian Steppes!

I'm telling the story with humour. But in truth, at the time I found it all deeply distressing; very unnerving and devastatingly sad. I hadn't a clue when I met her, but what I very soon learnt was that in her heart Tara P-T's just a sweet, daffy, desperately insecure girl. What I've gleaned about her over the past few weeks is that she apparently has a history of being seriously used and abused by men. On top of that, the girl's only just out of rehab in The Meadows and has known me for roughly six weeks. The people around her, many of whom I've learned are apparently still addicts of one sort or another, are clearly having themselves a whale of a time, winding her up tighter than a trussed-up Christmas turkey. It seems that a lot of sick folk out there just plain can't stand to see others happy. And when they've got a 'nasty habit' of their own to contend with and one of their best mates has finally managed to kick theirs, *and* been lucky enough to have found a man who finally makes her feel that 'all my Christmases have come at once' to boot, something really strange evidently happens.

They don't like it.

So though it hurts like hell to admit it, frankly the objective part of me can see Tara's crazy point of view. For all she knows I might truly be the UK's latest answer to The Yorkshire Ripper meets Montgomery Clift's character in *The Heiress*. Yet a voice of reason cries out from somewhere deep within my soul: 'What's all the bloody hysteria about? Talk to the people that know me! O.K! I've got a history! So what? Hasn't every bloke? I'm just a nice, normal guy with — OK — slightly oversized testicles in his trousers!'

I vacillate between melancholy and ironic humour. The deepest irony for me being that for the first time in six years I was finally just about ready to be serious about a bird. What I hadn't counted on was (a) how bloody famous she was, (b) how many hidden enemies I had both personally and professionally just waiting for the perfect opportunity to crawl out of the woodwork like sadistic vermin and stab me viciously in the back, and (c) the intensely self-protective venom of certain sections of English blue-blood society once they suspect that they maybe have an imposter in their midst.

I have somehow been transformed overnight into some kind of bizarre sexual folk-hero/social pariah. Ordinary working men come up to me in the street, chuckling, shake me wholeheartedly by the hand and ask me, 'What's the big secret?! 'Ow the 'ell do ya' do it then, mate?', while women either avoid me like I'm some kind of leper, or stare after me in dark fascination.

'Ooh, it's him! I wonder what he's like! He must have a few amazing tricks stashed away somewhere inside his jockey shorts!'

The inevitable questions rattle around in my brain, as I walk over to my local for a pint: 'How did all of this happen? And why did this happen to me?'

December 8, 1967

I'm ten years old, and for the first time I'm in love. Her name is Julie Smith. She may speak like some horny little slapper from Bethnal Green, but she's the most gorgeous thing I've ever laid my innocent, pre-pubescent eyes on, and there's no way I can snap out of my intense romantic/erotic reverie, as we sit holding clammy hands in the back of the school coach taking us up to Wembley Empire Pool to see 'Puss In Boots On Ice'. (Appropriate title, I think, as I stare longingly at her cute polka-dot, fur-lined booties.)

My initial foray into the magnificent, sensual arena of 'love' has so far gone very well. It seems that Julie, just like yours truly, has a profound, heartfelt passion for pear drops — those highly addictive red and yellow sweets that give you a high like you're sniffing aircraft dope as you suck them. Ever attentive to my sweet lady's wishes even at this tender young age, I've cleverly managed to wangle a wicked half-pound stash in the school playground for the pair of us to consume en route into the metropolis.

What I am not to know until some years later is what a Godalmighty bloody idiotic thing I've just done! The pear drops were procured via a swiftly concluded transaction with one of my best mates — a trade. I wanted Julie, and hence the aforementioned precious pear drops, more than life itself! So I was not exactly in what you might call a 'strong bargaining position'. All I happened to have on me at the time was a set of personalised autographs from a group of young men who at that stage of my life were entirely meaningless to me. Four members of a new band my dad was working with, called the Beatles. And these I traded for my precious booty! (Five years ago I told this story one night to Paul and Linda McCartney at their East Hampton hideaway, and having recovered from a massive fit of giggles, Paul said: 'You always were a good businessman, weren't you Greg?')

Julie meets Greg turns out to be a short-lived affair. But it's deeply meaningful nonetheless, as it marks my initiation into the strange new world of male/female sexual idolatry. Three weeks later Julie falls over in the school playground and is carried off to hospital with a hairline skull-fracture. Destitute, missing her terribly, I take up with a different kind of girl altogether, from the wrong side of the tracks, with a distinctly unsavoury reputation that borders on the salacious. No matter! Casanova lives! And he must experience!

September 3, 1999

Last year a fascinating book was published in this country: *Casanova, The Man Who Really Loved Women*. An unusually sympathetic defence of the mythical great lover by an eminent female psychologist, the book proposed an interesting theory. The hypothesis ran that, far from being the archetypal 'serial sexual-predator', (read 'the Greg Martin of the Italian Renaissance'), Casanova was in fact a sensitive, deeply romantic chap, whose innumerable intimate relationships with the fairer sex throughout his life were largely misconstrued and/or incorrectly documented.

Casanova, the book states, had been deeply loved by almost all the women in his life and had remained with many of them for a substantial amount of time. He had fathered their children, raising them well and lavishing on them all a great deal of love, material support and affection. Moreover, the myth of the prodigious, callous, hard-hearted serial philanderer had primarily arisen as a result of one or two deeply unhappy, rejected ex-lovers who in their dotage had somehow managed to get together to concoct a malicious but highly-effective character assassination of our hero.

'Hmmm,' I thought to myself, as I re-read the passage. 'Sounds familiar.'

There is, of course, a lot more to the esteemed author's theory about the reality behind the myth of 'the great lover'. One point in particular interests me, given my own recent experience of sexual and moral slander revolving around my allegedly heartless treatment of women: Casanova's apparently very close, and loving bond with his mother.

In fact, I personally happen to believe that Freud was more than likely just a severely repressed, randy old bugger! But something about this revelation of Casanova's deep, heartfelt relationship with his dear old mum prompted a degree of serious speculation in my mind as I began to ponder over any flaws in my own character that might have led me to this sorry pass.

I had always loved women, and had succeeded for several years at marriage. I had stuck the course, producing a happy, healthy son, subsequently fighting my way through the harrowing, and destructive scenario of divorce, somehow coming out of it all smelling like a rose. And I now had a positive, mutually supportive relationship with my ex-wife. I had experienced countless affairs with women both before and after my marriage and, moreover, had managed to keep the majority of those women as very close friends. Yet still I had not managed to sustain a permanently intact relationship. Why?

Forget all the macho bullshit. That's a crock. Even the die-hard womaniser deep down in his heart nourishes a hidden desire to 'get it right'.

July, 8 1969

The Beatles are recording their last album, *Abbey Road*, and one day I visit their legendary studio and receive a profound lesson that is to stand me in excellent stead for the future. It is my first, indirect, experience of just how strong and forceful certain women can be when they happen to be of a particular nature and are more than one thousand per cent fixed on damn well keeping hold of their man.

The record, which McCartney in particular was absolutely determined should be a fitting finale to the band's incredible career following the absolute debacle of *Let It Be*, turns out to be largely a collaborative effort between Paul and my dad, (apart from a pair of incredible songs from George Harrison, 'Here Comes The Sun' and 'Something', and Lennon's pieces, 'Come Together' and 'I Want You (She's So Heavy'). George seems most of the time to be only half there, while Lennon is at this juncture in his career pretty much totally obsessed with Yoko.

On the day I visit the studio I overhear a chat between Paul and George. John has just vanished to the little boy's room, and Yoko's gone with him.

'Christ, she won't even let the poor bastard take a piss on his own!'

Lennon, during The Beatles' earlier days quite a well-built, almost chubby man, has by this time become painfully thin. There are photos of him taken during the *Let It Be* sessions where he looks like a refugee from Auschwitz. This was the result of Yoko's unshakable conviction that the pair of them should adopt and religiously maintain a macrobiotic diet.

Recording a rock 'n' roll album is typically an arduous experience: long hours with a gruelling workload, performed under the constant irritant of overwhelmingly loud music played back at 3 or 4 a.m. Not in any way the glamorous image of the life of the rock star or producer the public is sold.

An ardent lover of Cadbury's milk chocolate since his youth, my dad would typically keep a half-pound bar on hand at the recording console, to keep himself sane during the course of the endlessly long nights. As I was about to leave that particular evening, I saw John sneak up to my dad's side (Yoko had been called away for a moment to the phone) and I sidled over to listen. This is what he said:

'Slip us a piece of choco, would you George? While Yoko's not looking.'

August 10, 1999

I'm marching up the Great Wall of China with international entrepreneur extraordinaire David Tang, his girlfriend Lucy, Tara, and ex-supermodel Lauren Hutton, a close friend of Tang's who's tagged along for the fun of it. Ms. Hutton's a gorgeous fifty-something, I can't fail to notice, and adds a nice little touch of older feminine mystique to the dramatic scenery, as we plough on up the endless trail of polished stone steps. It's a treat to be striding up this Great Wonder of the World alongside such a smart, foxy, one hundred per cent woman who made such a splash years ago propositioning Richard Gere's character in *American Gigolo*.

Tara's largely been a fabulous, highly entertaining joy from day one, and Tang's been extremely generous, putting us all up at his glamorous China Club, the first 'western-style' resort in Beijing. So I'm basically having myself a jolly good time. But the skin at the back of my neck is beginning to itch. I don't know why, but I sure as shit soon will do. Little do I know the shock that awaits me when I arrive back in Beijing and the first onslaught of nasty, scurrilous press clippings are faxed through to Tang from his UK office. Perhaps now is as good a time as any to explain just how this ill-fated, whirlwind, celebrity romance caught alight. I'm not going to offer a typical pathetic male 'defence' of this one. I fucked up. No doubt about it. We all do. Typically guys more often than gals. But this time it wasn't in the usual way (i.e. not for a second was I even contemplating the possibility of having sex with another girl). Far from it. I was actually smitten with what I saw as the sweet, innocent daffiness of the little lovely. My mistake was far more simple than that. It turned out I made a major miscalculation of the strength of a certain young lady's character, while unwittingly crossing the heart of another.

July 25, 1999 (Part One)

Oh, how I love irony! I have to love it. So far my life's been positively riddled with the bloody stuff! And in this instance the mysterious, supernatural force was operating with an overwhelming energy and cunning.

You see, I'd been asked to Mick Jagger's birthday party by a sweet, adorable lass called Sabrina Guinness, an ex-It girl from another era, and at first hadn't felt the least desire to go. The problem for me was simply Sabrina herself. How do you tell such a gentle, tender, delightful lady that you're frankly not in the least bit interested in her very obvious sexual advances when she's clear as daylight absolutely potty about you almost to the point of some kind of 'magnificent obsession'?

A close buddy of Mick's, though she was extremely pleasant, cultured — very sweet and attentive — she just wasn't my type physically. So I had absolutely zero intention of venturing anywhere in that direction. Don't get me wrong. I liked Sabrina. I liked her a lot. She had class, style and sensitivity. She just wasn't the kind of gal who sent my kabumba quotient rocketing skyward in any major kind of way. Sabrina, as women so often do, evidently had other ideas. A veritable cornucopia of them! And eventually, just like a bloody fool, I relented.

We were the guests of Jessica De Rothschild for the night, another sexy, young blueblood vixen. As we pulled up to the Rothschild Riviera country seat pre-party time, I hopped out of the cab with interior designer Nicky Haslam (the die-hard, party animal extraordinaire of the London nobs scene), and Sabrina promptly showed me to her own room at the top of the house.

'Very forward of the old sow, don't you think?' Haslam offered by way of an ostensibly 'friendly' observation. ('Friendly', I might add, to Sabrina, whom Haslam repeatedly claimed he adored.) 'I'd watch myself there if I were you, dear boy. She's clearly got her sights firmly fixed on you.'

'No problem. I can deal with that one,' I thought. I'll just get myself pissed as a lager lout at Mick's party and do my absolute utmost to be conveniently 'out of commission' later on, unable to rouse the old man into action.

To tell the truth, I was already more than a little bit nervous around Sabrina. I liked her company a great deal, but I was clearly getting myself into a bit of a bind. Her sights were, indeed, clearly firmly set on yours truly. So, ever the master of courtly male-female strategy, I'd begun by attempting to implement the classic 'gentlemanly parry technique' all of my fervent students out there will know so well from my first book: 'Casanova Reincarnated's Manual Of Dastardly Courtly Seduction'.

Doing my best to ignore the obvious earlier on in the weekend, I'd politely declined the initial proffered invitation when she'd tried her best to persuade me to hop out to Mick's luscious pad in the Loire Valley the day before the bash so we could all trip down together to the Cap in his privately chartered jet. I avoided this one by claiming that I had business to do in Paris and couldn't make the plane. This was at least a half-truth. In actuality though I *did* have business, I also had a couple of stunning birds to do in Paris! One an absolutely knock out blonde; a former Miss World candidate, and a truly bodacious babe. A gorgeous, sweet, hot-as-a-chilli-pepper-ridden-chicken-vindaloo beauty! Her only drawback was her absolutely robot-like loyalty to to some US cult religion or other.

(A note to my pupils. As a general rule at all costs stay away from girls involved in religious cults. Sweetness of soul, some kind of inner life, spirituality are all fine. But there's nothing less sexy than making love to some gorgeous woman while she's praising some weird, oddball, con man wannabe guru at the top of her lungs! No way! Get that rascal out of my sack! If I'd wanted a threesome I'd have picked up some other bird!)

Vis-à-vis the situation with Sabrina, I much preferred hopping on the super-fast TGV down to the Riviera on my tod the next day instead. I love trains. They're so phallic. Gives me a hard-on every time I hear that hugely erotic 'da-dud, da-dud, da-dud'!

Firmly locked away inside the garret at the top of the house, I nervously assist the lovely Sabrina pick out her outfit for the night's frolics ahead. And while I'm pleased she's apparently a long way from your typical neurotic, spoilt 'poor little rich girl', (i.e. she doesn't choose to put me through the archetypal parade of endless frocks and 'come-fuck-me-pumps'), inside I'm feeling like an edgy bloody cat on a hot tin roof, locked away in the loft with a seriously horny woman whose fervid erotic sights are so clearly firmly locked on my now notorious Cupid's Torch.

I'm in desperate need of a shot of something nasty to calm my nerves, and we descend to the pool outside, where a glass of watery Pimms is thrust into my hand by ex-deb supervixen Jessica. A further boring, endless hour is whiled away with Saab, Haslam and Jess vying for the title 'World Champion Name-Dropper'. Haslam eventually wins hands-down for somehow managing to cram Tom Cruise and Nicole Kidman, Tony and Cherie Blair, Princess Margaret, Posh Spice, Gary Glitter, Johnny

Vaughan, Camilla Parker-Bowles, Ricky Martin, Elton John, the Pope, Madonna, Glenda Jackson, Michael Portillo and Kevin Keegan into one brisk sixty-second sentence. Then the taxi arrives and, little does sweet, innocent old me know it, but I'm off to meet my female Waterloo.

Mick's bash is held at a sumptuous waterfront villa owned by a guy called Johnny Pigozzi, an art collector/financier pal of M & J. An extremely charming chap and a warm, elegant host, Johnny does his best to make everyone feel very much at home as he swans around his own Mediterranean back yard with Mick, Jerry, the kids and their assembling throng of admirers. As more guests pour in, Don Juan scours the landscape in search of any potential victims, while naturally doing his best to shower oodles of gentlemanly affection on Sabrina. There's already a nice little selection of likely prospects looming into my sights — the typical bevy of Eurotrash baby bimbos your archetypal ageing rockstars love to surround themselves with. But there's also an attractive gaggle of slightly older, at least superficially elegant *femmes du monde.*

I knock back the rest of my Absolut on the rocks, growl softly, long and low, like a sleek, black jungle puma about to embark on the hunt and turn and head towards the bar for a little more light refreshment.

En route I skirt past Haslam, in deep, pseudo-meaningful conversation with some dopey-looking, incredibly beautiful young boy with skin of pure alabaster. Nicky's sporting his latest look of 'Liam Gallagher meets Bob Dylan, meets Dave Stewart on Quaaludes'. I've got to hand it to the old love. He looks pretty amazing. A lot younger than sixty. Nevertheless, I wish he was smart enough to realise that cargo pants maybe shouldn't be hung quite so low at his age.

'Blend in, old son. Blend in,' I keep telling myself, as I slink across the floodlit lawn towards some incredibly foxy Russian countess in a clingy, strapless red Armani number. I feel like a weird mixture of James Bond and Inspector Clouseau. The party's hotting up, and it's going to be a lot of fun later on when the music starts. Given my background, I'm well used to show-biz glitz 'n' glam, and there's thankfully a good smattering of 'normal', unpretentious types around, like Bono and his wife, the beautifully nutty Ronnie Wood, and Tom Stoppard. But by and large it's all a bit plastic. I have a wicked desire to ask for a pint of Boddington's and a packet of cheese and onion crisps the next time I make my assault on the bar.

The Russian countess is beautiful. But *boring*! As I wade my way politely through an interminable conversation about the current price of Fabergé eggs, all I can think about is her own stash of eggs tucked away somewhere out of sight, like some fantastic, entrancing hoard of sexual pirate's treasure under that awesomely wicked red silk frock.

A feminine arm slips its way quietly through mine. It's Saab. 'Dinner's served,' she smiles sweetly. Then she turns and fixes a set of classic 'Fuck off, bitch, the stud's mine' eyes on the countess. Women are absolute masters of telling their own kind to piss off when their sexual territory could be at stake. Men, by contrast, are like retarded kindergarten children. Ninety-nine point nine per cent of the women I've ever known have had the utterly chilling ability to communicate their cold-blooded willingness to sever another woman's head from her body at the drop of a hat when they consider the loyalty of their man's noble tool might be under any kind of attack.

'Where the hell do they learn all that stuff?' I muse to myself, as Saab hauls me off to an awaiting table. 'Must be bloody genetic.'

I spy an absolutely amazing looking girl with long brown hair, black eyes you could drown in, and a body designed to make any grown man weep, and can hardly believe my luck as Sabrina seems about to plop me down right at her side. Uh-huh! No way

in hell that's gonna happen! Not with Mary Whitehouse in charge
of the seating arrangements! Instead I'm guided to the head of the
table with Mick's brother, Chris, on one side, and some ageing,
ever-so county duchess with a voice like the Queen on the other.
I sit down and help myself to a healthy glass of some of the very
nice vintage red plonk sitting on the table. Turning to face the
duchess, my face falls. Her nobbly old hand has already found it's
way onto my thigh.

The food is a bit weird. A really strange mix of unremarkable
Chinese, Mexican and French. I down my plateful as rapidly as
possible in between brisk snatches of superficial chit-chat with
Chris Jagger and the ageing nymphomaniac duchess. Then I
hastily excuse myself for a quick fag amongst the rhododendrons.
(Funny how for these types smoking is now pretty much always
considered a 'no-no', while hard drugs are sometimes still maybe
O.K.) I'm joined by a bizarre nicotine-addicted duo: Tom
Stoppard and Ron Wood. Together the three of us inhale our
Marlboro Lights like naughty schoolboys at the back of the
bicycle sheds. Ronnie is blissfully insane. A truly crazy sweetheart
of a man, he talks in a swift, harsh, razorback rasp, like a
rattlesnake crawling across gravel. I watch him as he regales Tom
with yet another hysterically funny tale about life on the road
with Mick, Keith and the boys.

'Life's a funny thing,' I can't help thinking. Ron's so superbly
'normal'. One wrong turn and you can see how he and his lovely
missus could've so easily wound up running a pub in Bermondsey,
with old spikey-hair playing a wicked blues set on his Fender
Stratocaster every Saturday night for the locals.

The amazing young lady with the long brown hair swans
over, and sexily lights up a Sobranie. My blood gets up, as she
starts to flirt with me outrageously. I check my shirt pocket,
putting on my sleek, hungry panther look, eyeballing her
furiously (technique numero uno for seduction par excellence —

the eyes, the eyes!) I smile, my hand quickly finding the small stash of business cards I've cleverly remembered to bring along with me. I pull one out and slip it to her, as I quickly check over her shoulder to see Sabrina's safe out of sight. I don't know this beauty. And it's a risk. She might be one of Sabrina's godchildren, who seem to be everywhere tonight, and all of them young, nubile, and *incredibly* fucking gorgeous. But risk is all part of the thrill for any budding 'scumbag serial philanderer'. It's like the weird fact I later learn that private dicks get their biggest kicks out of sitting in a pub, striking up a normal, everyday conversation with the very person they're secretly tailing.

'Brown Beauty' works at Sothebys. Like a lot of the younger birds here, she's been to Beadales, Sherbourne, Roedean, Stowe, or whatever other contemporary St. Trinian's is currently top of the list for the mummies and daddies of every self-respecting, up-and-coming It girl. When she opens her mouth it's a bit like listening to high-class chalk being scraped down a blackboard. But who cares? She'd probably love being bound and gagged. Most of her sort are into some kind of weird sexual behaviour or other.

'At least there'll be no need to cover her head with the proverbial brown paper bag,' I think to myself. 'She's sexy enough to make a bishop want to throw himself through a stained-glass window!'

Her eyes dart down to my crotch, as she playfully runs my business card over her luscious lips. She giggles silkily, as a skinny, mangy-looking young male blue blood in bright orange trousers, multi-neon-coloured Hawaiian shirt, and pink loafers lopes across the grass towards us. He looks just like a young Miami hood on holiday at Butlins.

'That's my boyfriend,' she whispers furtively in my ear in her odd, seductive, high-pitched whinny. 'Got to go. See you later, maybe...' She holds up my card. '... in London.'

The blue-blood comes closer. I recognise him as a trust-fund baby financier and very much a wannabe 'serial philanderer' along the lines of yours truly. Only one problem with the dear old love. He's as queer as a chorus boy in a Christopher Street production of *Les Miserables*.

'Him?' I can't resist asking her. 'I thought he was...? You know... '

'Gay, darling? Oh, sure he is. You know it. I know it. But he doesn't. And he's so fucking rich!'

She turns, vanishing into the steamy summer darkness back towards the house with an unnerving, sickly smile that makes her ravishing, ultra-foxy features morph into a warped, Bozo-like clown mask. As I watch her svelte body melt away into the night, I get an odd, brackish taste in my mouth, like I've just taken a swig of stagnant, rancid water from what looked like a pristine, sweet, virginal pond.

Something's going to happen tonight, and I know it. It might be good. It might be bad. It might be both. But it sure as shit is going to happen!

A frantic rustling from the bushes behind me makes me turn. It's followed by the distinct sound of heavy breathing, sexual groans. I can't resist. I carefully part the branches. There, naked as the day God made them, and in a *very* interesting position, like a pair of Calcutta contortionists, are a very famous rock star, and another very famous rock star's wife. Plus ça change, plus c'est la même chose!

September 29, 1999

I spent last night with a close friend. Her name's Isabelle; a lovely, smart, sexy Latina lass without a grain of selfishness in her voluptuous body. As we're sipping our late night cocktails with a couple of her pals, there's a knock on the door. Isabelle opens it up and in walks 'me'. I don't mean the me sitting there on the couch with my stunning pal, sipping my drink, dreaming of what might turn out to be the long, sensational promised night ahead. I mean the 'me' as in the character I unwittingly became via Nigel Dempster and various other members of the popular press on that Black Monday back in August.

'Oh, hi.' The words slide out of his mouth with a slimy, lop-sided grin. 'I know it's late. I was just passing. Mind if I come in?' Late? It's past 2 a.m. on a wet Tuesday night in the darkest depths of Bayswater! Isabelle stands aside and lets him pass, shooting an 'Oh fuck the weirdo's back, sorry' look my way. Mr. Seedy sidles past and plumps himself down on the far side of the couch. He's about fifty, with a thick shock of grey hair, dark, furry, Beelzebub eyebrows that rise and fall at will, like a pantomime villain, and a wicked beer belly cunningly concealed beneath his Marks & Sparks V-neck sweater. For all the world it's like sitting in a room with Terry Thomas. Any minute I'm expecting him to whip out a fake handlebar moustache, stick it on, give it a sinister twirl, and mutter to Izzy: 'I say! You're looking stunning, old girl! What do you say? Let's leave these rotters! They're an absolute shower!' And true to form that's almost precisely what he does! Lasciviously ogling her lovely Mediterranean tan, his mouth leers open. 'So your holiday obviously agreed with you, my dear. You're looking ravishing.' His eyes sidle on down to her boobs. 'Tanned and *very* fit!'

The torture of enduring Mr. Seedy's presence thankfully doesn't last that long, and I'm prevented from grabbing him by the scruff of his M & S sweater, and hurling him out into the filthy London night by Isabelle's protracted yawns and decidedly pointed comments, such as, 'Gosh is it that late? Oh well. Time for bed!'

Once this latter-day Jack The Ripper has slinked his way off into the pouring rain, she tells me who is. It turns out this charmer's infatuated with a relative of hers, an apparently gorgeous bit of recently divorced stuff, and that she and other members of her family have nicknamed him 'The Stalker', on account of the fact that he somehow uncannily senses every time the woman is due back in town. Hence his sudden appearance here this evening, like some sort of Hooray Henry Bela Lugosi, out of the bleak London night.

'So what?' I hear you say. 'London's just like any other major metropolis, isn't it? Chock-a-block with grubby, chintzy con-men seducers on the prowl.' True. But this one is such a caricature. And indeed the very spitting image of the dirty, rotten scoundrel Greg Martin splashed across the pages of the *Mail On Sunday* last month. It's been a bit like meeting my doppelganger face to face: the 'evil twin'.

Not that this lad 'doth protest too much'. It's just that I wish some of the other journalists had at least had the decency of Pete Clark, who wrote in the *Evening Standard* while offering an admittedly somewhat dubious defence of my character in which he described me like some kind of exotic sexual flower, as 'belonging to that mighty, great, perennial tradition of the world's greatest lovers, from Lord Byron to Jack Nicholson.' No matter. As that other great 'serial-womanising scumbag pig', JFK, once said: 'Forgive your enemies, but never forget their names.'

I cross to my kitchen window and stare out at the throngs of passing 'normal' shoppers trooping in and out of Harrods Food Hall, wondering what it must be like to live without a radically over-sexed piece of meat between your legs. 'Bloody awful!' I'm forced to conclude.

I check my messages. There's yet another painful one from Tara, a girl whom I've by now been forced to admit to myself is deeply in the process of slowly being led well and truly off her rocker by many of her so-called friends. It hurts like hell, but I recognise there's absolutely nothing in the world I can do about it. Zero! Zip!

'It's clearly not her fault,' I keep telling myself. 'She's getting it left, right and centre. It seems she can't so much as take a bloody pee without some malicious wanker or other tossing his two pence worth of phony, slimy slander about yours truly into the pot.' The current message makes me really sad. In the frantic voice of an incipient 'bunny boiler', she trots her discovery that I apparently dated one of her best friends years ago in LA. Now the 'truth' about me is out, and the knife well and truly in, the girl wants to meet with Tara to 'dish the dirt' on me woman to woman and congratulate her on such a narrow escape from what would surely have been a fate of eternal marital misery at the sordid hands of old bugger-lugs.

I pick up the phone and call Ms. P-T's mobile. She answers. There's the sound of Italian voices yelling and dishes crashing. She must be supping soup in San Lorenzo's, her local welfare kitchen, I surmise. She acts pissed off to hear my voice, but like the classic woman scorned, clearly can't resist leaving her villain alone.

'What do you want?! I'm told you were in this restaurant last night! Don't come here ever again! Nobody wanted to serve you! This is *my* territory!' By this point I'm feeling it's well and truly a losing battle, so I'm doing my best to get beyond the sense of sadness. I was thankfully born with a decidedly black sense of humour. So I laugh. We've known each other a month, but it's like we've been married for years and we're getting divorced! The laughter goes down like a cup of cold sick. But what other possible reaction can I have? In truth it's been heartbreaking. Really heartbreaking.

'I'm just responding to your last message, Tara. Tell me, who is this friend of yours?'

'Her name's Gabriella De Lisle. She's Black Jack De Lisle's daughter. We were at Sherbourne together. I've known her for years. She agrees with everybody. You're the ultimate conman! I'm going to see you fucking dead for this, you scumball!'

I've no idea who this young woman is. I've never so much as

heard her name. But I'm naturally curious. 'Tara. I have had a *lot* of girlfriends in my time, but even *I* tend to remember their names. I'd certainly remember Gabriella's, because I find it so sexy.' By now miserable with the absolute insanity of it all, my patience is wearing decidedly thin, and I can't resist pouring a little playful oil on such ridiculously troubled waters. 'Who is she? Tell me something about her.'

'She's married to Eric Fellner. Oh, what's the point! Fuck off, Greg! You're such an absolute bastard!!' There's a click, and her voice vanishes from the line.

'Hmmm. Eric Fellner,' I muse to myself, as I casually flip through the latest editions of *Hustler, Knave* and *Skin* magazines. He's one half of Working Title, the most successful film company in the UK to date. Now that *is* interesting. It's also potentially very serious. The rot is spreading deeper, into my professional life, way beyond the initial panic of my investors.

Eventually the penny drops. As I mentioned in my *Daily Telegraph* interview with Elizabeth Grice, I suppose it's sort of flattering to find I have so many enemies.

August 8, 1970

Abbey Road's out on the market and it's a phenomenon. As usual there are the secret drug allusions in the album's lyrics, and one day Stephan, the major school addict, collars me in the playground during the lunch-break.

'Hey man,' he leers at me through his oily, red-eyed haze. 'I hear your dad was the amazing dude who made *Abbey Road* happen. Tell him from me it's the best tripping album ever. And by the way, ask him if Paul's dead.'

When the Beatles first met my father they assumed, given his BBC accent, he was an ex-RAF Spitfire pilot. In fact he was born in the East End and taught himself to speak 'proper' phonetically at the age of sixteen. Ever the dutiful son, I convey the message to my father who utters a crisp, terse public school response. 'Tell the young man he needs help.'

The next week I report back to Stephan.

'Hey man, I thought your dad was cool until now. This is fuckin' rubbish! I s'pose next you'll try telling me 'Lucy In The Sky With Diamonds' was about some stupid painting John's son did at school.'

'Ummm, well actually, yes. Yes it was, Stephan. Julian painted it the month before the song was recorded.'

Stephan stares at me, bleary-eyed. 'Your dad's a fraud, man. Paul's dead. Everyone knows it. He died in a car crash years ago. You can hear the words on *The White Album*: "Paul is dead! Paul is dead!" And every song John's written since is about drugs.'

July 25, 1999 (Part Two)

Amused at my discovery in the Pigozzi hedgerow, I mosey on back up to the terrace where things are finally about to heat up. The music's going to start any minute, and an ashen-faced, plump, bearded man, looking like he buys all his clothes at BHS, is fumbling around, trying to plug an amplead into a guitar. He's a bit like an overweight, gawky computer nerd in his crisply starched, tieless pale blue shirt firmly buttoned up tight at the neck, wrinkly brown cords and dockers — which it turns out is precisely what he is. His name is Paul Allen, billionaire founder of Microsoft, and the third richest man in America.

It turns out that Mr. Allen, whose personal wealth has been estimated at over $20 billion, is a frustrated rock star in the guise of a bumbling genius. Which is why he's smart enough to own the rights to the complete catalogue of songs of Jimi Hendrix, along with The Portland Trail Blazers and The Seattle Seahawks. And, if the rumours are true, he will also shortly own the rights to the soon-to-be-single Jerry Hall! Rubber Lips and the boys ritually allow him to get his rocks off by jamming along with them at the odd celeb bash.

So here we are. To kick off we've got Mick and Bono on vocals, the Einstein of computer software on lead guitar, and the insanely paralytic Ronnie Wood on drums, (not his native instrument, I hasten to add, as the members of his fawning, blue-blood audience is about to find out.) As the band crashes into action, I turn for a moment to check out Sabrina's whereabouts. She's gotten herself distracted, and is for now in deep confab with two other latter-day It girls, (probably planning her strategy for 'the seduction of Gregory' later on in the evening back at El Rancho De Rothschild). My predatory eyes make a swift sweep of the room, in case any late-appearing potential victims have put in an appearance.

A chubby chap in a crimson suit with a thick mop of ginger hair and glasses is standing chatting with another younger man, and what looks to me like the most gorgeous piece of crackling I've seen in years. She's wearing nothing but a sexy little pink bikini under a see-through white sarong, and a very cute little pink pair of 'come-fuck-me pumps' with a pair of adorable, fluffy pompoms on top. 'Agent Provocateur' beyond a shadow of a doubt, I quickly note.

(Technique numero dos de seduction par excellence — always pay close attention to the ever-changing positions in the league tables of women's underwear shops! AP is definitely currently top of the division, a niche it unquestionably deserves, being as it is naughty, provocative, and *very, very bad!*)

It's Tara. She arrived last minute along with Elton John and his boyfriend, David Furnish, looking hotter than a July afternoon in Death Valley, which unbeknownst to me is precisely the place I'm now headed.

Funny how us silly male sods can never fathom if, when, and how a given relationship is going to go pear-shaped. Girls always seem so much more naturally in tune with the subtle undercurrents of it all. As opposed to us blokes, who, let's face it, are forever primarily pretty much always focused on the simple, straightforward 'ins and outs'!

When I first laid eyes on Tara I thought I'd died and gone to Hog Heaven. She looked fantastic! Ravishing! Nothing like the sad, sorry pictures I recalled having seen in the American press of her depressing entrée into a rehab clinic in Arizona. I'll be saying this until my dying day, but I might as well repeat it now. When I initially saw her, I didn't really have a clue who the hell Tara Palmer-Tomkinson was! I mean, of course I had some vague idea. But Tara P-T and her fellow tribe of It girls are an English phenomenon, and I'd been living in the States for the past fifteen years. I knew one thing though. She looked like a bit of alright! And whatever else I'd heard clearly hadn't filtered through. Because unlike her and the rest of her chums, I never paid that much attention to the gossip scene pages of the press. Having said all that, of course, I *must* confess at least *some* of the nasty news about the lass must've somehow registered somewhere deep down in the nether regions of my grey matter. Last week I picked up an an early draft of one of my film projects currently in development, a sweet little romantic-comedy with an environmental theme about the state of male-female roles at the millennium written by yours truly. Therein I discovered a character I'd created called 'Tara Cutcliffe-Jones'. A sexy, sweet, but desperately insecure young vixen, the girlfriend of our hapless hero, the lass spends most of her spare time shopping at Gucci, Chanel, Joseph and Prada, and basically wants nothing more out of life than to nail 'Charlie', the aforementioned deeply sensitive, and as it happens, very wealthy hero.

Now that is *weird*! I wrote that over a year ago, forgot I'd named her 'Tara', then met the very model of the character in the all-too-willing flesh and, like a total prat, fell for her myself at Mick's fifty-sixth birthday bash in the merry old South of France.

If there *is* such a thing as fate, that fact alone would be enough to make me sign up as a fully paid up card-carrying member of the 'Serial Mystical Reincarnated Philanderer, Scumbag and Seducers Club'!

(Speaking of clubs, I recall for a second that fateful night tearing my eyes away from Tara to check on Saab again, only to find her whinnying away with another ex-It girl. She looked just like one of those female members of that weird club down in the New Forest where the men ride their lassies around the room in black leather stiletto booties, saddles on their backs, and sprigs of holly stuck up their arses! Never heard of it? Stick with me. You'll hear about this and a lot, lot more!)

The trick now was somehow to make contact with the lovely Tara without Sabrina honing in on my plan. Not a simple feat, given any predatory woman's unerring ability to spot a potential rival at ten paces. Thankfully it turned out Tara was just about as game as I was. We made the initial sexual eye contact, then managed our first erotically loaded chat in the middle of the room. I remember the words as if it was yesterday.

'Hi, Tara. My name's Greg. You look bloody gorgeous. I don't know much about you. But what I do know, just from looking at you, is that what you need in your life is a good, strong, solid man.'

'And what you need is a naughty girl!' she giggled, salaciously.

That was all it took. It was over.

'Hello,' I thought to myself. 'I don't know who this one is. But she's one hell of a cracker!' It was a clear-cut case of instantaneous kabumba.

People have probably got the wrong idea about Tara Palmer-Tomkinson. I've seen her up close and personal, at intimate quarters inside her family home, where the insecure, attention-seeking party girl vanishes, to be replaced by a normal, slightly wacky country lass, who basically wants nothing more out of life than to play Chopin nocturnes, sing some silly karaoke songs of a night, and walk her dogs. Photos of Tara as a child are adorable. She's a cute delectably sweet little girl with an overwhelmingly attractive, eternally wicked glint in her eye. A large part of Tara's charm is her innate, innocent mischievousness. She's the archetypal St. Trinian's naughty sweetheart. You can just imagine her in her gymslip, black stockings and suspenders, stretched out flat on her back in some haystack, doing something really bad to the poor, drooling hunk of a local farmer's son.

At the time she was the equivalent of death on a plate for a man like me. To begin with I've got an in-built weakness for Latin girls (Tara's part Argentinean). Then when you add in her delicious sense of fun and decidedly off-kilter personality, for a chump like me you've basically got what amounts to the equivalent of a female neutron bomb. I didn't know it then. But I sure as shit was to know it within the next forty-eight hours. I was done and dusted. Stitched up. Flambéed, like a stag roasting over a pit of fiery, red-hot coals!

On the way back up the hill to Chateau De Rothschild, Haslam, clearly relishing the thought of my long night ahead in bed with Saab, giggles, doing his best to deal with my onslaught of questions about Tara. He warns me that if I toy with her, I'll be 'a dead man'. I'm used to being taken for the definitive, heartless, womanising bastard. Any half way good-looking, single man who isn't gay or neutered in London, New York, or come to that any other major world metropolis, tends to be labelled a lecherous Don Juan these days. But nothing in my wildest dreams could have possibly prepared me for the surreal assault of public slander that lay ahead.

We arrive back at the house, Sabrina swiftly leading the way up to the sexual garret at the top of the stairs to commence 'the ravishing of Gregory'. I trip and stumble as best I can, slurring my words like a raving drunk from the Gorbals, trying every single trick in the book I can possibly think of to make her believe I'm biologically completely and utterly incapable of the deed. Nothing works! The noble tool of this 'seducer par excellence' betrays him. My entire army of troops rebel, causing my star performer somehow to suddenly rise to the occasion in meteoric, and quite unwished-for style.

Sometimes it seems life's just one gigantic metaphor. Sabrina swans out of the bathroom in an extremely naughty see-through, white negligee, plumps herself down on top of me, and the bed promptly collapses beneath us with an ominous, creaking groan, like a female rhinoceros in labour!

CHAPTER TWO

ROGUE AND VAGABOND

'Older women are best because they always think they may be doing it for the last time.'
Ian Fleming
'I never make love on a wooden table. It goes against the grain.'
Jack Yelton

September 4, 1999

When I was just five years old my father walked out of the house one day and never came back. No one ever explained why. I spent the next twenty years of my life thinking it must've been something I'd said. My mother never stopped loving my dad. In fact, she loved him desperately. So much so that it was a bit like growing up in a house of mourning. She told me once that for over a year after he left she couldn't sleep at night without holding onto his clothes. I can remember as if it were yesterday bursting into floods of tears one day when I was six, just a year after my old man had hopped it, when the little girl next door told me I was stupid: no way could I marry my mum to try to take her pain away.

I mention this not in order to provoke a chorus of bleeding-heart 'mea culpas' amongst my readers. God knows, it's a familiar enough story. A broken home is about as common today as a white Christmas in Siberia. I recall the event now only because of the profound emotional reaction it provoked in me as a child, and what, on reflection, the experience may have subsequently led to regarding my pattern of voluminous sexual interaction with women as a man.

Casanova, as you may recall from chapter one, adored, revered and worshipped his old mum. According to our eminent female shrink, he was forced to take care of her due to the psychologically difficult and complex circumstances of his childhood. In doing so he developed a unique sensitivity to his mother's needs. In other words, Casanova the kid grew up with a singular, built-in *understanding of women*. He *loved* them, as well as *relating* to them. Which is a gift that means a hell of a lot more when it comes to doing the nasty than all you super-macho blokes out there might imagine. (We'll get to this later on. Having trouble between the sheets? Turn to Chapter Nine: 'The Subtle Art Of Seduction'!)

Now, if you link that kind of acute, exceptional awareness of the feminine nature to one hell of a powerful male libido, you've got a pretty much fail-safe recipe for the creation of a potentially extraordinary male lover.

No worries! This isn't about to turn into some boring, turgid psychological treatise on 'the childhood roots of the serial sexual Casanova complex'. If I can't get a good laugh out of both my former 'spectacular life of crime' along with the horrendous, malicious slander campaign I went through, I might just as well give it all up now and become a milkman in the Outer Hebrides! Hang on to your hats! You've embarked on a rollicking, crazy charabanc ride through the spectacular hills and valleys of my copious sexual memories! But I'd be doing both myself as well as any of my budding 'student scumbag philanderers' out there a huge injustice if I didn't pay careful attention to the fundamental interior bedrock of any man who truly loves women.

Remember, this book *is* a caper. But it is also a *defence*. Calling a man of major passion a 'scumbag, serial sexual predator' just because he's slept with fifteen times more women than you have is a bit like labelling D.H. Lawrence a pornographer because he wrote more profoundly sensual books in the English language than any other author, dead or living. There's a subtle, but crucial distinction to be made here that seems to have somehow gotten conveniently lost amidst all the mud-slinging, slander and abuse. A cad uses women. He devours them, chews them up, sucks them dry, spits them out, then moves on. A lover adores women. He lavishes them with care, attention and affection *because that's the way he was raised*. He loves them both physically and mentally like they've never been loved before, worships them, reveres them and cherishes them. A lover will stay with his woman until it's clearly pointless to go on. *But if it is right, he will stay with her forever.*

May 14, 1971

'Pizza!' The word thunders like a herd of careering wild buffalo through my brain, and instantly I feel a warm, tingling sensation, like an explosion of soft, melting jelly in my crotch. I'm fourteen years old, and whether or not I realise it at the time, I've just experienced my first orgasm inside a woman.

I say 'whether or not I realise it' because (a) I'm pissed as a fart on way too many pints of rough cider, (b) I'm scrunched up on a Restoration couch half the size of my body, clumsily sprawled across a half-naked Spanish woman three times my age, and (c) her 250-pound heavyweight boxing champion husband has just walked in through the front door of their home carrying a deluxe, mighty-meaty pizza.

I beat a hasty retreat through the back door, Levi's dangling from my ankles, as the woman desperately tries to rearrange both her body and the room into some state of normality. Outside, I shoot off into the night on my Puch Maxi 50cc moped, howling at the fat full moon, like a drunken English pirate who's just looted a prize Spanish galleon laden to the gills with doubloons and gold bullion.

'Yee-hah!! I've fucking done it! I'm a bloody man!'

There's a sudden screech of burnt rubber, the moped slides out from under me, like an eel wriggling out of a fisherman's net, and the next thing I know I'm flat on my back in a hedgerow, staring up at the bemused eyes of a fat Jersey heifer.

July 26, 1999

I'm back in London after the Jagger party. Ms. World has been staying at my Knightsbridge flat while I'm away and has a few well-grounded complaints to make to me about my recently hired PA, Richard Griffiths. (Griffiths, it later turns out, was the primary source for one of the most damaging articles of all that appeared in the *Mail On Sunday* upon my return from my trip with Tara to Hong Kong. Twenty-five thousand pounds for a crock of slander! We'll have more to say about him later on!)

It turns out ol' Ricky's been treating Ms. W. like some kind of unwanted intruder into what was to Griffiths the fragile and apparently private world of Gregory and Richard, and my film and television production company.

I do my best to calm the storm, as always trying to give any employee of mine the benefit of the doubt. But it does seem to be getting a little bit weird with the dear old love. He appears very confused. While frequently dressing and behaving very flamboyantly, he exhibits classic signs of on the one hand deeply revering, while on the other deeply envying my prolific success rate with women.

'I don't like her!' he hisses venomously to me one day behind Ms. W.'s lovely back. 'Trust me, Greg. She's just like all the others. Every bitch you meet has her own secret fucking agenda!'

Now, I can't deny the likelihood of a possible 'agenda' with any of the sexy Susans I come across. Women are, after all, much smarter than us silly male sods, being as they are principally typically ruled by their heads, hearts *and* private parts, while, like some kind of sick joke perpetrated upon us by our Creator, we men tend to be almost genetically pre-programmed to let our cocks lord it over our corpus colosums and all the other ancilliary areas of our anatomies. However, I can't resist the nagging thought there may be just a wee bit of psychological projection going on here with ol' Ricky.

I swiftly duck out with Ms. W. into the London night, meeting the foppish Haslam and a bunch of his tepid gay pals for dinner. We move on to China White, where Haslam's cellphone suddenly gives a frantic ring at the precise moment I'm out on the dance floor doing a killer bossanova with the lovely Ms. W. Haslam calls me over, cups the phone with his hand and shoots me a strange, and in retrospect, decidedly ominous grin.

'It's Tara. She's mad as hell because you haven't called her. Apparently she's already announced to the whole world, including her family, she's met the man she's going to marry.'

I stare at him in shock.

'What? I only just met her last night, Nicky! We spoke for about ten minutes. That was it! She's cute as hell alright, but she must be a little bit off her rocker! What the hell am I going to say to Sabrina?'

Haslam gives a deep, throaty chuckle, and just shrugs. 'God knows, dear boy. I did warn you the old sow had her sights firmly set on you. Besides, I wouldn't worry too much about Tara, if I were you. She *is* a little crazy. But, by God, she's gorgeous as hell. Don't even think about it. I've heard her say she's met the man she's going to marry more than a hundred times before.'

He grins and hands me the phone. Tara's voice booms down the other end of the line in a breathless, sexual pant.

'Greg! It's Tara! Where have you *been*? I've been going *mad* because you haven't called me!'

Something about the completely insane sweetness of the girl's intense, heartfelt ardour gets to me, and like a fool I completely forget about the darkly portentous comment that's just slipped from Haslam's mouth.

'Hi. I'm sorry. I've been quite busy today. When are you coming back into town?'

'Tomorrow! I'm going to get to the airport *four hours early* so I don't miss my flight! Will you send someone to meet me?!'

Four hours early? Woh! My God, this one's keen!

'Um, okay. Yeah, sure. What time does your plane get in?'

'Six o'clock. You *will* send someone?!!'

I laugh gamely.

'Sure. I'll come and meet you myself. We'll go to some hotel if you'd like. It would be nice to get to know you a little bit better. Where would you like to go?'

'I don't care!' she wails dramatically down the line. 'Anywhere! A bed-sit in Brixton!' (With hindsight, it would've been fun to have actually taken Tara to Brixton for our first love tryst. This is the kind of girl who I later learn has a history of never deigning to lower herself to date a man worth less than a cool million. I'd maybe have saved myself a whole lot of trouble from day one if I'd pulled that one!)

I hang up, turn to Haslam and hand him his phone. The strange grin appears again at the corners of his mouth. 'I'm going to need your help with this one, Nicky. She's obviously a fabulous-looking girl, but I don't know her.'

'I warned you, darling. She's one in a million — but a trip. This is Tara Palmer-Tomkinson we're discussing, not some dirty little Iranian girl from Knightsbridge. You started it. Now you've got to finish it.'

'I gave her my business card, Nicky. And now we're apparently already getting married.'

He just laughs, blowing a boozy kiss to one of the lovely boys seated across the room.

'Right. Where shall I take her?'

'Relax. Enjoy each other. Explore her. Get a suite at The Savoy, old boy. "Hole up", if you'll pardon the slightly slutty pun, in the room with her for the weekend with lots of room service. Tara's the kind of girl who's used to being surrounded by all of her creature comforts.'

'*But what about Sabrina?*'

Haslam shrugs again.

'Just tell her. You've only seen her a couple of times. I'm sure she'll understand.' But the eerie, foreboding grin comes again. Somehow I just don't believe him.

November 5, 1973

I'm in the doghouse. Having narrowly missed expulsion, I'm banned from school for a month (ask me if I care!), following a particularly brutal session with the cane. The reason? I ran my favourite girl's bra up the flagpole instead of the Union Jack on Remembrance Sunday. My stint at my senior school makes *Tom Brown's Schooldays* look like 'Seven Years At Club Med'. But I'm having fun!

St. Albans is supposed to be for particularly bright boys (Stephen Hawking was an ex-pupil), but my theory is they took me in for sheer amusement value; the deadweight comic chocolate in the box. Having barely scraped through the entrance exam, (my answer to the question: 'Who was Marie Antoinette?' 'A sexy, young French film star — the next Brigitte Bardot!'), I excel at three things: acting, writing — and sex.

This latter activity might actually have been the cause of a lot more than mere expulsion for yours truly, should the truth have ever really come out. The bra prank was a result of a state of intensely triumphant sexual euphoria induced in me the night before via a rather naughty, pre-planned, 'ill met by moonlight' encounter with the rather ravishing, but bored wife of one of my least favourite teachers, at the school's rugby playing fields on the far side of town.

Freezing, drunk as a skunk on more than half a dozen pints of Wadworth's 6X and too many dark rum and blacks, I fumbled in the bitter darkness of the dank, sodden, gloomy changing rooms to unbutton my fly, as she lay there, prostrate on a wooden bench in her black silk slip and heels, like an English county 'Venus On The Half Shell'.

Now it could have been the booze, the icy, glacial wind biting into my shrunken, arctic-blue testicles, or just the weight of sheer bloody nerves that went along with the knowledge that, although finally over the age of consent, I was about to give the wife of the man I hated and feared more than life itself the bloody shafting of the century. Whatever it was, for fifteen minutes it was like trying to shove a wizened, shrivelled-up, old marshmallow into an ice-cold telephone coin-box.

Finally recovering from what was my first psychologically bruising encounter with brewer's droop, I mounted the nubile lady, only to find myself locked into one of the most cripplingly painful sexual positions I've still to this day ever experienced.

Frigid concrete, nasty, rough wooden benches, and a sub-zero wind-chill factor are hardly the most conducive conditions for passionate copulation. Within thirty seconds I had a splinter up my arse the size of a toothpick! Then I was suddenly hit with a brilliant idea. The baths!

There was no 'karma sutra love oil', no sexy wild strawberry-scented bubble bath to hand. But there *were* candles, and lashings of steamy hot water. And within fifteen minutes of torrid oral sex, my least favourite master's wife and the naughtiest lad in the school were at it, like a pair of horny, turbo-charged ferrets, in the first fifteen's communal bathtub.

I learned a lot that night, and it was an experience that leads me to deliver the hearty recommendation to any game young buck that at the earliest possible opportunity he try a majorly serious dabble in the mysterious, deeply alluring and instructive world of 'the older woman'. I guarantee you any girl I've been with since has in one way or another benefited from the intensity and awesome power of that experience. What neither I, nor the borderline-nymphomnaiac wife of my miserable old teacher had counted on that night, however, was the old school games keeper doing his rounds with his trusty old twelve-bore shotgun.

It's a funny thing about sex. It *is* like a drug. And if you get it right, it becomes *the* most amazing, mind-blowing narcotic in the world. That night was one of those nights. My first. Unfortunately for me I lost all sense of time and space, and 'tripped out' off into my own personal sexual Shangri-la. That haven, as many of you I'm sure know, is a Nirvana like no other known to the human animal, and once you've reached it you *definitely* do *not* want to go home.

Bang! Smash! Bang! Smash! Bang! Bang! Smash! Smash! A series of bullets shattered both the windows above our heads, and the glorious ecstasy of our illicit bliss. And within thirty seconds flat the darling lady's lovely lobster-pink bottom had vanished from the tub, and she was sprinting for dear life towards the back door, like a bat out of hell. As it slammed shut behind her, the front door creaked open and there stood old Mr. Geoffrey Clutterbuck (yes, that *was* his name!), eighteen stone, with a crimson, vein-stubbled, pudgy, pig-eyed face. A butcher by trade, and a butcher by nature, Clutterbuck's gnarly old hands clutched his faithful old CCF twelve-bore.

I stood slowly, freezing hands clutched delicately around my privates, like some terrified, randy teenage Adam having just had his first succulent taste of the awesome terrible fruit of the tree of carnal knowledge. Clutterbuck chomped down furiously on the sodden Silk Cut dangling from his lip, growled, then gestured nervously with the gun for me to raise my hands. I nodded, eagerly complying with his wish, and his bloated face suddenly turned ashen, his mouth falling open in an awful, stunned silence, revealing a set of nasty, nicotine-stained teeth.

'Christ, lad!' he whispered in stunned shock. 'Where in God's name did you *get* that thing?!!'

July 27, 1999

It's 5 p.m. and I'm stuck in an appalling traffic jam on the M4 on my way out to Heathrow to pick up Ms. T-P-T, which gives me plenty of time to think over just how I'm going to handle the coming encounter. I'm very attracted to her, there's absolutely no doubt about it. And her wonderful wacky side is something I find extremely appealing. But all this about a wedding announcement to her family and friends before I even know anything about the idea, I find just the slightest bit disturbing.

'What the hell, she's probably just kidding,' I try telling myself gamely, as my BMW crawls along the motorway at a snail's pace. 'She's more than likely just a highly overexcitable, sexy girl. A gorgeous piece of foxy stuff simply very hot-to-trot; a lovely piece of major crackling with big-time ants in her pants.

I eventually pull into the short-term parking at Terminal One, and walk on inside to the arrivals gate. The flight from Nice is late. But that's okay. Gives me time for a swift pint and more time to think. But *why* am I thinking so much? That's not like me. Not in a situation like this. I dismiss the question, like the stupid twit I've already somehow unwittingly become, and stroll back on down to the gate. (Technique numero tres for the budding serial philanderer par excellence — never ignore the inner voice. If you're behaving abnormally, there's some angel scratching away at your brain, frantically trying to tell you something — probably something crucial. Pay attention! It's a built-in early-warning signal any Casanova reincarnated ignores at his utmost peril!)

I snoop around a bit as the British Midland flight from Nice finally lands and the passengers pass through customs. There are a couple of guys in a corner with cameras. But it simply doesn't register. I know it may sound naive, but I repeat: not for one second did I have the slightest idea how bloody famous Tara was in this country! Eventually the doors slide apart, and Ms. T-P-T strides on through in her tight-fitting Gucci pants, Prada sweater and booties, closely escorted by a member of British Midland security personnel. I walk right up, give her a quick hug and a peck on the cheek, and am immediately blinded by the frantic pop! pop! pop! of flashbulbs exploding all around me. Tara turns and gives me a sweet, apologetic smile.

'I hope you don't mind. I knew at least some of them would be here. Let's get to your car.'

I take her bags, and guide her off towards the car park, the paparazzi trailing after us, like a bunch of crazed lemmings.

'Are you in love, Tara? Is it true? Is Gregory Martin really the man you're going to marry?' The questions spatter across our path, like bullets from an M16, as we head towards my car.

I'm actually quite phased, but manage to keep up a good

front. The last time I was subjected to this kind of exposure was fifteen years ago when a mini-series I starred in premiered in the States. And then it was my party. This time it's definitely Tara's. And, little do I know it, but I've just signed up as this month's guest star on the classic, long-running English soap opera called: 'The Tragic And Flawed Love Life Of Tara Palmer-Tomkinson.'

August 12, 1974

Summer in the city. I'm doing my first season with The National Youth Theatre, and for the first time in my life I'm officially let loose on the unsuspecting and exotic world of London. I'm having a ball, spending most of my nights completely out of my tree at the local hang-out in Euston, hobnobbing with not just the rich bevy of hot young girls up for the hols from the provinces, but also ogling the likes of 'real women' like Vanessa Redgrave, Helen Mirren and others. Sexy, intelligent, artistically mature females in their prime.

One night I get a call from Rachel, a girl I've had the serious hots for since the first day when I watched her slink into the theatre in a mini-skirt, black tights and thigh-high boots. It's late: 1 a.m. But she's begging me to hop into a cab and come round. And we *both* know what for. I don't need any persuading. I pull on my Levi's, grab a bottle of Stoli, stick a handful of condoms in my back pocket, and sprint out the door.

Rachel's staying on Sutherland Avenue in Maida Vale, sharing a flat with four other Youth Theatre girls. I'm feeling hornier than a three-balled tomcat, and as the taxi speeds through the sticky London summer night, my brain is filled with an awesome array of visions of a orgiastic night ahead. Just me and the five young lassies, going at it hammer-and-tongs into the wee small hours, like a gang of sex-crazed coyotes.

To my surprise I find the ravishing Rachel sitting alone in the flat, wearing a thick, woolly tracksuit firmly buttoned up to the neck. I crack open the vodka, offer her a swig, and ask where all her fellow harem members have vanished to. She tells me she's sent them out for the night. She knew it was time for the big showdown between the two of us, and wanted me all to herself. I grin and casually toss off my leather jacket, take her in my arms and give her a kiss designed to make her go weak at the knees. The kiss works like a gypsy charm, but something inside doesn't feel quite right. Why is she all trussed up, like Nanook of the North, on a balmy London summer's night? And what's the real reason why her pals aren't there? I know at least three of them have got the hots for me something rotten. And the five of us had whiled away many a drunken evening in The Rising Sun, joking around about having group sex. My answer comes when the Stoli finally hits and she plucks up the courage to drag me off into the bedroom. As she closes the door softly behind her and I yank off my jeans, she turns to face me, wearing a weird expression that can only be described as resembling a calf about to be slaughtered.

'I've something to tell you,' she mumbles nervously, as she pushes me back down onto the bed. 'It's gonna sound a bit weird. But I find you incredibly sexy, and I have to do it before we go any further.'

My mind races frantically. What can it be? Is she bi? Into animals? Is she in some other way I've yet to come across otherwise perverted? Christ! *Is she a man*?

'It's my body,' she finally wails, wracked with misery. 'It's... horrible!

I pull away. Scratch my neck. Pause a brief moment for thought. A myriad surreal images sprint through my brain at the speed of light. First-degree burns? Leprosy? Scabies? Clinical psoriasis?

'Look. I clocked you the first day, Rachel,' I tell her, grinning with comic lechery in an attempt to somehow humour the poor girl. 'You've got a figure to die for. You're stacked like a loaded deck at Las Vegas. You show me one single bit of your luscious bod that's naff, and I'll give you a thousand pounds.'

She turns away. Her voice drops to a weak, fragile whisper. 'Oh, my God! You don't understand! It's all of me!' she mutters in terrible desperation. 'It's *all over me!* I'm... I'm covered in... *hair!*'

As this last astounding word is uttered, she suddenly whips off her tracksuit, and my eyes are assaulted by the weirdest sight I've ever seen in my life. This gorgeous, poor young girl is indeed blanketed from neck to foot in soft, downy cappucino-brown hair. She looks exactly like a beautiful overgrown version of a sexy female chimp from Regent's Park Zoo. For once, I'm at a total loss for words. I stare at her like I'm a mad anthropologist, examining the fuzzy woolliness of her 'hide' in bizarre fascination. My zany brain suddenly kicks into serious overdrive, as a series of absolutely ludicrous and heartless ideas dash between my blown synapses at warp factor three.

Should I get out the teacups? Maybe quickly pop out to the all-night store for a bunch of bananas? Roll over, beating my chest furiously with my fists, while screeching frantically, like a sex-crazed gorilla? String up a mini-trapeze over the bed and swing her gently to and fro as we fuck? How shall I describe this one to all my mates over a pint in The Rising Sun? 'Rachel's a real "animal"! It was a bit of a "hairy experience!" '

Rachel is clearly going through sheer bloody hell, and I quickly snap out of it, as I begin to see the tears welling up in her lovely Neanderthal eyes. I reach out, pulling her gently down onto the bed beside me. It's a bit like cuddling a softly, whimpering puppy, as I stroke her 'fur', slowly beginning to enjoy the odd sensation of what feels like heavy-petting with a yeti.

'You can't deal with it, can you?' she suddenly blurts out at me through the endless flood of tears. 'God, I understand! How could *any* man ever find *me* attractive with my clothes off?'

'Listen, Rachel, I... I think you're...' (I search desperately for the right word) '... gorgeous.'

The part of me that's still attempting to assimilate the shock is struggling. But I'm a bit tilted anyway. Something about Rachel's 'quilt' is definitely slowly becoming more and more appealing. I clamber on top of her, and blow me down if things aren't suddenly starting to kick into action! I'm just about getting back to my normal self when Woody Allen suddenly swims into my consciousness, and from nowhere I'm assailed by a fit of terrible, uncontrollable giggles.

'Look on the bright side, Rachel. You've got a lot of plusses for a man. Hell, at least he'll never have to pony up any serious dosh for you to buy a fur coat.'

The speed at which her paw makes fatal contact with my cheek is mind-boggling!

July 28, 1999

I've chosen to ignore both Haslam's pseudo-'shi-shi' suggestion re checking in for the weekend to a suite at The Savoy, as well as Tara's obviously tongue-in-cheek comment about me taking her to a bed-sit in Brixton. Instead I've followed my own classic master seducer's instincts, booking the pair of us into The Waterside Inn at Bray just outside London, conveniently a mere stone's throw from Heathrow. A romantic gourmet spot owned by the fabulous master chefs, the Roux brothers, it seems the ideal choice for a quiet, intimate, little *weekend-à-deux*.

As the sun streams in through the window, I lie there quietly for a moment, listening to the ducks quacking on the river outside our room, then turn over, see Tara asleep beside me, and blink rapidly, recalling the torrid events of the night before. It was a wonderful beginning: by turns tender, passionate and fiery. At one point Tara very amusingly insisted on hanging upside-down by her legs from the steel, four-poster bed frame wearing nothing but her saucy g-string, like some kind of sexy, exotic, upper-class female chimp! And later on the same naughty garment is adapted for use in what I'm to discover is evidently one of Tara's preferred sexual games. (Put it this way. I don't exactly travel around with a set of silk ropes in my pockets!)

But I somehow still haven't gotten rid of the strange sense of apprehension I'd felt the previous night at China White when Haslam had made the decidedly weird comment about me having 'started it' simply by giving Tara my business card, and that now I would have to 'finish it'. She's evidently already told most of the western hemisphere I'm going to marry her, before I've so much as had a chance to give her a bad dose of snog-rash. And there's a menacing sense of foreboding hanging over me about this rapid, potentially star-crossed affair. It's as if Murphy's Law is on the point of taking over my life to the nth degree, and for the first time in my life. I've somehow managed to enter the sexual lion's den minus not only my spear, broadsword and mace, but also my flame-thrower, bazooka, Kalashnikov and limitless supply of titanium-coated dumdum bullets.

But I must admit, I do love danger. And Tara's lovely, tilted wackiness is one of the very things I find so attractive about her. In a few ways we seem to be quite alike. She's obviously more than a bit of a risk-taker, just like yours truly. And an exciting, spitfire of a woman like that just happens to be one hell of a turn on for me. I've always believed that men and women who lead intense, passionate, sexually charged lives are almost always inevitably risk-takers. I know for a fact that I am.

For my own amusement I recently completed a quiz in *Time* magazine designed to reveal the tally of any given reader's innate 'risk-factor quotient' on a scale of 1–20. And wouldn't you know it, I came out with a set of the highest marks possible, which puts yours truly within a deliciously impressive category, alongside the likes of Ghengis Khan, Alexander the Great, JFK, Malcolm Forbes, Richard Branson, Churchill, Hitler, Orson Welles and, naturally, Bill Clinton, amongst others. Now I've no idea how many babes Ghengis, Alex The Great, or Hitler bedded in their primes, but I'm sure most of us must have a pretty good idea about the sexual score sheets of the rest of the bunch!

In *The Times* yesterday there was a fascinating article on people addicted to risk, claiming it has been proven beyond the shadow of a doubt that the unique character trait is linked to a specific gene labelled a D4 dopamine receptor (DP4), aka the 'novelty gene'. And just take a wild guess at whose picture I find there at the top of the front page? Right! T-P-T herself in splendid living colour, alongside Tony Blair and Rod Stewart! And while it's admittedly kind of hard to imagine our Tony fooling around in the front room of Number 10 with some overweight intern from Brighton and a rather large Monte Christo cigar, you can hardly picture ol' Rod-the-Mod being willing to play the role of second fiddle to yours truly!

Tara by now has awoken, and when Tara wakes up, it's definitely a case of 'all systems go'. Being a daft, insatiably incurable romantic, and there being no room for us at the inn the next night at The Waterside, I had arranged for us to drive down to another intimate and beautiful haven, Bailiff's Court in Sussex. But this idea apparently doesn't appeal to the young lady. Instead, she immediately wants to introduce me to her mummy and daddy at their plush country seat in Hampshire. We should drive to London, pick up a change of clothes at my flat, and hurtle off down the M3 to be there in time for supper.

I'm by no means sure I'm ready for this precipitous first meeting with Ma and Pa P-T, but as we've already established, for some strange reason my most precious and effective romantic fail-safe equipment appears to be severely malfunctioning, à la Murphy's Law. So I foolishly bite my tongue, instead deferring to the highly excitable young lady's heartfelt wishes. We drag on our clothes, I pay the bill, and within an hour we're back outside my

London bachelor pad.

And what do we find waiting for us there, camped, like a pack of rabid hyenas right outside my front door? Right! More paparazzi! A veritable shit-load of them! The blood slowly drains from my face, as I hear: 'Give us a smile, Tara! Come on! Just one snap of the happy bride-to-be!' As we trot up the steps, like a perfect junior 'Stepford wife', Tara turns, grabs my arm, and the flashbulbs explode again in a frenzy, just like a miniature version of one of the biggest nuclear tests on Bikini atoll.

December 15, 1977

It's the end of my last term as a senior drama student at RADA, and there's much cause for celebration. To begin with I'm told I'm among what is considered to be a 'golden group' of actors, a phenomenon they figure happens about once every ten years. But the real icing on the cake has been the extraordinary array of exceptional female talent! It's massive! It's prodigious! It's everywhere! And it's horny as hell!

As a rule I learn in later years by and large to avoid getting myself involved with either actresses or models. The majority of them are innately way too self-centered. They have to be. It comes with the territory. But at drama school I have found things to be different. The 'business' hasn't yet got its teeth into them, with its utter dependency on all that ultra-superficial schmoozing and socialising. The girls are still largely quite naive, and if they possess even the slightest modicum of a gift, they tend to be somewhat super-charged with a fabulous, insane sexual edge. It's enough of a turn-on to make a pimp out of the Pope. I have myself a very healthy slew of extremely close encounters with a veritable cornucopia of nubile young ladies aspiring to the thespian trade, but manage to get myself sexually stuck with one particular girl, now an extremely prominent British stage actress in her prime, when she confesses to me one dark, stormy Kilburn night her fundamental belief that she's somehow suddenly morphed into a die-hard, incurable lesbian in disguise.

Eventually boring of the interminable round of bonking with an ever-increasing, neurotic panoply of would-be bisexual divas, I finally hit what I consider to be major pay-dirt one sunny Monday afternoon inside the YMCA gym on Tottenham Court Road. I'm just on the point of finishing my final, punishing round of stomach-crunches, bicep-curls, bench presses and push-ups (technique numero quatro de seduction par excellence — keep fit, my lad! Keep fit!), when I spy myself a *particularly fit* young bit of stuff in a pair of *very* hot pants watching me intently from the far side of the basketball court.

I stride across, flexing my biceps eagerly, like I'm some kind of UK version of Sly Stallone in *Rocky*, strike up a conversation, and within minutes she and I are seriously deep-throating each other in the front seat of my Renault van. The sweet young lady's name, she tells me, is Linda. After Linda Lovelace of *Deep Throat* fame.

'This alone bodes well,' I think to myself, as I shove my little blue Renault van into gear and head off into the night towards her place. She's an extremely foxy young lass from Newcastle recently arrived in the big city along with her sister. The pair of them are 'dancers', and together they've just formed a fantastic new double act, Linda tells me enthusiastically. As she hauls me on inside the building, her even more gorgeous older sister lunges towards me, grabbing me ferociously by the balls, as if testing my sperm count. Then the pair of them immediately drag me upstairs, tear my clothes off, and begin the kind of raging assault on my body that can only be compared to the sexual equivalent of the Siege of Stalingrad.

Forty-eight hours later, when the mighty campaign is finally over, and all my brave, loyal troops are spread, dead as Dodos, across the wasted battlefield of Linda's bedspread, I ask her a question.

'Your act, Linda. What's it called?'

'Orgazmatraz!' she leers at me with a sexy, depraved smile. 'Do you like it, love?'

To my mum and dad's disgust, I decide to move in and set up shop with the pair of lovelies in their plush Islington squat. I consider it a rebellious, bold move, and my testosterone levels soar, as I begin to enjoy what was probably the randiest, most depraved year of my life. It was a bit of a naughty little dream come true for me. If I was thoroughly pissed off and had gone through a lousy day, I'd come home and Linda and sis would put on a splendid little show. And with these particular pair of nubile young strippers, the only audience member was me — *and* I got to shag them both something rotten afterwards!

Things begin to go a little sour one day when, by way of helping me take my mind off the intensity of my work, playing the leading role in Molière's *The Misanthrope*, Linda suggests I come and watch her 'work' one Saturday afternoon at some seedy little pub in the Balls Pond Road. It turns out to be one of the biggest mistakes I've ever made in my life. Let's just say the thin 'veil of glamour' that had initially so entranced me — i.e. the fact that I was finally living with my own personal harem — was brutally rent asunder in the course of an excruciatingly tortuous forty-five minutes, as I stand there at the back of the smoky public bar, choking on my pint of Worthington, watching Linda do for a bunch of sad, depraved seventy-year-olds exactly what she did for me in the privacy of our own bedroom, regular as clockwork, night after night.

Deeply depressed and sadly disillusioned, I do a stupid thing. I pick up the phone, make a date with a gorgeous piece of stuff from the year below me at RADA, have myself a major kabumba session and wind up giving myself the nastiest case of NSU I've ever encountered. For two dreadfully painful weeks thereafter every time I take a leak, it's like the very raging fires of hell themselves are streaming out of my sorry Adam's Arsenal.

Luckily, University College Hospital, which in those days had one of the best venereal disease departments in London, is just a hundred yards down the road from the college, and I pay them a very hasty visit.

So there I am, sitting, quiet as a deeply humbled lamb in the waiting-room, flicking my way through a tattered old copy of *Woman's Own*, when I suddenly spy an extremely familiar face directly sitting opposite me. At the time a very famous English classical actor, he's also, fortunately for young bugger-lugs, a man who just happens to be currently running one of the biggest and most prodigiously successful repertory theatres in the country. And yours truly has coincidentally just gotten himself an audition there the very next week!

So, what do I do? Right! Like the complete jackass that I am, I decide it might perhaps be in my best interests to strike up a friendly little conversation with the geezer.

Wrong!

'Hello! I recognise you! You're... '

'Um, yes. Yes I am. Ha, ha,' He nervously interrupts me before I'm stupid enough to blurt out his name.

'Great to meet you! Let me introduce myself. The name's Greg Martin. I'm a senior student at RADA, just down the street from here. I'm in my last term, and I've got an audition with you next week!'

'Really?' By now the poor man's looking *seriously* nervous. 'What a coincidence! And what a strange place to meet!'

'Yes! Isn't it!'

And I continue to rattle on like this for what must easily be a good fifteen minutes, like a total dork. I'm somehow completely oblivious to the fact the poor sod's squirming miserably in his seat the entire time, like some helpless fish suddenly caught on the line (the gentleman does, after all, currently have something of a pretty major television profile). Eventually, to his obvious and overwhelming relief, he's called inside by the nurse for inspection.

The next week, still blissfully clueless to the enormous professional blunder I've just made, I hop on a train up north to do my audition for the chap's splendid theatre. It's a gorgeous day, and I'm keen, confident, sober, and more than ready to completely blow them away with my two phenomenal speeches, one classical, one modern. But as the door to the auditorium opens and I stroll cockily on inside to speak my piece, I'm once again assailed by an insane attack of unadulterated idiocy. I see the poor man directly across from me, sitting with a group of his esteemed colleagues in the front row of the stalls, promptly open my big, fat mouth, and say: 'Hi there! How are you? Remember me? We met at... '

'Yes! Yes! Of course I do! Well, let's see what you've got to show us today, shall we?' is his rapid response.

Needless to say, I didn't get the job.

July 29, 1999

My arrival at the Palmer-Tomkinsons' country seat has been greeted with heartfelt warmth, and I'm immediately very graciously made to feel like I'm part of the family. Tara's siblings are markedly different from her. Santa, the elder sister, is a very grounded, classic English beauty bearing a slight resemblance to Princess Diana. She works for Ralph Lauren in London, and has recently married Simon Sebag-Montefiore (what is it with all these bizarre monickers most of the nobs are saddled with?), a prominent, highly intelligent journalist and historian. James, Tara's brother, works in the City and is married to a sweet young lady called Sos. The pair of them have an adorable little girl named Honour.

Mum and dad are both extremely pleasant and amusing, and treat me with great politeness and decorum. Patty, Tara's mother, is a very attractive, well-read and witty woman of grace and charm who clearly 'runs the ship'. Tara's dad, Charlie, is an eccentric, funny old guy who seems to enjoy spending the bulk of his time either playing tennis, or running around the 12,000-acre estate making sure all's running smoothly 'down on the farm'.

After dinner Patty and I while away a happy few hours together solo, getting better acquainted. She's a great talker, a charming lady with a marked gift for rapid, challenging repartee. As the evening wears on, I get to know a little bit more about the difficult background of the lovely Tara. It seems the drug thing kicked in during a particularly damaging relationship some years ago. He was hooked on coke. Tara had never touched the stuff. At the time she had a regular nine-to-five job working for the Rothschilds. The gallant chap apparently spent a lot of his time taunting her for not being able to keep up with the hectic pace of his social life. One night she relented and took her first hit of the fatal white powder. And the rest was history. It's by and large a sorry tale of an essentially nice, very lost, deeply insecure girl searching desperately for approval.

I'm a writer and actor as well as a film producer and entrepreneur, and I have a deep-rooted fascination for human psychology, as well as a fair degree of compassion. I don't recognise it at the time, but my in-built need to nurture and protect, borne from the peculiar circumstances of my childhood, is in the process of being fired up big-time. The fatal curse of having watched my dear old mum go through such crippling, painful shit as a boy is kicking in, and for a brief moment following this frank conversation with Patty, I manage to delude myself into thinking there's maybe something more to this odd, speed-of-light flirtation than I've hitherto allowed myself to imagine.

I've been divorced for six years, and have had more than my fill of an endless round of 'relationships' built on the unstable quicksands of immediate sexual fulfilment. In other words, this stupid twit feels he's maybe finally at that astoundingly mature point where he's ready to admit he's prepared for something more. Who knows? It could just be Tara. I excuse myself politely and turn in for the night.

Upstairs I find something very odd awaiting me. Tara's lying in bed, arms folded, a strange, sultry pout on her lips, like Scarlet O'Hara having just watched Rhett Butler vanish off into the Virginian night.

'What's up, love?' I ask cheerily, as I tear off my clothes and leap gamely under the covers.

'It's my mother. You've fallen in love with her, just like every other boyfriend I've ever had! I hate you!'

November 11, 1979

The torrid affair with exotic dancer Linda has surprisingly lasted, on and off, for almost a year, but the rot begins to set in when I nab my first primo acting gig playing the role of Edmund The Bastard (typecasting, it seems) in a production of *King Lear* at the Young Vic, travelling abroad for a week to Hong Kong. I've already had one major, disastrous fling during my spell with one half of the high-class nightclub act, 'Orgazmatraz', with a sweet, budding opera singer who had the disconcerting habit of shrieking forth an aria or two from Puccini's *La Bohème* every time upon reaching the point of orgasm. She had been devoted enough to yours truly to travel all the way out to the darkest depths of Worcester to witness me performing the leading role in Richard Brinsley Sheridan's *The Rivals*, only to find me 'performing' with an extremely foxy young actress in an entirely different manner one night in the dressing-room after the show. But it's the Young Vic trip to the Orient that proves to be the event that puts the final nail in the sexual coffin.

To begin with, let me explain that any exotic tour abroad for a young actor has to be one of the headiest experiences imaginable. You're suddenly let loose, along with a gaggle of your own unique and typically insane kind, fooling around playing make believe for the sheer blissful fun of it every night in some superb foreign locale. *And* you're being paid for it! It's madness! Brilliant, incoherent, innocent madness!

Lear himself is played by James Bolam of *The Likely Lads* fame — a great guy and a true, die-hard boozer extraordinaire — and the entire bloody company nearly gets thrown off the plane in Bombay due to the fact that the pilot has sent back a crate of champagne for our consumption since he's such an avid fan of dear ol' Jim's. What the pilot doesn't know is that Bolam is a truly serious drinker with a ferocious fear of flying, and both he and the actor playing The Duke of Gloucester have already indulged themselves in some major tanking-up inside the appropriately named Shakespeare's Tavern at Heathrow Terminal Three prior to take-off.

We calm Jim down and manage to dissuade him from topping the only very effete male trolley-dolly member of the cabin crew simply because the poor old love asked Jim to 'please stop swearing at me, and return to your seat, sir', and eventually land at our Oriental port of call safely in one piece. Arriving at our hotel, deliciously placed directly above the enticingly-named Red Lips Bar, I check into my room, discover the amazing qualities of 'Tio-Vite', a unique and truly awesome hangover cure stashed away in the fridge of every self-respecting Hong Kong hotel room, and then head off out into the night to prowl the dark, mysterious streets.

Chinese girls, I very quickly discover, are lovely, but by and large decidedly reserved and conservative, and for a day or two there seems to be the distinct prospect of very slim-pickings on this theatrical Far Eastern charabanc tour. Until one day I suddenly hit on the brilliant idea of picking up the phone and calling a woman whom I shall call Elfreda, a close old friend of my mother's whose wedding I had attended many years ago, as a mere infant. (I still have some old cinefilm footage of me trotting around at her reception in shorts and a dashing little bow tie!) It turns out, to my great excitement, that Elfreda has by now turned into a typical, forty-year-old 'colonial wife', whose hubby is constantly on the trot around the globe. She's therefore more than delighted to hear I've arrived in town totally out of the blue, and eagerly promises to come to the first performance of the show the next night at Kowloon Town Hall.

'And since you're single, Greg, I'm going to bring along one of my foxy female friends,' she says sultrily, dangling the fatal sexual lure right in front of this horny young devil's perpetually sniffing nostrils.

The show goes down a treat with the locals. There's a simultaneous Chinese translation of the play projected onto one of the walls, and we play hard on the dark ironic humour of the piece, which provokes a ripple of amused, but at times disconcerting Oriental tittering that tinkles around the auditorium every time one of us manages to hit the proverbial funny bone. At the end of the performance the cast are asked to line up, just like the visiting squad at Wembley, to do an official meet-and-greet with the latest incarnation of Bruce Lee currently bringing in maximum box-office returns to the Far East via Hong Kong-produced kung fu movies.

I've done my ferocious best to make both the chillingly choreographed broadsword fight with my brother, and Edmund's death at the end of the play as realistic as possible. But it's still Shakespeare, and it's a tough task faking your last, bitter gasp while spouting forth an endless slew of gorgeous iambic pentameter. So I'm kind of interested to hear what ol' Jackie

Chan has to say when he finally gets around to me.

Our Oriental Arnold shakes my hand in an intense, vice-like grip, then flicks his steely glare onto major high-beam, his eyeballs attempting to penetrate mine with the power of an ancient Zen Buddhist monk.

'Mr. Martin,' he says with a chilling look. 'Very good death! Excellent! But one thing, if I may say. In China, we like to *see* the *very moment* of death! Like this...!'

His hands suddenly leap up to his neck, seizing it with the raw, naked brutality of a starving vulture landing on a bloodied carcass in the desert. And he promptly proceeds to give himself the ultimate ultra-dramatic throttling, complete with an horrendously loud death rattle that would make the biggest English ham actors of the nineteenth century turn over in their graves.

It's a truly memorable, deeply silly moment, and I'm thankfully saved from what seems like an uncontrollable fit of overwhelming giggles by the appearance in the green room doorway of two very tasty-looking birds indeed in their early forties.

It's Elfreda and her ultra-nubile, very fit-looking gal-pal, Sarah. Ho, ho! I'm a happy chappie once again! The pair of them look as hot as a couple of exotic dancers from Stringfellows. And Elfreda, in particular, is absolutely smashing to look at — a veritable feast for my hungry male eyes.

Quick as a flash I hop out of my bloodied battledress and tights, and the three of us vanish into the steamy Hong Kong night for what swiftly turns into a fabulous, all-night session of drinking, dancing and debauchery in the Red Lips Bar. We make one hell of a threesome. And later Elfreda astonishes me by almost exhausting my sexual reserves. She's also *very loud*! Louder, I'm astounded to discover, than even the aria-spouting opera singer back in Worcester. And it's only by way of me turning on a bout of majorly serious charm with the night manager back at my hotel that I manage to prevent the three of us from being heartlessly tossed out into the pouring rain at 4 a.m.

The next day I decide to visit Elfreda at her home in the New Territories, the area backing onto the Chinese border, and am fascinated to find that she and her old man are apparently very much into 'alternative sexual practices'. Wife-swapping, for example, I'm very quickly told, is virtually completely *de rigeur* in these parts, especially amongst the ex-pats. The lovely Sarah is evidently much more than just Elfreda's pal. Elfreda has one hell of a treasure chest of very naughty toys and other sexual goodies stashed away in a room at the bottom of the house she very cutely calls 'the dungeon'. I borrow a wicked-looking set of handcuffs, and we're back in the sack once again in under fifteen minutes flat, this time the very fiery and wilful Elfreda plucking up the courage to ask me if I would please be so kind and bold enough as to give her the occasional, hearty slap or two as we screw.

'No problem with that one,' I'm thinking, as I bring my hand down firmly on her ample backside. Except that's apparently not exactly what the doctor ordered. She actually wants me to slap her on the face!

Now my hand has never made physical contact with a woman's face in my life. That sort of weird, kinky, violent stuff thankfully just isn't built into my DNA, and I find the request decidedly disturbing. A little passionate rough stuff, the odd bit of slap and tickle, is fine. But this dark, nasty business is simply not my game. It's a case of venturing into an area of perverted territory I just doesn't want to enter.

'Go on. Do it!' she tells me. 'Please! Just one good, hard slap on my face, as you do me!'

'Um, I'm... I'm not too sure about this, Elfreda. I'm a big lad, you know. I'd *really* hate to hurt you.'

'You won't! Go on! Do it! Please! Please! Please! It'll make me feel *so* good! Just like this!' And she takes her hand, slapping it extremely hard across my cheek.

'Fuck!' I reel, smarting from the stinging blow.

Kinky Elfreda giggles beneath me. 'It's wonderful, isn't it? C'mon! Now it's your turn!'

I shake my head. Heave a heavy sigh. 'OK. Alright. If you really insist. But if it hurts, don't blame me.' I raise my hand and bring it down firmly, giving her a crisp, hearty slap across the cheek.

She gives a shrieking wail of agony, suddenly cursing worse than a drunken sailor. 'Christ, Greg! You absolute bastard! I didn't mean *that* bloody hard!'

One final very amusing incident during my first Far East sojourn was to make a significant contribution to this volume of my sexual memoirs — a trip to the massage parlour for a classic all-over body rub. No journey to the land of concubines could ever be complete, I thought, without my sampling this tempting, enticing experience. So me and a few of my more adventurous mates from the *Lear* cast and I decided to hit one of the 'health spas' run by the convivial and accommodating owner of the Red Lips Bar one afternoon in the seedier part of the city.

I manage to pick myself out a veritable contemporary Shanghai Lil from the gaggle of gorgeous Chinese girls presented for our delectation, and within minutes I'm flat on my back buck-naked in a private room at the back, with the sexy little thing rubbing a sweet-scented sudsy soap-bath all over me. She's wearing nothing but a very saucy G-string. And for over thirty minutes I'm dispatched to a sexual nirvana, the likes of which I had not experienced since my foray into the enticing world of 'Orgazmatraz'. Then Lil abruptly stops.

'You want wanky-wanky now?' she asks me, ever so politely.

It's a bit of an abrupt transition. But I grin gamely, like the proverbial Cheshire cat about to devour a couple of dozen plump, juicy mice. 'Oh, yes. Yes! Yes, my love! Abso-fucking-lutely! That would be just... mmm puurrfect!'

'I come back in five minutes.' And she climbs off me, smiling sweetly, and leaves the room.

'Christ! This is it!' I think to myself, salivating, like a horny bloodhound. 'This is what I came for! The ultimate experience! This is going to be the fucking dog's bollocks!' For more than five interminable minutes I lie there, picturing in my lascivious mind the coming event, only preventing myself from drooling over the prospect, like some horrible, dirty old man, by reminding myself that 'to drool ain't cool'.

Five minutes later, right on the nail, the girl walks back in through the door, chillingly transformed, wearing a pair of dirty old jeans, sneakers, and a hairy, tatty sweater.

'You finish now?' is all she says.

July 30, 1999

The long-standing conflict between Tara and her mother is a place I definitely do not want to go. I don't like being handed the rap for someone else's problems, least of all those between a mother and daughter. Frankly, if I'd still had even one tenth of my brain cells functioning at their full capacity, I would have clearly seen enough of the proverbial warning signs by this point to have beat a polite but hasty retreat back to my wolf's lair in London. But I didn't. One reason was quite simply that I've been well-bred, and it's not in my make-up just to suddenly vanish from someone's world, like a puff of smoke. Another is that I have a fatal weakness in that I frequently fail to realise I've bitten off far more than I can chew. And apart from the fact that I was still very much entranced with the young lady, there was something in the nature of the challenge of the situation that frankly very much appealed to me.

The final very simple and straightforward reason was that, apart from the perpetual display of dazzlingly red flags my stupefied brain was doing such a fabulously bang-up job of ignoring, I found myself adoring Tara's family. I was actually having myself a jolly good time!

It is the tail end of that spell of incredibly hot weather we had in 1999, and I am pleasantly whiling away the days either lazing besides the P-Ts' very English pool, (i.e. lots of moss coating the sides and bottom, and an extremely rickety, dangerous-looking diving-board), or taking long, romantic walks with Ms. P-T in the family woods. The nights are typically spent either listening to Tara take a series of very amusing, but none-too-tuneful stabs at the family's new Karaoke machine, or slumped on the couch, watching videos.

Tara's brother is a budding amateur movie-maker and has done quite an impressive job recording one of the family's fascinating, very amusing summer jaunts on the Latsis boat in Greece with Charles, Wills, Harry et al. It's odd, watching your future king frolicking around in his speedos with the kids, just like our old uncle Frank on holiday at Blakpool! But also somehow mildly reassuring. They seem pretty much like 'normal' people, and the pair of young lads — Wills and Harry — are both utterly winning and charming. Everyone seems to be having a rare old time, and the boys obviously think Tara quite a trip. (Her mum described her relationship with them as: 'A bit like that of an elder sister.') But I must admit I'm a little shocked when we get to some footage of Tara going topless sur la plage and flashing her pair of lovely, ripe avocados at them. Young studly Wills looked more than interested, but poor little Harry just blushed and turned away.

No one in the room watching seemed in the least bit phased by the incident. And in the weeks to come I'm to learn why. Titillating Tara apparently has this habit of flashing her boobies at plenty of other folks besides a pair of adolescent Royal sons. She'll pretty much show them off to any family friend she considers worthy of their attention! And why not? They may be a little on the small side. But in my very studied and seasoned opinion, they're a smashing set of gazonkas!

It's later on, in bed, where the trouble seems to be brewing. It's not of the sexual kind. No, no: she and I are doing very nicely in that department, thank you. It's her Achilles heel: the mother/daughter issue again. I've been taught to be courteous to women. Yet every time I attempt to strike up even so much as a simple civil chat with Patty I'm clearly risking bringing the almighty wrath of Tara down on my head like a ton of bricks, and getting myself a thorough bollocking merely for being polite. It's as if there's some strange, deep-rooted rivalry between the pair of them. And principally, because of her youth, it's clearly on Tara's part. The same accusations made against me on my first night at Dummer are reiterated to me over and over again.

'You've fallen in love with my mother.'

I try protesting that I'm simply behaving politely to the sweet old girl, just as any bod would — particularly given the fact that Tara's told most of the entire civilised world she's convinced she's just met the man she's going to marry and hopefully spend the rest of her life with.

Nothing works. Tara's clearly convinced herself within twenty-four hours that I secretly fancy Patty. Oy Vey! There's definitely one hell of a weird psychological family dynamic going on here. 'Could this be the source of Tara's innate need constantly to seek so much public attention?' I later muse to myself, in a quiet moment of reflection.

I do my very level best to ignore it, but the thing once again rears its ugly head the following day when, at a tea party arranged for me to meet Tara's aunt from Argentina in London, Patty and Tara suddenly get into one hell of a spat because Tara's insisting on what seems to me to be the slightly excessive idea of having a snow-machine at the wedding she's evidently now planning for mid-December. (It's a bit nuts! Still, no one has bothered to ask yours truly.) Tara's anger with her mum is once again sent rocketing full-force in my direction when her cellphone rings, just as I ever-so gently remind her we should probably get going. There's a dinner planned that night with my father and his wife.

'Quiet! Can't you see my phone's ringing!' she suddenly snaps at me in front of both her mum and aunt, like an overindulged, spoilt child.

There's something not right with this picture, and I'm going to set it right. I'm a pretty patient type, particularly when I care for someone. But when really pushed, I've got a temper that can blow like a thermonuclear reactor. Still, I don't really like scenes unless they're clearly necessary. So I sit on my anger until we get into the car. I'm silently fuming inside, trying to figure out the right way to deal with this one, as we drive down the Fulham Road back towards Knightsbridge.

'What's the matter with you? Why have you suddenly gone so quiet?' Tara asks me, nervously.

'I'll tell you when we get back to my place. I'm angry with the way you just behaved. It was childish and rude. But I'm not going to get into a fight with you while I'm driving.'

But she definitely wants to drag it out of me, and eventually I decide to give it to her full-on, in cold, crystal-clear terms. 'You won't speak to me like that again, Tara. Others may tolerate it from you. But I won't. I'm not your servant, nor your dog for that matter. You're adorable. But from what I've begun to observe you're a girl who needs a straightforward, good, firm slap on the backside every once in a while.'

'What?'

'You heard me. It's very simple. You're a very sweet girl most of the time. I think you're fabulous. But frankly, you're spoilt.'

'That's it! Stop the car! You're an absolute bastard! I'm getting out right here!'

To her astonishment, I meekly oblige, pulling the car over to the curb in order to allow what I come to learn is the classic, full-blooded 'Tara drama' to unfold. She shoves open the door, tears flooding down her face, slams it shut in my face, and stalks off down the street straight toward Joseph presumably for some instant retail therapy in her cute pair of little pink Prada booties. I don't follow. Grown-ups aren't into those kind of games. But I do put a quick call in to her sister's husband, Simon Sebag-Montefiore.

'Well done!' he says cheerily. 'At long last we've got a man in our midst who's prepared to stand up to Tara! Don't worry. She does this kind of thing all the time. Santa and I will find her. You've done just the right thing! Cheerio for now! Can't wait to meet you!'

He's right. Within less than an hour she's back at my flat, repentant. Typically I find that sex after fights is always rather good. And with Tara it's definitely no exception. But as I lie there on my bed early that evening in post-coital repose, that odd feeling of trepidation is gnawing away even more persistently at the back of my mind.

And again, like a fool, I ignore it.

CHAPTER THREE

NEW YORK, NEW YORK

'Hickeys are like PG-13 movies. You think they're pretty hot stuff after being limited to G. But you never bother with them once you're seriously into R.'

Judy Markey, *You Only Get Married For The First Time Once* (1988)

'There was scarcely a woman alive, it seemed, who could resist the urge to haul men down onto beds, car seats, kitchen floors, dining-room tables, park seats, parlour sofas, or packing crates, entwine warm thighs around them, and pant in ecstasy.'

Russel Baker, *Growing Up* (1982)

October 17, 1999

A large part of this magnum opus is being written on a deserted little island in the Outer Hebrides. When you've lived through the kind of insanity I've experienced over the past months, it helps the necessary healing process to get the hell out of the lunacy of London, and off into the wilds for a spell. Sheep, stags, eagles, duck and snipe don't gossip, at least not to my knowledge. I spend many an afternoon staring out of the window trying to imagine one sheep whispering furtively to another: 'Have you heard the latest about Doris? She was shagged rotten last night by that caddish serial philanderer scumbag ram Hercules. Daisy's absolutely raving, fucking mad! She's starting a witch-hunt. All of us girls who've failed to nail him are clubbing together to have him run out of the pasture!'

Sexually, believe it or not, I've actually been at a red light. For a good few weeks my entire carnal equipment has shut down in one massive sexual general strike of epidemic proportions, as the overwhelming impact of what has clearly been a united front of 'Greg's been nobbled. What the hell! Let's all jump on the bandwagon and put the boot in!' took its toll. Now that normal conditions have been somewhat restored, I'm saved from going mad as a hatter and running out at night in frustration to ravage some poor, lonely sheep on the moors by the therapeutic presence of a gal pal. We're up here doing an extensive fix-me-up project on an abandoned hunting lodge she owns. A friend of her family is along for the ride, and the guy turns out to be a real Godsend, being as he is an expert in construction/renovation (as opposed to yours truly, whose rather rudimentary schooling in that particular arena frankly leaves much to be desired!)

The chap's recently been through a none-too-dissimilar experience from my own, having been slandered and pilloried by a slew of his 'friends' because the poor bugger's marriage is on the rocks and all of the above have chosen to don their honourable wigs and robes of judgment and firmly side with his soon-to-be-ex-Mrs. I watch him closely, feeling deep sympathy, as he tells me his sorry story over a few pints of velvet, several very strong screwdrivers and the odd glass or two of ten-year-old Malt, my heart frankly bleeding for the very obvious amount of pain the poor sod's had to go through. It's etched in every line of his face. A barrage of philosophical questions races through my mind, as I take another healthy slurp of my Highland brew.

What is it about us sorry human beings that makes most of us (a) love to gossip, like chattering hyenas, about the hard times of others, (b) frequently enjoy their pain, and (c) want to ravage and destroy any given man or woman so intensely if the feeling happens to so take us once we catch the smell of their blood on the wind? Is it some weird, depraved genetic throwback to the Dark Ages? Or perhaps to a time a great deal further beyond, in the deepest recesses of history — to the primitive days of Australopithecus or Neanderthal, maybe?

In my opinion scapegoats are fundamentally *very* convenient. The frantic moralistic bloodletting that follows the outraged cry of 'scumbag', 'cad', 'seducer' or 'bounder' somehow enables us to rid ourselves of our own dark side without the need to confront it within. 'Judge not, that ye be not judged.' Or, in the words of Eric Clapton, 'Walk a mile in my shoes.' Know why? Because whichever twit it is who's so quick off the mark to judge another is typically, in secret, riddled with a sackful of the very nastiness they're projecting onto the 'bad guy'.

Alright! Enough of my soapbox preaching, and on with the romp!

April 7, 1980

My spell with the *King Lear* company is followed by two very delightful gigs. The first is a season with the Bristol Old Vic; the second, performing the role of a deliciously sadistic Nazi in the world premiere of *Bent* at The Royal Court, with Ian McKellen, later *Sir* Ian.

The Bristol jaunt is particularly merry. There's quite an

esteemed company of thespians, including Pete Postlethwaite and a very young Daniel Day-Lewis in his first professional role. There's lots of boozing, bonking, partying and general fun, along with some delectably funny incidents both on-stage and off. During a performance of *Guys And Dolls* the actor playing Detective Brannigan falls fast asleep in his dressing room one afternoon during a matinée and completely misses his entrance, leaving Pete, myself and the other thugs standing on stage like a bunch of ham sandwiches at a Jewish wedding, with absolutely zero to say.

A nervous stir gets up in the audience. Then I have a sudden, brilliant idea. I turn stage left. 'Quick, fellas! Brannigan's coming!! Let's get the hell out of here fast!!' The rabble of gangsters follow me off into the wings, like a herd of terrified, stampeding rhinos, and we stand there for what seems like an eternity, making desperate, frantic gestures of 'Where the hell is he?' to the stage-manager. Brannigan still refuses to show so, having no better ideas, I lead the way back across to the other side of the stage with more cries of: 'Quick! This way! He's right behind us!' Nathan Detroit, Nicely Nicely, Harry The Horse and the rest have suddenly turned into a West Country English version of the Keystone Cops. We do this a few more times, until eventually the severely shaken, seriously drunken Brannigan finally shows up on stage, sweating like a pig about to be slaughtered, and trembling with the worst case of the shakes I've ever seen.

Later on, at the Edinburgh Festival, the same burly actor, now hopelessly miscast as the mighty Greek warrior Ajax in Shakespeare's *Troilus and Cressida* manages to fall off the stage during the famous duel scene with Hector before he's even so much as taken his sword out of its scabbard! It's one of those productions riddled with humorous, rib-tickling incidents. An actress swiftly gains a well-deserved reputation as the company's 'rusty old bike', and the night after I do the nasty with her myself,

I collapse on stage in a fit of helpless giggles, as I hear the actors playing the Greeks shout, 'The Trojan's trumpet!' and on walks the company bicycle!

Bent turns out to be quite a bit of a departure for yours truly, being as it is a play about the plight of homosexuals in the concentration camps. The company is consequently riddled with lads who do a lot more than just bat for the other side. I'm sure my audition was deeply impressive, but I'm equally certain the way dear old Sir Ian had pictured me looking in jackboots and full SS regalia did a lot to help me bag the role.

Thankfully there are a couple of other straight chaps in the cast, and avoiding both Sir Ian and the other devoted members of the fluffy brigade's seemingly ever-roaming eyes at all costs, the three of us make sure we constantly hang out together as a tight little unit backstage, talking very loudly in exaggeratedly deep voices, and vanishing to the pub next door at the speed of light, as soon as the curtain's down. Being an intensely ardent lover and pursuer of the female sex while having to undergo the alien attentions of a bunch of fellas whose inclination is decidedly otherwise is a decidedly disturbing experience for this devotedly heterosexual animal. But in a way, I suppose, it's a good one. For once, the predator gets to feel precisely what it's like to be the prey. It's a very weird sensation being such a die-hard womaniser while knowing some member of your own sex is lasciviously eying you up and down, wondering about the size, nature and shape of the enticing equipment stashed away inside your boxers.

Speaking of homosexuality, when people ask me if I have any stories about the strangeness of growing up around the phenomenon of the Beatles, I'm frequently reminded of my first brush with that other world, via something that happened one night at Abbey Road Studios. When I was told the story it was the first time I properly understood exactly what a gay man was.

There were always rumours about John Lennon having

possibly had an affair with his manager Brian Epstein way back when. God knows whether or not it's true. All I know is that Lennon was definitely the kind of guy who'd try anything once, if only for the experience. They certainly had a close relationship. But despite his prodigious talent and intense sensitivity, Lennon also had a side to him that could be very nasty at times if provoked. Like any great artist, he was a complex man. Oh, yes, if you caught John Lennon at the wrong time, *anyone* was fair game for the biting wit of his acerbic tongue!

Epstein was essentially a very lonely man and, it being the Sixties, homosexuality was still very much a no-no within many circles. By 1967 the Beatles had stopped touring, and his role as a manger was more or less over. What Brian would habitually do at this point at nights was to go to a club like Tramps until the place shut at around 3 a.m., and if the band was recording late into the night, bring a beautiful young boy he'd met at the club out to Abbey Road to impress the kid.

One night Epstein walked into the studio with his latest toyboy in tow. Lennon was on the floor recording a solo vocal track. My father, the engineer and the tape-operator were up in the control room. Epstein swanned across, leaned over my father's shoulder, pushed the button on the panel that enabled him to talk to Lennon and said, 'Johnny, I've just signed a contract with a publisher to write my autobiography. What do you think I should call it?'

Lennon looked up at the control room window, adjusted his famous flowerpower glasses, and without even pausing for breath, like a jaguar going straight for the jugular, shot back: 'What about *Queer Jew?*'

October 18, 1999

My mother calls me up in the Outer Hebrides, telling me some articles have just appeared in the *Daily Express* and the *Daily*

Mail apparently having bit of a go at Tara for doing an exclusive with *Tatler* based around the alleged notorious incident between her and Prince Wills in Greece when she's supposed to have put her hand down his swimming trunks. My mum's in a rare old mood. None too happy with having her boy defamed in public, and seriously disappointed with the way Tara and her family have turned against me merely because of all the nasty gossip, she wants 'justice' and is therefore understandably more than happy to see Tara apparently hoisting herself with her own petard.

Patty, I know from experience, would have been more than a little upset at Tara's decision to do the *Tatler* interview. She made it one hundred per cent clear on several occasions in front of me she wanted to see the end of those days of exposure merely for the sake of exposure for Tara, if only for the sake of the family. It strikes me as such a goddamn shame. Why does Tara still feel the need to do all this crap? There's so much there inside her just waiting to be correctly used. She's basically got a fabulous, winning personality. All it needs is focus.

Later on my sister calls to read me some of the *Tatler* article over the phone. There's more of Tara's jokey references to her now famous 'love rat' and a few silly comments about me supposedly having 'more wives than Henry the Eighth', as well as countless illegitimate kids scattered across the globe. She says she doesn't know if anything she's been told about me is true, but she is 'so exhausted by the whole thing', she doesn't want to waste her time hanging around to find out.

I'm at the point by now where some healthy degree of detachment is thankfully beginning to settle in, and at times I feel very sorry for her. She's naive enough to believe this absurd fiasco was really all about me — completely ignorant of the inherently nasty nature of a lot of her own kind. I'm afraid my name could have been Jesus H. Christ, and I guarantee you that some sick bastard or other out there would've sponsored the creation of some malicious fantasy about my having spawned more than twenty-five illegitimate kids via Mary Magdalene, plus hosted a series of seriously debauched gang-bangs with my twelve horny disciples in a back street Jerusalem brothel!

On a more serious note, I'm getting a little bit tired of seeing myself constantly referred to in print as the 'serial-philandering, scumbag love rat'. I just thank God my lovely little boy, Connor, is not here to witness it. What exactly is a 'love rat', anyway? You've got me. At one point recently Tara appeared on a UK television chat show saying she calls me a 'love rat' because I apparently 'ratted' on her. It doesn't make a blind bit of sense to me. Doesn't 'to rat on someone' mean 'to spill the beans'? What did I tell? To whom? No matter, just like Sam Goldwyn, Tara, I understand, has become somewhat notorious for her malapropisms. That too is a shame. She's actually quite bright, but at times it appears like a large piece of her grey matter's gone majorly AWOL. This, after all, is the girl who asked me not only what Tiananmen Square was famous for, but also what the capital of China was one day while we were driving through downtown Beijing. And who later called me from Anouska Hempel's yacht in Spain trying to find out which country Barcelona was in.

Let me explain the etymology of the 'love rat' thing as I understand it. In one of the super-lurid press pieces on me published during my ill-fated Hong Kong trip with Tara, the writer recounted a brief, silly affair I had a few years ago with Kara Noble, prior to the famous Sophie Rhys-Jones photo scandal. At the time Kara was one of the top DJs for London's Heart Radio. One of Kara's buddies on the morning show had met me and come up with a highly amusing description of yours truly as 'Thor, the Love God'. (At the time I did have a *lot* of hair, and admittedly looked a lot like Tarzan-meets-Conan The Barbarian.) The joke caught on and it very quickly became a regular feature on the breakfast show pretty much on a daily basis.

'Thor, the Love God!' the guys would intone sombrely, as loud, sweepingly romantic music played over the air-waves, followed by a stream of endless jokes about Kara's latest searingly torrid romance. 'I saw Thor yesterday morning, actually, Kara. Yeah, he was driving his chariot around Trafalgar Square. You know, that ultra-sexy one with all them really sharp swords coming out of the wheels!'

Then the whole thing went decidedly pear-shaped, as Kara clearly started to want to use who I was for her own personal publicity ends. My father was chairman of the radio station at the time, so she jumped right on the old PR bandwagon. That was the first time I found myself appearing in the *Daily Mail*'s venerable Nigel Dempster society column — as DJ Kara Noble's toyboy! She hadn't even bothered to consult me, so I very rapidly decided to pull the plug on the affair. The upshot was a short, brutal burst of on-the-air jokes from Kara and the boys for the next week or so along the lines of it all being over because she never had any idea where ol' Thor was 'going to park his chariot'.

In Hong Kong Tara, Tang and Lucy read the above-mentioned nasty piece and the three of them decided it was actually a very appropriate name for yours truly. (Perhaps this was to be considered flattering. I don't know. I suppose at the least it speaks highly of my elevated testosterone count.) Then, when we got back to London and the shit was really starting to hit the fan with the virulent Richard Griffiths article suddenly showing up in the *Mail On Sunday*, Tara apparently decided I was actually a 'rat' in disguise, hence the origin of the phrase 'love rat'. (Tara's favourite movie is *Breakfast At Tiffany's*. She likes to see herself as a sort of an latter-day English Holly Golightly. Remember? In the film, Holly travels to New York to meet and marry a millionaire, and constantly refers to the men she's met in Manhattan who've treated her badly as 'rats'.)

Here's an odd thing about men who are publicly known to

have had a lot of women: girls secretly adore the idea, and are somehow fascinated by it. I remember quite clearly the first time Tara called me a 'rascal'. She said it with a funny, very sexy smile, almost as if she actually found it very attractive. (Who knows? I was more than probably some sort of massive relief after the endless slew of super-rich, chinless-wonder, trust-fund baby Hooray Henrys she'd worked her way through.) It's like the weird way I've found women occasionally looking at me in the street since this whole thing erupted, if they happen to recognise me. As I mentioned earlier, while a good few of them admittedly stare at me in askance, as if I'm the latest incarnation of The Boston Strangler, others are quite definitely more than just intrigued.

In fact, I recently encountered a sweet young lady from the Seychelles and decided I might just as well inform her up-front precisely who I was, my fabulous newfound reputation, etc., as well as the kind of things her girlfriends might say about me once they found out we'd had the odd date or two. To my complete surprise what she came back with was: 'Oh, no. No, they don't believe a word of all that crap in the papers about you. All they want to know is are you as good-looking in person as you appeared in the photographs!' Ho hum! You never know with women.

I take a quick peek at today's edition of *The Times*. There's an article about some smooth-operating Arab con man who somehow managed to dupe Cher into believing he was in reality a super-rich oil sheik, or something. 'Now *there's* what I'd call an expert and truly accomplished "cad",' I think to myself. 'Better watch out, Tara, the *real* 'love rat' himself could easily come sniffing around your door in next to no time!'

Right on cue my cellphone rings, and it's the lass herself, having left another very bitter, sad message chock-full of another series of fantastical accusations. The grand finale is truly absurd. Apparently some fresh blue-blood wing-ding has now convinced both Tara and her entire family that I spent seven years inside a lunatic asylum. Ha! The only loonie bin I ever had the misfortune to spend any serious time in was called the city of Los Angeles!

January 21, 1982

It's always been one of my biggest ambitions to live and work in the States. I want to be a writer, film producer and director as well as an actor, and now I'm finally en route there, via a brief stop-off at my father's recording studio on the idyllic island of Montserrat in the Caribbean.

It's my birthday, and who should decide to show up on the happy day to check out the new facility, but Mick and Keith of the Rolling Stones. Mick has a lovely young Texan beauty called Jerry Hall in tow. Little do I know it at the time, but I'm destined to recall this very day some eighteen-and-a-half years later, when I'm invited down to Mick's fatal fifty-sixth on the Cap by Sabrina Guiness. I'm a strapping, healthy twenty-five years old at the time, and let's just say, ever so politely, that it's not just ol' rubber lips who has a well-deserved reputation for the proverbial wandering eyes!

Over dinner the conversation comes around to the tragic murder of John Lennon outside his Manhattan home just over a year previously. I recall a comment Paul McCartney made at the time *vis-à-vis* public sensitivity and the extremely unpleasant way a man's words and actions can today sometimes be twisted by certain unscrupulous members of the popular press in favour of a story. At the end of that fateful day, McCartney had been cornered by a bunch of journalists pressing him for a comment. Deeply distressed, the only words he could possibly muster were: 'It's a drag.'

Paul, a man who despite all the difficulties between them, loved his ex-partner deeply, was of course referring to the way the press kept on so relentlessly hounding him. The next day a headline appeared in a major English newspaper: 'Paul's only comment on John's tragic death — "It's a drag".' This conversation had profound reverberations for me years later during my own now notorious press debacle.

The studio is absolutely top-of-the-line. Probably the best in the world at the time. And while my dad shows M & K around the superb, high-tech facility, I do myself a little bit of seriously flirtatious chin-wagging with the gorgeous Jerry over a couple of very stiff vodka martinis. The result is that she slips me her private New York number surreptitiously under the table. She's definitely one hell of a babe, and I'm not only extremely willing, but able, and very hot-to-trot. The only drawback is I'm not too sure about the politics of the situation, particularly given that Mick's presumably here to do some kind of deal with my dear old papa about working at the studio.

Mick, Keith, Jerry and their entourage are spending the night on the nearby island of Antigua. And I'm spared from any of my trepidation at the prospect of a possible future dalliance with Jerry by my father's obvious disappointment as the group take their leave. Mick shakes his hand, shoots him one of those incorrigible Jagger grins and says:

'Lovely studio, George. But I'm afraid it's a bit too slick for us, mate. We kinda wanna get back to our roots right now.'

I wave a friendly goodbye, and that night enjoy a fabulous dream of Jerry and me doing the deadly deed together in a hot tub inside some incredible Manhattan penthouse.

August 11, 1999

David Tang, Lucy, Lauren Hutton, Tara and I are back at Tang's gorgeous Hong Kong apartment from our whistle-stop tour of Beijing, arriving to find the first slew of ultra-scurrilous press-clippings re yours truly freshly arrived from London. My initial reaction is mixed. On the one hand it's an extremely unnerving experience — completely unexpected. On the other it all somehow seems ludicrously funny. The title of the main article is 'Watch It, Girl!', and the basic gist of this initial full-frontal assault seems to be that Tara needs to be careful: her latest man may not be precisely all that he seems. Tang chooses to sit on the fence. And why not? He doesn't know me from Adam, and it's clear as daylight that both his relationship with the Palmer-Tomkinsons and his close connection to St. James' Palace mean a great deal to him. An erudite, witty, and highly creative businessman and entrepreneur, he's won a great deal of respect from me in the short few days that I've known him. He's generous to a fault, gracious, and has Tara pegged to a tee.

'No drama!' is his constant refrain. And after all, why should he rush to the defence of a man who might very well indeed turn out to be a consummate con man? Yet he's evidently decent enough to make a vaguely positive comment in my direction. 'Never ask a hero his past,' he says pointedly to Tara, as we sit down to another splendid five-course Chinese dinner.

Tara, however, is clearly more than a little disturbed by the press articles, and in the course of our meal leans over to ask me, in between snatches of her classic, very amusing party tricks, if it's true that, as was apparently mentioned in one of the newspaper articles, my father disapproves of my lifestyle.

'What lifestyle's that?' I ask her by way of response.

Lauren Hutton says nothing. She's a unique, mature individual who's spent long spells of time doing really interesting things, such as living with American Indian tribes, and seems more than a bit of a fish out of water amongst this crowd. While Lucy and Tara spend ninety-nine per cent of their time shopping, Lauren's quietly reading books on ecology, and the history of the indigenous peoples of some of the remotest parts of China. In other words, the lady clearly has a great depth of soul. At one point, while Tara's doing one of her amusing turns, I catch Lauren watching her. There's an expression on her face that reads: 'I like you very much, young lady. But you have a lot to learn.' After dinner she picks a moment to pull me discreetly to one side. 'Take each day as it comes,' is all she says.

Later, as I roll into bed with Tara this particular night she's obviously homesick and is on the phone with her mum on the Latsis boat in Greece with Prince Charles. I listen in to the tail end of her chat.

'No, Mummy, it's OK. We're having a great time. Greg's already had his first attack from the papers. But he's dealing with it. We're all fine.'

Tara's already told me she thinks we should probably do an exclusive interview on our brief, whirlwind romance with *Hello!* magazine as soon as we get back to the UK. 'They'll give us at least one hundred thousand pounds,' she tells me, excitedly. 'Isn't that cool? I'll split it with you.' I know if we did the interview it would make her mother very unhappy. If she wants to do it, I tell her, that's her business. But *she* has to take the flack with her mum. Next thing, I hear her say:

'Mum, if Greg wants to tell the story of our engagement to the *Sun* or some magazine, that's his decision. I can't stop him.' This is not good. It's like she's already setting me up to be the fall guy with her mother. I have a brief chat with Patty, in the course of which, referring to all the nasty press, she asks me, in what I find to be a refreshingly reassuring, cheerful tone:

'What have you done then, Greg? Killed someone?' Then I hang up the phone. I turn to Tara.

'Tara, I'm afraid I overheard some of your conversation with your mum. You can't do that to me. If *you* really want to do the article with *Hello!*, then I'll do it. But *you're* the one who's going to have to admit to your mother that it was *your* idea. I like your mum, and I basically agree with her attitude about you and the way you should conduct your life. I'm not going to sit back and take the rap for you. I've already told you, I don't give a toss about all that publicity crap.'

She smiles at me sweetly. 'Don't worry, darling. I'll take the blame. I just want Mum to know you're your own man. And that when you do have something to say, you'll say it.'

March 1, 1982

I've been in New York one month, and I'm having the time of my life! Jerry Hall hasn't been in town yet, but ask me if I care! Randy old bugger-lugs has been let loose in one of the wildest, most exciting towns on the planet with money in his pocket and a lot of healthy sperm in his testicles! It's the Reagan era, when the confidence of the country is at an all-time self-deluded peak, and oodles of excessive fun is the name of the game in the Big Apple. Via a connection I've made back in London I'm being pursued by a talented manager who's set me up with one of the top agencies, and within three short weeks I've managed to land my first job doing an off-off-Broadway show. It's a slick production of an English 'street' play. And amongst the cast is a talented young American actor — a lad called Kevin Spacey.

Spacey hails from California, but manages a killer cockney accent. The cast has a ball, and the theatre is packed every night. One of the black actors in the show decides to give us a very entertaining time one evening after the performance when we travel the New York subway system until 4 a.m. just for kicks. At one point an old bum gets on the train, sits down next to us, and my newfound Harlem-based pal performs what I consider to be an awesome feat. For the next sixty minutes he hosts a non-stop, hilarious conversation with the bum using only three expressions: 'Right on!', 'No static!', and 'I hear you!' I'm deeply impressed, and am left wondering what the English equivalent might be. Probably something like: 'Yeah!', 'Right!', and 'Fucking straight!'

Kevin is a real blast to hang out with — incredibly funny

and, like me, quite an accomplished mimic. We spend one hilarious evening together in a Soho bar creating an imaginary conversation between Dustin Hoffman, Johnny Carson, Richard Burton and Laurence Olivier. But another member of the cast for some strange reason seems a little out of the loop. He definitely has a hard time relating to the female gender. Eventually I clock what's probably going on with him as I stroll homeward one drunken night with his best buddy after closing down another Soho bar and he suddenly grabs me and literally tries to stick his tongue down my throat.

It's the first, and I'm glad to say the only time in my life I've ever been physically accosted by a gay man, and I don't exactly take to the experience like a proverbial duck to water! Summoning the strength of ten men, I shove the lad off me, and ram him back up against a brick wall.

'Who the hell do you think you are?' I ask him.

'What does it look like?'

'It looks like you're what some of the more unsavoury types I know back home would doubtless call a bottom-bandit, that's what!

'Correct.'

'OK. Well I'm sorry to have to tell you that you're barking up the wrong sphincter, my old son! This man's bod is strictly for the birds, if you catch my drift. To put it slightly more succinctly, I'm about as straight as the Manhattan grid system!'

The next day I inform Kevin of what happened the night before. He just smiles that spooky, all-knowing smirk of his, and says, in his inimitable Johnny Carson voice:

'That's cool. One word of advice, though. If I were you I'd watch my back in the dressing-room.'

The off-off-Broadway gig with Kevin is followed by a couple of highly entertaining theatrical divertissements — one in New York, and the other at the Tyrone Guthrie Theatre in the wildest, frozen depths of Minneapolis-St. Paul. The job in Manhattan is the US premiere of a rock musical called *Lennon*, a show that subsequently had a very successful run in London, about the life and times of the famous ex-Beatle. For some odd reason one of the roles I'm asked to play is sweet, little old Ringo, while a bald fella who doesn't bear even the remotest resemblance to my dear old man is given the task of impersonating him!

The show is produced by a man called Sid Bernstein, a tubby little Damon Runyon-esque character, famous for two things: (1) he produced the famous Beatles Shea Stadium concert, then subsequently turned down the chance to represent them in the States; (2) whenever he gets nervous he apparently grabs his assistant and embarks on a two-hour, non-stop shopping spree around the best pastry shops in Manhattan.

My dad's in town for the Grammy Awards and pays us a visit during rehearsals. There's a very interesting expression in America: 'Even the President has to shit!' It's a bit odd when you know your old man as just a regular kind of guy with the same basic set of problems we all have, and yet he's treated like some kind of an icon. The cast loved the time he spent with them. And he apparently thought the music sounded great. *Lennon* turns out to be a great show, but for some reason the box-office is not good, and the night before the thing's due to close, a desperate Sid tells us he's decided he's going to go on stage to make an announcement.

'Ladies and gentlemen,' he intones sombrely, as the curtain falls. 'I loved John. *We all* loved John. This show is a tribute to his life. This talented group of magnificent young performers have put their very hearts and souls into this piece because *they* loved John. Now I'm not gonna deny it. There have been problems with *Lennon*. The critics were not kind to us. The reviews did us a lot of harm. But I'm convinced in my heart that if we can somehow keep this show open just one extra week, we'll be home free, and *Lennon* will run forever. So I'm gonna ask each and every one of you to put your hands in your pockets tonight, and please, for John's sake, give us whatever spare change you have to keep... '

Sad Sid's voice is suddenly drowned out amidst the furious wail of catcalls and cruel jeers from the assembled audience. I cringe, along with the other cast members, as a half-eaten ice-cream cone hits him right on the nose. Poor old Sid begs the audience for money one more time, then beats a hasty retreat back into the wings, as a massive barrage of empty popcorn bags is suddenly hurled at him from all sides. Sid consults quickly with his PR strategists, then tries a final, last-ditch attempt to salvage his investment just as the cast are about to leave the theatre. We're asked to assemble in the auditorium.

'Guys, gals,' Sid begins in a mellifluous voice of ultra-sincerity. 'The PR fellas and I have come up with a plan. We're just not gonna let this baby die. No way. Tomorrow night is officially our last performance. We want you guys to stage a 'mock bed-in' protesting the closing of the show, just as John and Yoko did for world peace in Amsterdam all those years ago. It'll be great copy. We'll get all the press here, and... '

The stage door slams loudly behind us, as the entire cast troop out of the theatre and out into the dark Manhattan night.

Some people never learn. Lennon must've been turning in his grave.

The jaunt to Minneapolis was a different kind of event entirely. For one thing the Guthrie is a major regional theatre in America, and I had been assigned the monumental task of playing the title roles in both *Hamlet* and Ibsen's *Peer Gynt*. For another, I had to endure the entire run of both plays while having the worst case of pubic lice I could ever possibly imagine. It wasn't my first encounter with the dreaded critters called crabs. But it was by far the most awkward to handle.

Generally, if you've caught a nasty dose of these particularly irritating, horrible bastards, you can afford yourself the occasional sneaky scratch every now and then without anyone around you clocking your frantic wrist action. It's a different matter entirely, however, if you're on stage in front of more than two thousand people night after night, attempting to pull off a pair of the most notoriously difficult and challenging roles in the entire canon of classical dramatic literature.

As Hamlet I used simultaneously to dread the soliloquies, (particularly 'To be, or not to be' because it required so much goddamned stillness and silence!), and long for the mad scenes and the fights, when I could finally rant, rave and scratch away to my heart's content. With *Peer Gynt* there was a built-in 'rest area' to the piece. The scene in the troll kingdom, where Peer is so desperate to be accepted by all the dirty little Nordic beasts, who are itching away like scabrous, flea-ridden cattle anyway, that the odd hearty rub in the area of the groin by yours truly was simply seen as part and parcel of young Peer's frantic quest to be part of the family.

I had figured there was no way in hell I was going to get away with it scot-free, however. Not with the intensity of my condition and the rather lengthy time I faced alone on stage in both productions. While in a sense it worked to my distinct advantage with certain female members of the audience whose eyes were of necessity frequently drawn to the area of my crotch (although I was hardly in a position to capitalise on this solitary plus after a performance due to my helpless state — after all, a true gentleman would never dream of passing on such a venomous condition to a lady!) the critics, as anticipated, had a veritable field day.

'Mr. Martin gives an intense, truly heartfelt rendition of the tragic tome,' one local columnist wrote. 'His Hamlet is magnificent. By turns beguiling, mad, passionate, compassionate, and deeply virile, he manages to penetrate right to the very core of the student's torment. One wishes, however, his performance were slightly less mannered. Mr. Martin's obvious and constant need to draw the attention of the female members audience to his genital area, for example, one finds a little distracting and frankly unnecessary.'

A major US nationwide periodical was slightly less tactful and kind, particularly in their review of my Peer. 'Gregory Martin clearly has the potential to develop into a mighty classical actor. One more than capable of scaling the dizzy heights of the great male roles of world drama in years to come. His Peer is powerful, rich, deeply moving. Yet why does he insist on constantly touching his own groin throughout the play? It is an odd, disconcerting choice for an actor to make as a part of his character's physical business. Mr. Martin is, after all, playing Peer Gynt. Not Elvis.'

The way I caught such a nasty, relentless case of the dreaded little vermin was none too pleasant either. At least, had I been single, as on other occasions, I might have possibly had myself a bit of fun in the process, perhaps picking up the pests as a result of a merry tumble in the hay with some actress playing a buxom young serving-wench backstage during a dress rehearsal, for example. Sadly, for me, that was not to be. My bird at the time, who had joined me briefly from New York for my six-month term of penury in the frozen Midwest, had flown back home for Christmas, and had very sweetly brought the little sods back with her as a rather unusual New Year's gift. When I cross-examined her, she confessed she'd 'gotten lonely' one night, and had wound up screwing some kid on a beach on Maui, while yours truly was freezing his poor nuts off in Minnesota. Nice!

August 13, 1999

We're out at David Tang's Hong Kong country retreat, and the unnerving momentum and bizarre ferocity of the press articles regarding yours truly are faxed daily to us from Mr. Tang's London office is slowly growing in intensity. For the first time I'm forced to contemplate the chilling possibility there may be 'something rotten' in the state of certain English society types whom I may have unwittingly pissed off by becoming involved with the likes of a girl like Ms. Palmer-Tomkinson. But who are they? Who might nurture the degree of implacable hatred towards me that would fuel such a vicious attempt at character assasination?

I remember Richard Burton, with whom I starred opposite Faye Dunaway in the CBS mini-series *Ellis Island*, recounting to me one afternoon on the set the incredible public uproar over the start of his notorious affair with Elizabeth Taylor during the filming of *Cleopatra* in Rome. 'How the hell did I know the woman was so bloody famous!' he reportedly said at the time. 'She knocks Kruschev off the front page!'

I'm not an insensitive man, and there can be little doubt there's a decidedly weird vibe building within the Tang Hong Kong stronghold. It's as if they're slowly starting to actually believe all the garbage. Tara's mood, in particular, has very clearly undergone a massive sea change.

But then, sadly for me, so have some of my feelings for her.

To start with there's the frantic, non-stop shopping. Now I know a lot of girls love to while away a lot of their free time running from one latest fashion boutique to the next, and I've no particular objection to a girl wanting to indulge herself in this arena. As I say, love of shopping seems to be almost universally endemic to the female of the species. (A current gal pal, who happily seems to be more than a million miles away in character from the classic 'wallet-piranha', gets turned on by going into

DIY stores!) But there comes a point when even the most patient and understanding of men gets thoroughly pissed off!

My own gasket finally blows one rainy afternoon when Tara, egged on it must be said by Tang's girlfriend, Lucy, manages to find herself what is apparently the most expensive designer top of all time. I tag along dutifully after her, like a complete idiot, to the Amex office so she can access her account and see if they'll maybe extend the credit line on her Platinum Card. It's no go. She then turns to me, staring at me with her puppy-dog eyes, and asks me if I'll please 'loan' her the money.

Now, it's clear as daylight to me it's a test. If I cough up the money, buying the dreadful, ludicrously overpriced piece of schmutter for the little lady without so much as asking her to pay me back at a later date, then I'll pass with flying colours, and I'm on to the next level in the non-stop Super-Nintendo version of 'Are You Man Enough (read Rich Enough And Stupid Enough!) To Keep An It girl?' If not, then it's all over, and I might as well just hop on the next Virgin flight back to Heathrow without so much as a 'how's your father'!

I decide to call her bluff, telling her I'll give her the money if she buys me something nice in return. She naturally agrees. What else can she do? But she's obviously not a very happy camper. I'm not playing the game. At least not the game she's used to playing.

The next item on my agenda that's a cause for concern as far as my own feelings for her are concerned is as follows. Tara had tried to explain to me during our first few days together that she has a weird habit of pushing away anyone who's nice to her. While admitting to myself that could be quite a problem, I basically read it as a simple, clear-cut case of insecurity — the 'I don't really believe I'm any good inside, so if you treat me kindly I'll reject you' syndrome. In a way it probably hails from roughly the same area as 'the shopaholic syndrome': 'I don't really believe I'm worth anything. There's not all that much to me in reality. So

I'll keep on giving myself an endless feel-good fix via my poor, exhausted Amex Platinum Card.'

The trouble was things were beginning to get astonishingly personal. While on the one hand proclaiming her undying love at night, she'd then suddenly turn around the next morning and assault me with a veritable litany of physical insults.

'Are you aware your jaw clicks when you eat? You need surgery. From now on I'm going to call you Love God the Clicker.'

'Your teeth are really foul, darling. What's living in there? Do you ever bother to brush your tongue?'

'You should dye your hair. You'd look much more handsome as a brunette. And by the way, I'm not overly fond of those love handles.'

Eventually things reach a peak when at 3 a.m. one morning in our bedroom I find myself in the middle of one God Almighty row. Not good! Three weeks into our relationship and we're arguing like George and Martha out of *Who's Afraid Of Virgina Woolf?* Tang's insisting we stay on a couple of days longer. But Tara's decided she's had enough and wants to go home. That day Tang's secretly pulled me to one side, telling me in no uncertain terms that I have to convince her to stay. So I'm caught. The guy's our host. We can't really say no. It's only two days. Surely that would be impolite to the very man responsible for putting her through rehab, and such a generous, friendly chap, to boot. I tell this to Tara, and she explodes.

'You don't give a fuck about me!' she screams, dramatically. 'All you care about is David! I'm sick of watching the way you suck up to him!'

'What the hell are you talking about? I was simply trying to be polite!'

I decide I've finally had enough and figure it's probably about time I took a gentle pop at her weird stream of personal criticism. I know Tara hates one thing about her body. Her ankles. She's obsessed with what she considers their ugliness. That's why you always see her in boots.

In truth they're not quite so bad. And given the rest of what the Good Lord has given her, she can't seriously have grounds for complaint. But be that as it may, I'm by now pretty much fed up to the back teeth of her constant harping on what she sees as my vast array of physical imperfections, and decide it's time I finally gave it back to her in spades.

'Tara, I've said it before. And I'll say it again. In my humble opinion, you need a good smack on the backside. I want you to feel exactly what it's like to have someone who claims to adore you constantly insult you directly to your face. Guess what? *You've got fat ankles!*'

'Aaagh! You bastard! I hate you!' she screams at me, like a raging banshee. And she picks up a hefty Prada bootie, hurling it straight across the room at my face. It misses. Touché, pussycat!

I give her a big, cheesy grin, the Rhett Butler in me suddenly coming triumphantly to the fore.

'Frankly, my dear, I don't give a damn.'

Softly, I close the door behind me.

CHAPTER FOUR

L.A., SEXUAL INSANE ASYLUM (PART ONE)

'Californians try everything once.'
T. J. MacGregor, *Kill Flash* (1987)
*'Show business is like sex. When it's wonderful, it's wonderful. But
when it isn't very good, it's still alright.'*
Max Wall

October 19, 1999

As I mentioned earlier, the level of absurdity the Chinese
whispers about me ultimately reached would have been truly
hysterical, if it hadn't been so damaging at the time. One of my
favourite stories was the one about the anonymous, well-
connected young Miss from Paris I'd apparently asked to marry

me just weeks before meeting Tara. Evidently I was supposed to have already met her mum and dad, bought the ring, set the date — everything!

OK. So if this scumbag is so into preying on wealthy, vulnerable, well-connected women, why the hell didn't he marry Ms. French Anonymous, taking her right out for all she's worth? Come to that, why didn't he stick with dear Sabrina? After all, she's higher up on the '*Tatler*'s 250 Most Wanted Party Guests' list than Ms. T-P-T these days!

No one, it seems, ever bothered to check into my past properly. Sure I've had numerous affairs with a lot of lovely ladies in my time, some of them very famous. But I've never lived with any of them. Let alone married them! In fact, if the truth be told, with most of them it was typically me who wound up picking up the tab!

Now someone was having a ball out there at both my and Tara's expense, mercilessly toying with the unfortunate onslaught of insecurity that followed her notorious aborted engagement to Matthew Freud Communications PR guy, Kris Thikier.

November 29, 1983

I'm submitted by my agent at ICM for an audition on a movie being directed by Susan Seidelman called *Desperately Seeking Susan*. The star of the picture is an unknown singer/dancer/actress who, I'm told, is 'just about to break', called Madonna.

The audition is held in a warehouse in Greenwich Village, and as usual when I arrive a little late for a meeting it turns out I perform much better than usual. Experience has taught me it's better not to think too much before an audition. It kills all sense of spontaneity. The role I'm auditioning for is that of Madonna's boyfriend — a bit of a dork as a character (what bloody idiot out there just chimed in with typecasting once again?) — and at the start of the scene, which I'm reading with the lovely lady herself, I'm supposed to surprise her somehow. So I cheerily decide to sneak up behind her, and give her one Godalmighty whack on the bum!

Though my defence is quite simply that the gesture is entirely in keeping with the character, Madonna clearly's none too pleased with the impact of my right hand on her superb buttocks. But she grits her teeth like a true pro, and carries on with the scene. I'm asked to hang out for a few minutes after the audition, and I put my feet up in a waiting room with the lovely Ms. M herself. She spends most of the time on the phone, chatting away to her agent and various gal pals, and gives absolutely zero indication of any interest in yours truly.

Eventually I'm told I can go, and the next day learn that although they loved the audition, they'd decided to go with some guy a little shorter and uglier than yours truly.

'Oh well, that's that,' I thought to myself, and began preparing for the next round of meetings I had the following week. 'I fancy that Madonna chick, though, whoever the hell she is,' I later mused, as I supped my Bud in the local tavern. 'She seems pretty talented. I wonder if she's going anywhere?'

About two weeks later, I'm hanging out in a seedy little theatre dive in the Village one night, when I spy a very cute piece of stuff sitting at a table across the room from me. As I watch, another young lady joins her from the bar, and to my surprise I recognise her as Madonna. (In retrospect, I'm to realise this was about the time of the 'Material Girl' single. Call me silly, but it was very early days for the lass, and I simply wasn't clued in to Madonna's 'Village scene'.) To cut a long story short, we recognised each other, got talking and, away from the pressures of the audition scenario, quickly established a very strong mutual kabumba report. Madonna back in those days was already establishing her reputation as a wild one in her social circle, a description she well and truly deserved. That night was directly pre-Sean Penn. Her hair was red, and all in all her whole image was that of the quintessential female rebel. We quickly adjourned to an East Village club where copious amounts of booze were imbibed, and then headed for home and a nice warm bed.

As I mentioned earlier: 'In matters erotic, I'm straightforward, not exotic.' In other words, I'm basically far keener on a simple, regular, one-on-one passionate encounter with a lady without any of the frills and frippery of the world of kinkiness, so this steamy close encounter with The Material Girl, although not my first encounter with handcuffs, is actually my initiation into both a veritable orgy scenario as well as into the utilisation of some of the other more far-out tools of the sexual trade! And, by God, did I ever enjoy it! Put it this way, once Madonna locked the cuffs around my wrists, I would have happily followed her to sing-sing, Wormwood Scrubs or the fiery depths of Dante's Inferno. Later on that night there were three other of her incredibly willing and gamely adventurous female pals who chose to join us in what became a feast of sexual passion and game playing. Every tool and costume in Madonna's considerable erotic war chest was employed. Madonna was a veritable virtuoso! I can recall not closing my eyes until mid-afternoon the following day!

Madonna in her business life is a fascinating combo — a brilliant artist with the soul of a clever, driven businesswoman. Much like that other great diva of music and movies, Barbara Streisand, she's creative, but practical and grounded. For her public that's a large part of her sensual allure. And, take it from me, the same holds exactly true, according to my memory, of her extraordinary and fascinatingly diverse abilities between the sheets! The night seemed endless, yet passed within the twinkling of an eye, such was the fervour of physical passion between us. Madonna, much like yours truly, proved to be a relentless sexual athlete with the stamina of a marathon runner. In addition, she had the gutsiness of a true-born sexual connoisseur. She loved to experiment.

Sadly for me, the fabulous night was never to be repeated. Unknown to me, a highly gifted young man called Sean Penn was already hovering in the wings of the fabulous diva's life, and her career was on a roll. Madonna, forever incredibly driven and disciplined, was also in love. She vanished, like a will o' the wisp, from my life, just as she had so suddenly appeared. It was one brief, torrid night, and chances are the lovely damsel today doesn't even remember it. But yours truly will never forget. Take it from me, and if you don't believe it take a peek at the wonderful dangerous, highly-explicit tome she published a few years ago entitled *Sex* — the public image of Madonna is the reality. With this gorgeous, gifted, deeply spiritual lady, what you see is definitely what you get!

August 18, 1999

It's one of our last days in Hong Kong and Tang has very kindly offered to take us all on a day trip to Macau, the old Portuguese colony. It's hot as hell, and although Tara has made all the right noises about the proffered visit to what is actually quite a fascinating place, it's virtually impossible for her to conceal the fact that she'd secretly much rather be out shopping back in Hong Kong with Lucy.

On the ferry across I get chatting with the beautiful Lauren Hutton again. She truly is an extremely interesting woman who's clearly lived. The unique vibrancy of her inner world is obvious if only from the fact that she's still so beautiful in her mid-fifties without having had so much as a single piece of 'work' done to her physique. We share a lot of interests: American Indians, ecology, shamanism. I can tell Lauren's recently embarked on some kind of spiritual quest of her own design. She's all in all a thoroughly great combo. Feisty and tough on the one hand, she's also sensitive and kind — the type of woman you can instinctively tell would be at home dining in a palace with the King of Buthan, or slumming it inside a tent pitched somewhere in the middle of the Sahara Desert.

What makes her of even more interest to me now, given my current odd situation, is that she's clearly once been where Tara is now, but on a much larger scale. She's lived through being somebody based entirely on your looks alone, and lived to tell the tale. Lauren was one of the first supermodels. Yet she's managed, in her fifties, to transform herself into a fascinating, sensitive woman of the world.

I ask her what she meant when she told me the other day to 'take each day as it comes'. She looks across at Tara chatting away with Lucy, the pair of them flipping through the latest copies of *Hello!* and *OK!* magazines, and from the compassionate expression on her face I can tell she sincerely hopes that Tara is one of those girls who, like her, will one day be able to make that transition.

'Listen,' she says to me softly. 'I don't know you. But I can tell you're a good man. Forgive me, but from what I can see you've managed to land yourself in a bit of a mess. It may take you a while to get out of it, and it may be a little messy. But you don't belong there, and, believe me, you will get out.' She smiles. I give her a friendly little peck on the cheek and return to my seat.

We arrive in Macau, grab a quick bite of lunch, then head out to the older part of town. It's a truly charming place. An old colonial haven slowly being eroded away by the relentless influx of casinos and ugly, ultra-modern hotels. Tang suggests a visit up to the three-hundred-year-old remains of the original Catholic Mission. It's quite a sight. But when Tara and Lucy begin to whine about the heat (read: 'We're bored and want to go shopping!'), Tang relents, and we return to the port for a truly spectacular helicopter ride back across to Hong Kong. That night we enjoy one final, fabulous meal chez Tang, then retire to bed.

By now the joy of sex has pretty much fizzled away. Tara flicks off the light without so much as a 'good night'. The next day we're leaving anyway, and I'm frankly glad of the chance of a good night's sleep. But I don't sleep so well. And the next day the weather gets worse.

On the way out to the airport Tara decides to throw what I've come to call one of her 'pouty moods'. It's her own version of the classic silent treatment, except that with Ms. T-P-T there's the occasional snappy comment thrown in for good measure. Once we've said our goodbyes and passed through immigration and on into the departure area, I ask her kindly to tell me what it's all about. She tells me it's apparently because I refused to make love to her last night.

'But you clearly weren't interested,' is my very simple, direct response.

Tara's reaction is to flounce off on another shopping fix, buying herself yet another silly, ridiculously overpriced Prada handbag. And when she returns, and I suggest that she maybe might want to back off a bit on the purchases since apparently she's currently so strapped for cash, she replies that 'it won't be a problem'. We're doing our piece for *Hello!* as soon as we get back. If we split it, that'll net her a cool £50,000. I say nothing, astonished that she's still thinking everything's just handy dandy between the pair of us, when it's so clearly not. As we sit waiting to get on the plane, she can't resist delivering a couple of comments about the state of my teeth and clicking jaw. But I'm too tired to rise to the bait. We finally board the plane and get into our seats. The 747 lumbers slowly into the air. And that's when I snap.

As the stewardess comes round with our drinks, I'm quietly working away on my laptop and say to her: 'Can you set it there, please?' It's probably the sole occasion since I've been with Tara that I've neglected to add a 'thank you', but she leaps on it.

'Sometimes you're so bloody rude, darling! You could at least have said "thank you" to the girl.'

I gently close down my laptop and turn to face her.

'Listen to me, Tara. I'm fed up to the back teeth with your destructive, constant harping. You nag on at me like an old fishwife, and I've come to realise there's a side of you that's just plain nasty, pure and simple. I'll fight with you if you like. But you don't fight fair. You can dish it out. But you can't take it. All this engagement crap is bollocks. You're so desperate to find some poor idiot to march you down the aisle, you couldn't even wait for me to ask you. If you can't learn to grow up, and behave like an adult, I think you and I should call it quits.'

She stares at me for a moment in shock. Then she grabs the cell-phone at the side of her seat and frantically tries to run her defunct Amex Platinum Card through it.

'What are you doing?'

'I'm calling my friend, Normandie Keith, in London. She can pick me up. You're horrible to me!! I've never been treated so appallingly in my life! I never want to see you again. *Ever!*'

The card doesn't work.

Tara furiously pushes the button for the flight attendant. When the girl arrives, she asks to be moved to another seat.

There aren't any other seats available.

Tara curls up into a ball and starts to sob. She refuses to speak to me for the rest of the flight. And by the time the plane touches down in London, the writing's well and truly on the wall. It's the last thing I wanted. But if it goes on like this much longer, it's clearly very soon going to be well and truly over.

January 18, 1984

The other brilliant rumour, about my having spent half a dozen odd years in some loonie bin, happened to be much closer to the truth. To me LA is, and always will be, just about as close as you can get to an urban insane asylum on this planet! The route that led me there was via a superb piece of good luck that came my way one day I managed to get myself cast by CBS in the leading role of Marco Santorelli, the Italian immigrant who makes good as the first immigrant State Senator in turn-of-the-century New York in the mini-series *Ellis Island* opposite Richard Burton and Faye Dunaway.

But fate very nearly took an entirely different turn for me a couple of months earlier when I unwittingly auditioned on tape for a starring role in the hit night-time soap *Dynasty*. I say 'unwittingly' because this was one of those occasions when an actor is put on tape under the clever guise of what he's been told is in fact just a simple, straightforward 'general meeting'. (i.e. I wasn't told what shows the casting director happened to be currently working on). A week later a call comes through to my manager's office in Greenwich Village — the producers of *Dynasty* have decided they want to do a deal with me. Now it may sound weird to a lot of you out there, but you have to be one hell of a strategist, as well as an innate opportunist, to be any kind of a successful actor. The road to fame and fortune is littered with the carcasses of young men and women who've made notoriously bad choices in their careers. I'd always felt that television, unless it was some truly exceptional piece of work, should be an absolute no-no for me.

Cinemas to me are like cathedrals. Mysterious palaces of worship where the audience has to put its hands in its pockets and cough up dosh before being privileged to watch their favourite stars acting out their fantasies on a massive screen. Television, by contrast, is decidedly domestic. Your public gets to watch you right there in the comfort of their own living-rooms, on a comparatively tiny screen, and pay virtually zilch for the experience. It's all very psychological. That's why I feel so few television stars ever manage to make a truly successful transition to the big screen. Their persona has just become too well-known as a 'domesticated' animal, as opposed to something exotic and otherworldly — fundamentally unattainable.

This is the thought that is very much in my mind when the offer comes through that day from LA TVland. The role sounds great — very charismatic. A sort of Lady Chatterly's Lover to Joan Collins as Alexis. And the kind of money they're apparently prepared to throw at me to tale the part is just plain silly. If the role plays for over three years, I'll make more than US$1 million, and have plenty of hiatus time to do any features. But it's still television, and I'm happy as a clam in New York, which is where the LA feature world comes to find the best 'real' actors anyway. It's true I'm not exactly rolling in dough, but I know that'll come to me with time. I'm currently doing the classy New York premiere of a new Harold Pinter play with Diane West off-Broadway, and Pinter himself is along for the ride. I check in with my manager.

'OK, Greg. Look, I know you're about movies. You wanna star in 'em. Write 'em, produce 'em, direct 'em. The whole shebang! But why don't you just me play around a little and let me see how much money I can get for you outta these assholes? It could just be your mealticket.' I give him permission to go ahead and fool around with the deal, and within twenty-four hours he's come back to me, telling me they've more than doubled their offer of money. Well over US$2 million over three years!

Now I may fundamentally have the soul of a creator and performer. But I'm also a born businessman. And I'm certainly not stupid! This is very serious dosh! I relent, the deal is signed, and the following Monday morning I'm booked on a United Airlines flight out to LA to do the obligatory formal screen test. The first sign that I've maybe just made one hell of a massive boo-boo comes as I find my seat in the First Class cabin.

'I envy you, man! I know you! You're gonna have a *lot* of

fun! There'll be half a dozen real super-hot chicks goin' out to LA to test with you. And *you'll* be the only guy!'

My manager, an archetypal Jewish wiz at promoting his clients, is a married man who tends to enjoy my tales of my endless round of erotic adventures. I ask him if he knows any of the girls' names. Maybe they're actresses I've already bumped into here in the city.

'Nah! Nobody you know will be there, I guarantee you. They're mainly red-hot supermodel types.'

When I get to my seat there are two pieces of admittedly quite delicious crumpet sitting either side of me. But neither one of them is what I'd in any way term a 'red-hot supermodel' type. By now let's just say that I've been around the block a few times, and can tell a class act from a hustler. These girls both definitely fall into the latter category. It's more like sitting next to a case of 'Orgazmatraz' redux. I get chatting with the one on my right. Her name's Honey. There's no doubt about it, she's sexy as hell, but she talks with an irritating Texas whine that puts my teeth on edge, as I chug back my glass of 'shampoo' and munch away on my dish of up-market snackettes.

It turns out Honey was has appeared with a staple in her tummy in *Playboy*, and has been recently snapped up by some trendy new New York modelling agency that desperately wants to branch out into films. She's got a fascinating, very varied track-record, including the odd soft-porn movie and, sure enough, a brief, challenging spell working in Oklahoma City as an 'exotic dancer'.

Right from the start it's crystal clear Honey's very much up for it. But just for the moment there are more important matters weighing on my mind. Things just don't feel right. This is confirmed when we finally get to LAX to find there's no promised car there waiting for us. Eventually I make a call to ABC and receive a profuse apology. I'm told there's been a screwup.

Could the three of us please hop a cab to The Beverly Hilton? Then we get to the hotel and the next thing wrong is there's none of the promised script material waiting there for us so that we can prepare for the shoot the next day. I check into my room, already feeling like I've probably made a serious mistake. But the contract's already been signed. That's the way it's done. The screentest is just a formality. What can I do? There's a knock at my door. It's sweet little Honey. She's standing there in her bathrobe, wet hair swathed in a towel, grinning at me provocatively, a roll of tubing in her hand.

'It's my centrefold. I thought you'd maybe like to take a peek. Tell me what you think. I heard you played Hamlet. It's really very artistic.'

A crazy thought suddenly pops into my mind, as I allow her to enter my haven. How badly do I really want to get out of this? It's clearly not for me. There's no way in hell I'm going to be happy surviving for three years living in La-La land acting opposite a bunch of ex-*Playboy* bunnies! The only sure-fire way out is for me to totally tank the test tomorrow. That means me being as unmistakably bloody awful as possible, so ABC thinks, beyond the shadow of a doubt, they've made a fatal mistake and don't pick up the contract. And what's an absolute dead-cert way of my being bloody awful tomorrow, while having myself one hell of a blast in the process? That's right! By having a ball of a time all night long with little Honey, and getting at the most maybe one hour of sleep!

I'm now a man with a mission, albeit a rather strange one. I see it as a bold decision, and one that I'm very happy I made the next day. I get to the sound stage thoroughly bleary-eyed, walking like some cowboy who's been stuck in the saddle for well over six months, only to find a man who regularly helps shoot episodes of the series itself, sitting on his fat arse inside his trailer watching an epic of great cinema history on his VCR called *Donkey Dick*. It's without a doubt the most disgusting piece of filth I've ever seen in my life! And it doesn't just involve donkeys. Sheep, goats, hens, a bull — they've all got starring roles somewhere in there!

'Man!' I think to myself. 'Did I ever make the right move!'

This lad is quite simply just not into animal porn. It does nothing to me, punches absolutely none of my sexual buttons. I'm your basic, everyday man to woman material. One on one. Always have been. Even with threesomes and upwards these days I somehow find my mind starting to wander. It's as if I quite simply like the intensity, the focus of a good old-fashioned, down-to-earth 'famo-a-mano'. But this little incident does clearly signal for me, apart from the fact that I'm unquestionably right on in my decision to tank the test, that I'm about to enter a world where kinkiness is decidedly in vogue.

LA, as I'm about to discover, is the true home of sexual extremes, and has been since the good old days of Charlie Chaplin, Fatty Arbuckle and Errol Flynn. Not that other cities don't abound with elements of fetish, S&M and the like. London today is actually riddled with the phenomena. A lot of people I know subscribe to mags like *Skin Two* and regularly attend the famous October 'Rubber Ball'. But LA always has been, and surely always will be, a veritable world mecca for perversion. And the movie and television industries seems to maintain an irresistible flirtation with the subject.

Tanking the *Dynasty* test with just one hour of sleep and a marathon of shagging with Honey under my belt is a doddle. I effortlessly manage to bring my game down to the level of the ladies around me, generally acting like a total moron, at one point even appearing to be almost helplessly gay as I trip over my shoelaces, the furniture, anything I can possibly find. At the end of the day the guy with the animal porn fetish takes me sombrely to one side and very sweetly tries to reassure me about my 'performance'. 'Don't worry. It'll all be OK.' But I know myself.

I've very happily done a first-class job of shooting myself in the foot.

To celebrate, I take my six seductive 'supermodel' sirens out to The Polo Lounge, then on to a slap-up feed and a late night visit to a fabulous strip joint called The Garage. And it's there that I first start to get the full picture of the seedy decadence of this essentially very suburban town. A sultry, ravenesque vixen called Mother Theresa in a black rubber mini-dress and sporting a nasty-looking whip takes us home to her pad way up somewhere in the Hollywood Hills for a night-cap and what she promises will be a bout of 'serious, strict education'.

Once inside her little home-sweet-home which looks like some cross between a torture chamber inside Dracula's castle and The London Dungeon, she disappears downstairs with the girls, leaving me alone with my glass of Jack Daniel's, inspecting the magnificent array of weird 'equipment'. A nasty-looking steel recliner chair complete with chains and a device to keep the victim's legs firmly spread wide open. A body-suit with metallic spikes strategically positioned in all the right places, plus one hell of a dildo attached to the crotch. And a truly spectacular array of spike-heeled black leather boots next to some deadly looking gray six-foot long rubber tubing.

Eventually Mother Theresa and the girls re-emerge from the lower depths, and I'm astonished at the transformation. It's like I've somehow suddenly been transported back to the last days of Sodom and Gomorrah! Wearing a set of rubber nuns' outfits and gas masks, each one carrying a whip, they slowly approach me, as 'Fire' by The Crazy World Of Arthur Brown begins to scream out over the stereo system. It's a little bit on the disconcerting side, but I decide gamely to play along with it anyway. What the hell! You only live once!

'Be gentle with me,' I plead in mock supplication, as they grab me and haul me bodily across to the awaiting steel reclining chair, locking my arms and legs firmly into position with the chains. 'Please! Be gentle with me!'

October 20, 1999

I'm still up on the deserted little island in the Outer Hebrides communing with the local wildlife. The tilted nuttiness of human beings and their bizarre preoccupation with 'social status' seems like a million miles away. But next week I have to venture back down to London on business, and I have to say it's not an experience I'm particularly looking forward to. Trying to convince myself that what I already suspect isn't true, (i.e. that all of this is a manufactured slander campaign perpetrated by a bunch of sorry wankers who want me run out of the country) is pointless. The facts are staring me straight in the face. There's no escaping them. And at times I don't mind admitting it's deeply depressing. For over a year I've worked very hard at quietly building up my position in England in order to implement my dreams. And although most of the hip social world of London clearly believes otherwise, my motives are more genuinely rooted in a healthy desire to do good than the result of a pure ego trip.

I take a break from writing and attempt to divert my mind for the afternoon by picking up a recent copy of *Hello!* magazine. Not a very bright move. This week's issue is, as usual, chock-a-block full of splashy tabloid pictures of the very world I've just been so unceremoniously tossed out of. There's an article on a grand soiree thrown by David Tang for the Duchess of York, plus another on the engagement bash thrown by Tara's pals, Lucas White and Normandie Keith. There are all the blue bloods out on the town in their frippery and finery. And, wouldn't you just know it, amongst the others there's a smashing pic of Tara with her best buddy Tamara Beckwith, along with a pair of her ex-boyfriends, Robert Hanson and Morgens Tholstrup. England is unique in that the world of the aristocracy is so intimately connected with the fields of entertainment and big business. It's a two-way street, almost as if most of those born into wealth or influence in this country get some kind of odd reassurance of their personal worth by flirting with street-wise rock stars and actors from the wrong side of the tracks. While the performers, musicians and entrepreneurs, many of them in their own way typically riddled with a similar deeply rooted insecurity, somehow wind up making themselves feel better by hobnobbing with the likes of Lord This and Lady That, or the Right Honourable Cecil Ducannon Smyth Forbes-Willoughby, the Fourteenth Earl of Hellman's Mayonnaise, husband of the Grand Duchess Helga Van Tessvangarden of Heinz Baked Beans.

In America, by comparison, the concept of aristocracy doesn't exist. As an ex-girlfriend of mine from the LA film industry commented when I told her all about my recent, strange experience: 'My God! In Los Angeles you'd be a hero!'

I laugh and joke a lot, and generally do my best to have myself a jolly good time. But in truth I'm covering up a lot of unpleasant feelings deep inside. The world these people inhabit is way too close to my business. I know a lot of folk assume that because my own father's a bit of an entertainment icon in this country and has recently been knighted, that I've probably grown up with my own trust fund, plus a cornucopia of related social privileges. But in reality nothing could be further from the truth. Both my father and my mother came from poverty; working-class people with nary a brass farthing to their names. My mother came from what you'd definitely call impoverished beginnings. But even she was shocked by the hardship she saw in my father's humble home. So I'm very glad my dear ol' dad was always so tight with us when we were kids. It helped make me who I am today. A lot of your archetypal trust-fund babies are so screwed up they can hardly get out of bed in the morning and work their way through breakfast without hitting a bottle of Stoli, or hauling a line of coke up their noses — let alone be capable of starting their own business from scratch without a hefty influx of mummy or daddy's monetary assistance and heavy-duty social connections.

Which brings me back to the fatal weekend of my return to the UK with Tara from Tang's hedonistic, happy Hong Kong hideaway...

August 20, 1999

As I've mentioned before, one of my biggest weaknesses is that I've always hated seeing people being hurt, particularly women. I feel like I've been through this current scenario more than a hundred times before, and I hope to Christ I never have to go through it again. Some part of me now knows, beyond the faintest shadow of a doubt, that the relationship with the lovely Ms. P-T is probably over. But I can't bring myself to physically end it. In fact, in truth, I'm a little scared of ending it. There's a side of Tara that's frankly so loopy I simply don't know how she's going to react, or what she's going to do. To make matters worse, I know she has to be pretty much aware it's well and truly done and dusted too. But some part of her doesn't want to believe it. It's a no-win situation. I know someone's going to have to wind up being 'the bad guy', and the chances are, according to my experience of Murphy's Law, it's probably going to be me.

It's not a nice feeling. And, true to form, when we touch down on the tarmac at Heathrow, Tara opens her eyes, turns to face me, and does one of those disorienating 180-degree turns that some women seem so profoundly proficient at, and that we sorry male bastards always seem to find so absolutely impossible to somehow wriggle our way out of.

'I'm so sorry, darling,' she says, smiling ever so sweetly. 'It's all my fault. I know I can be such a bitch sometimes. I just don't know why. Let's go straight down to Mummy and Daddy's and have ourselves a fabulous weekend. It's Mummy's birthday, as well as little Honour's, too.'

I've bought some very nice gifts for all her family from Tang's famous Hong Kong clothing store. Half-a-dozen silk shawls in a series of fabulous colours for the ladies, plus two sets of beautiful Chinese tea glasses for Patty.

'What the hell. I might as well be hung for a sheep as for a lamb,' I think to myself idiotically, as I pull my BMW out of the Heathrow long-term parking lot and head down the M4 for Hampshire.

Our arrival at Dummer is greeted very warmly. Lots of kisses and hugs and friendly pats on the back. The ladies love their shawls, and I finally get to meet Simon Sebag-Montefiore, who's brought along a very interesting and charming journalist pal of his, Robert Hardman, Royal Correspondent for the *Daily Telegraph*.

Looking back on it, that final weekend at Tara's family home was incredible. It was as if I was suddenly operating within the confines of MI5. Not for a solitary moment was I allowed to believe that there was anything in the slightest bit strange going on. But boy, was I wrong! The facade the Palmer-Tomkinsons maintained throughout was flawless — impeccable. An endless round of superficially joyous breakfasts, raucous lunch parties and suppers — even a charming kids' tea party for the adorable little daughter of Tara's brother, which I dutifully filmed on my new digital video camera, purchased in Hong Kong. There were a series of long, chummy walks *en famille*, and also what turned out to be the last-ditch attempt to salvage the slowly sinking ship of my sexual relationship with the beloved Tara.

The group deception conceived that weekend was so magnificently complete that on the Sunday afternoon I found myself winding up taking a quiet, intimate stroll with Patty and having a long talk with her about her serious concerns for Tara's future, and how very pleased she was that the young lady had the good fortune to finally meet a man strong-willed enough to be able to deal with her decidedly 'challenging' personality.

Later on in the afternoon, feeling strangely on edge, I decide to take myself on a long run around the extensive perimeters of the Palmer-Tomkinson estate. I'm just halfway down the driveway, when I suddenly take a nasty tumble, like a complete and utter twit, tripping over my own training shoe laces. I fall badly, scraping my hand in a bloody gouge across the gravel.

(In retrospect this seems like an exquisitely appropriate metaphor for the bizarre situation I was about to find myself thrust into!)

I keep on running, as I know from experience that I most likely won't feel any real pain until I stop. And when I finally do, six miles later, the trail of blood dripping down my palm is spectacular. I walk into the P-Ts' kitchen looking for the first-aid kit. Patty enters, sees the blood, and quickly finds the iodine and plasters for me. It's a stark contrast to Tara's reaction when she walks into the kitchen two minutes later, spies my horrendous-looking wound, cups a hand to her mouth and blurts out:

'I've got to go the video store, and I'm leaving right now! I can't stand the sight of blood!'

The lovely Nicky Haslam turns up — superficially for cocktails, but actually, it turns out, to show off his now much-publicised recent face-lift. I smile and tell him how great he looks, but in truth I quietly find myself agreeing with Tara's dad, the eccentric, old Charlie P-T, who tells Nicky straight to his face with a lovely grin that in his opinion Nicky looks 'absolutely no different whatsoever from before'.

Haslam throws me the same cheery smile he greeted me with over two months ago when I first met him, and never for an instant do I sense that he is one of the very people who, while I've been away, has so fervently been laying the groundwork with

Tara's parents for my exile the following day.

'Hi, babe,' he says innocuously enough, as he kisses me on both cheeks. 'Good trip?'

'Super, thanks Nicky,' I reply. 'Love the face job.'

'I'm afraid I can only stay for a few.' He shoots me a sly wink. 'I've got some serious homework to do tonight. See you at my party next month?'

'I'll be there. Cheers, mate!' As I raise my glass of 'shampoo', I catch the briefest glimpse of a haunting smile flicking across Haslam's now taut, delicately reworked features.

After Nicky departs, I grab myself a quick sandwich, then hop in my car and pound on back up the M3 to the city on my tod. Tara has told me she wants to stay down in the country for the night to spend some quiet time with her mum and dad.

'Fair enough,' I think to myself. After the Far East debacle I could do with a good night's solitary kip.

Back at my pad I check my messages. There's only one I can clearly remember now. It stuck in my mind because of the nasty, churning feeling it gave me in my innards for the rest of that subsequently sleepless night.

'Hi, Greg,' the voice said. 'I take it you've had yourself a peek at the *Mail On Sunday*.'

CHAPTER FIVE

L.A., SEXUAL INSANE ASYLUM (PART TWO)

'A vacuum with nipples.'
Otto Preminger (of Marilyn Monroe)
'There are a number of mechanical devices which increase sexual arousal,
particularly in women. Chief among these is the Mercedes-Benz 380SL
convertible.'
P. J. O'Rourke

March 30, 1984

It's a cold spring Monday morning, and I've been sent along by my agent to the CBS building in mid-town Manhattan to audition for the leading role of an Italian peasant gardener who becomes the first immigrant State Senator in the new mini-series

Ellis Island. I think it's a bit of a joke at the time. I'm six foot three with blue eyes. I might barely pass for a native of northern Italy, but only if I had coloured contacts and my hair was dyed dark brown. Still I'm more or less game for anything. And I find the prospect of playing a great Latin lover on screen tantalising. For some strange reason today my blood's up, and I'm really in the mood to conquer, so I wind up giving a particularly hard-edged rendition of a passionate Mediterranean romancer, and later on that day get a call from my manager telling me that I've apparently bagged the role. Now I know why I needed to tank the *Dynasty* screen test so badly!

'What's the money like?' I ask my manager.

'Not bad. They'll pay you $100,000 for eleven weeks' shooting, plus you get some nice accommodation and a very generous per diem. And there's some more good news. Your co-stars are Richard Burton and Faye Dunaway.'

I've think I've died and gone to heaven. Working with Burton has always been a lifelong ambition of mine, and not merely because of his acting prowess. His deeply impressive reputation as a womaniser makes my own pale by comparison. 'It'll be like sitting at the feet of the master,' I think to myself. And in more ways than one!

And then there's the fabulous, sexy Faye! Alright! The show is also going to be shot principally in the UK, so it's a very nice way for me to return to the old mother country — with charismatic, sexy role under my belt. And even though it is television, it's a mini-series *shot on film*. Big difference!

I fly over a few days before my first day's shooting and find out the production company has been generous enough to set me up in a lovely little bachelor pad just off Oxford Street in W1. I pay a visit to the set right away and am delighted to discover not only that I'm amongst an amazing and talented cast, but also that the crew contains four British Academy Award winners, including the very famous cinematographer Jack Hildyard who won his Oscar for David Lean's classic *Bridge Over The River Kwai*. A cockney security guard, who introduces himself to me as Bill, shows me to my trailer and I spend the afternoon banishing my nerves and getting used to the concept of being on a film set for the first time.

The role of Marco proves to be incredibly demanding. Being an 'Italian stallion', I have been assigned the deeply unpleasant task of kissing more than half a dozen ladies on screen. I spend all my spare time boning up on my Marx Brothers 'you donta-lika-my-spaghetti' accent, learning meaningful lines such as: 'God didn't give me much, except women like to look at me, and I make-a love good. I'm crazy not to use it. Right?', and standing in front of my bathroom mirror practising my on-screen kissing technique.

Rehearsals with the principals are immediate, and my first is with the ravishing lady playing my mistress, Faye Dunaway. This turns out be my first encounter with Tara's famous illness, 'rumouritis'. I've heard many stories about Faye back in the Big Apple.

'This could be more than just interesting,' I muse to myself, as I roll up in my cab outside Ms. Dunaway's gorgeous Knightsbridge home. My opinion of Faye as an actress is high. I've been far more than just an avid fan of hers ever since the days of *Bonnie and Clyde* and *Network*, and at the very least I know working with her will be a challenge.

Faye at that time was married to the brilliant, and very ballsy English celebrity photographer, Terry O'Neill. Terry and I were already sort of acquainted via his connection with all the great rock stars of the Sixties, such as the Beatles and the Rolling Stones. A great, gritty guy with no side whatsoever, he struck me as the perfect match for Faye, who was not only absolutely smashing to look at but very charming, sweet and sexy as hell, to boot.

The next day, when I enter the make-up trailer for the first time, the gang working there immediately starts in with all their stories. (The hair and make-up wagon always tends to be the hub of gossip on a film set. It's traditionally the place where tempers can be vented and controversial opinions aired in a relatively secure environment, as the actor sips his coffee while being sweetly pampered, primped and preened.) But even the first tale I hear about poor Faye would have been enough to set any faint-hearted young male co-star's heart a-poundin' big-time had I not known any better. The rumour going around had it that one of the most difficult jobs the production company faced on *Ellis Island* was simply finding any hair and make-up people happy to work with the lovely Ms. Dunaway.

There's a handsome, very talented young Irish actor about my age playing the role of an IRA terrorist in the show. His name is Liam Neeson. Later on, one day in the early stages of the shoot, he and I are sitting down in a pub on location near Smithfields fish market over a couple of pints of cold Guinness when he suddenly turns to me and shoots me a sly smile.

'So I hear you get to make love to Ms. Dunaway in this one. Lucky you, boy.'

There's a tone of envy in his voice. And he's a man I come to respect. He evidently knows a hell of a lot about strong-willed actresses. At the time he's living with Helen Mirren — like Faye, one hell of an actress and reputedly something of a sexual powerhouse. So as we lock eyes on one another on that first day of rehearsal, I've done my best to block out all the stories I've heard about the dear lady back in the States from my mind. Faye, to me, is and always will be quite simply an extremely attractive woman and a great actress. She exudes confidence, elegance, wit and great sexual allure as we carefully run through our lines together that first morning under the watchful eye of Herr

Director, Jerry London. In fact, I'm very happy to say that I find her quite a massive turn-on. Which I feel bodes very well indeed for the amount of lusty, sensual contact we're due to have with one another in front of the cameras in the upcoming couple of months. Our first scene, however, is not up for another week, so as the party ends and I take my leave, I give her a sweet little peck on the cheek and politely tell her how much Don Juan is looking forward to working with her on set. (While in my mind I'm already secretly thinking how much I'd seriously like to do her!)

During the next few days I pay a visit to my dad's venue, AIR studios in Oxford Circus, where he's recording the album *Tug Of War* with Paul McCartney. Sting puts in a brief appearance, and a brief chat re. the recently much-publicised topic of his dabble with tantric sex leads me to the conclusion it's a matter that must, at all cost, be immediately investigated.

'It's all about control,' Sting intones gravely as he stares at me with his inimitable, steely-eyed glare.

The next day I purchase a hefty tome on the subject from Selfridges. I'm a quick study, and that night make my first attempt at putting the ancient and sacred theory into practice at the end of a date with a sultry young lady from Cyprus. All goes amazingly well for about fifty minutes, until my otherworldly Ravi Shankar sitar tape abruptly ends, at which point I immediately descend from my realm of ecstatic, spiritual bliss, and instantly morph back into the ferocious carnivore that I am apparently forever destined to be within the confines of this mundane, material world. Kabboooom! My personal Nirvana explodes, transmorgifying into a gorgeous moment of mortal splendour.

Before getting to grips with the fabulous Faye in the flesh, I first have to shoot a few highly charged erotic scenes with an American TV actress whom I find not only to be a truly talented thespian, but also a real fiery sexpot. There's a scene the two of us have to play in which her character comes to visit me at midnight at my campaign headquarters in an overt attempt to seduce me. In the film she finds me in the bath, buck naked, a result of me having to write some late night speech, and then proceeds in no uncertain terms to come on to me, big-time. The scene culminates in a kiss and, on the night the scene is being shot, the lady in question chooses to go for it with gusto, a gesture to which I dutifully wholeheartedly respond. We get into the spirit of things to such an extent that Herr Director is forced to yell out 'Cut!' more than just a few times at the end of the first take.

As the crew preps for the second shot, out of the corner of my eye I catch an odd-looking, overweight nervous guy, hanging around the very edges of the set. Mike, my seriously gay make-up man, fills me in while he's quite clearly getting off on daubing my tanned torso down with lashings of mock sweat from my bathtub.

'Try not to make it quite so real next time, sweetie. Take it from me. You're enjoying deep-throating the little lady way too much.'

'Why?' I chuckle cavalierly in response. 'She's a foxy babe. Given the chance I'd probably do her in a hot New York second.'

'Right. A foxy babe. That she is. And that tubby little character over there in the corner would *do you* in an even hotter New York second as a result! He's not only her manager. He's also her husband.'

He vanishes and I slowly turn to face the young sexpot's husband, giving him a friendly but nervous little wave, as the babe minces sultrily over for the next take. The guy just nods. But no way in hell does he look like Mr. Happy. My hair lady pops across to give me the quick once-over.

'Did Mike warn you? Did he tell you what's going on?'

'Yeah, I think I understand the situation perfectly,' I respond, my smiling, scared eyes stuck on the jealous husband in the corner.

'I don't think you do, love,' my hair gal adds, as she gives my barnet-fair one final, rapid sweep with her brush. 'The lady's hubby packs one hell of a mean-looking Colt-45 in his pocket.'

She slips away again back into the shadows, as the First AD calls out for quiet on the set, and my phenomenally sexy and very determined co-star moves back in towards me for the kill. I swallow hard, her searing eyes meeting mine in a look of sexually-charged anticipation.

In a mood of naked self-preservation, I make the next smooch nothing less than a strictly rudimentary exercise in the ancient art of 'theatrical kissing'. I suddenly feel like I've been plunged back in the Dark Ages of film censorship when actors were permitted merely to simulate tongue-action, or else fall seriously foul of the prevailing authority's mighty sword. It's not exactly as easy as it sounds, particularly given that the gorgeous lady's dander is most certainly up following all the intensely heated passion I very determinedly threw in to the first take. But at this point all I'm frankly thinking about is saving my own dastardly skin!

Later on that night, as I'm slipping on my glad rags in the privacy of my trailer, a knock comes on my door. 'Who is it?' I ask, as I fumble with my fly. The door swings open, and there stands my co-star, looking hotter than an August afternoon in the Sahara, in jeans, an absolutely killer pair of 'come-fuck-me' pumps, and a tight little crimson cashmere sweater that quite clearly bares all the worldly goods with which Mother Nature has apparently chosen so generously to endow her. Before I can so much as utter a word, she's slipped inside my private domain and closed the door firmly behind her. It very swiftly turns into a replay of the scene we've just finished shooting. She sashays over to me, shoves her arms around my neck and, almost as if still in character, utters a variation of her lines in the show.

'Don't you want me, Greg? I've wanted you ever since the first moment I saw you.'

I'm *so* tempted! But the angel on my shoulder comes into play in a decidedly forceful manner. Saving my arse from being riddled with a slew of bullets from her Othello's Colt-45, I respond in kind, quoting my own character as I gently remove her arms from my shoulders.

'Please. Go away.'

'Why?'

'Because I'm lonely just like you, and if I do this, I'll regret it the rest of my life.'

Yeah! No shit!

August 22, 1999

Even after the sleepless night, like a silly, trusting fool, I'm still blindly following the dictum of the Palmer-Tomkinson family to 'ignore' the press, and hence don't bother to read the article in the *Mail On Sunday* apparently based around a very unpleasant interview with my now ex-employee Richard Griffiths. Instead, I drive out to visit my dear old mum in Hertfordshire that Monday morning to show her the video footage I've just taken of my trip to Hong Kong and Beijing.

'I really don't want to worry you, dear, but I've got a very funny feeling about all this nasty press business,' she tells me sweetly in her gentle and inimitable, Scottish way, as we down our cups of Nescafé together. 'I have an odd sensation inside me that something awful's about to happen.'

I do my best to dismiss her nerves. But in my heart I know she's a bit of a wise old seer, and that she's seldom been wrong when she gets her 'feelings'. I tell her I want to come out to Hatfield to write sometime during the week ahead, and in return she gives me a knowing look, as if to say: 'There's something not right, isn't there?'

I peck her on the cheek, give her golden retriever a hug, and head on back into London. I'm meeting Tara at my flat at 1 p.m.

for lunch. There's the usual throng of press outside my humble abode. It's by now a phenomenon I've become used to. But this time, strangely, none of them ask me anything. Not a single question. And the funny way I see some of them looking at me gives me brief pause for thought, as I turn my key in the lock and push open the door. Tara's not there, and the apartment is almost spookily quiet. I check the mail, brew myself a cappuccino and flick through the *Daily Telegraph*. I wish to God that day I'd bought myself a copy of the *Mail*. At the very least I would've been mildly prepared for what was about to come down.

The phone rings. It's some guy from the *Telegraph*. The chap asks me if I'm interested in doing an interview with a very high-profile journalist, Elizabeth Grice, commenting on some of the scurrilous stories that have recently broken about me. Still completely in the dark, I tell him I'll think about it and ask him to call back in a couple of days. I hang up. The phone immediately rings again. It's one of my financial contacts, a man who brokers deals with a number of Middle Eastern finance groups. I think he's calling regarding the meeting we have scheduled for early next month with J&M, the major film sales company, and Coutts Media Banking Division regrading my upcoming production slate. This is how the conversation goes:

'Hi,' I greet him cheerily. 'How are you? When is our man coming down from Scotland for the meeting with J&M and Coutts?'

Dead silence from the other end of the line. Then: 'My God, Greg. You don't know what's happened, do you? I'm calling to tell you we're going to have to postpone everything until all this has somehow been cleared up.' I haven't the faintest idea what the hell he's talking about, and am prevented from asking him by a frantic ring on my doorbell.

'Look, I'm sorry. I don't understand, but I want to hear what you have to say. I'm going to have to go right now. Someone's just arrived. I'll call you back later.'

I hang up the phone and walk across to my front door. Tara's standing there, a strange look on her face, and a crumpled-up copy of yesterday's *Mail On Sunday* in her hand. She pushes past me, inside the flat, plumping herself down on my sofa. I close the door behind her and follow her into the room. The expression on her face is odd. Twisted into a painful, cynical half-smile. She shoves the paper down on the coffee table in front of me.

'I can't go on with this, Greg. You're a liar! An absolute, out-and-out, fucking scoundrel! The lowest of the low! Read this!'

June 1, 1984

For a brief period there after *Ellis Island* I was admitted into hospital suffering from what at the time was classified as 'nervous exhaustion'. Actually I was suffering from what can only really be truthfully described as 'an excess of exhausting erotic encounters'! And similarly, my short stay inside the hallowed walls of one of Manhattan's most respected medical treatment centres can only be truthfully described as literally 'going from the frying pan into the fire'! Every truly red-blooded male I know on this planet has this strange, in-built thing about nurses. Don't ask me why. Maybe it's just the uniform. Maybe it's the way they get to play around with you like a baby, and stick all manner of weird pieces of medical technology up each and every one of your orifices in the process! But it's most definitely there. And by the end of my sojourn in the hospital ward all I could think about was the great W. C. Fields' famous comment: 'I spent four weeks in hospital last fall, and at the end I took a turn for the nurse!'

My first day's shooting was fascinating. To begin with, old Bill, the security guard who'd very kindly showed me to my trailer on the first day, showed up on set as an extra dressed in the costume of a nineteenth century Rabbi! It turned out he was flogging fake Rolexes to all and sundry between takes! He showed me where he kept them — stashed away on his right arm under his cossie!

Then there was the lovely Faye...

A lot of women probably don't realise how when they get nervous around a bloke and they get 'frosty' it can be a real turn-on. Faye was nervous as a super-charged sex kitten on set. Magnificently edgy — testy in that quintessentially sexy, sultry way that can make even an experienced cameraman's lens fog up like the famous old London pea-soup at fifty paces. I'm still twenty-seven at the time, remember, and my hyper-charged libido is in seriously high gear. There seems to be just about the right amount of sexual tension between the pair of us to make it work, and the first day's filming passes like a dream.

The next day we get to our first bed sequence together and the old pro, Burton, quietly pulls me to one side over a can of Diet Coke as the crew are prepping for the initial shot.

'You're between the sheets with her today, then, are you?'

'Yup.'

'You realise that she's after you?'

I shrug nonchalantly and smile. 'Maybe.'

'Are you after her?'

'She's married to a great bloke. I like him. He's a mate. Look, if she was single I dare say I'd probably give it a go if the offer came my way.'

Burton stares at me with those incredible, rock-hard, turquoise eyes of his. He's been got to. He's heard the rumours and clearly doesn't like her. 'Five hundred quid says you won't once this scene is shot.' He nods sagely, stands, and vanishes mysteriously behind the arc light.

I turn and watch her make-up gal give the sweet, gorgeous Faye a final facial touch-up.

August 23, 1999

I've spent both the remainder of the past day and this morning meeting with various chums and supporters, going over the Richard Griffiths article in the *Mail On Sunday*. I've also consulted a lawyer. It turns out that it's such a clever and professionally woven tissue of lies, mixed in with just enough fact that it makes it virtually impossible for me to take him to court personally for slander. Whoever it is who's behind all of this garbage is a master.

One of the most socially damaging areas of the piece is Griffiths' accusation that I apparently returned from Jagger's party 'crowing' about how I was going to use Tara to 'cut a swathe through London society', and that I allegedly said to him: 'The next time you see me, I'll be skiing in Klosters with Prince Charles.'

The initially farcical turn of events, it seems, has now turned deadly serious for me. Before she fled the coop yesterday, Tara had mentioned that a number of 'individuals' have also apparently called various members of her family corroborating the series of alleged scandalous tales re. the character and negative moral credibility of yours truly.

'What the *fuck* is going on?' I ask one of my best and most lucid mates, as we down a few pints of chilled Guinness in my local (such an appropriate drink for me to be imbibing, I can't help thinking), and the potential gravity of the situation slowly seeps into my grey matter.

'You're getting nobbled, mate,' is his succinct reply.

'OK. Why? This is not only getting *very* weird. It's also now borderline scary.'

And it is. Truly. The general tone of the Griffiths article is that old bugger-lugs is indeed your archetypal 'scumbag, cad, serial womaniser' whose modus operandi in life is to ritually 'prey upon' whatever rich, well-connected women he can possibly lay his insatiable little paws on. Half a dozen of my so-called victims are noted in the article, including a girl I've since come to call Sophie the Sorceress, a young lady I had taken with me to Vancouver as my son's nanny when I initially met Griffiths.

Sophie the Sorceress's comments are particularly nasty, but hardly surprise me, given how I eventually had to deal with her. It's the sad fact that she actually felt the need to avenge her inevitable expulsion from my life in such a sordid, tawdry way that I find so disappointing. I knew she needed money, and was the type willing to do pretty much anything for it. But this? Sophie the Sorceress describes the act of going to bed with me as 'the most disgusting thing I've ever done'.

Funny, that's not quite how I seem to recall it.

My first thought is to call the three women he mentioned whom I know not only think the world of me, but with whom I parted on very friendly terms. I pick up the phone. Dial. The first two are out of the country until September or October and unreachable. Then a thought occurs to me:

'This is a waste of time. What's the point? What could they do anyway? Sell their stories to the *Mail* in response?'

My publicist is also out of the country, at the Venice Film Festival. I try in vain to reach her, but the phones to that part of Italy are well and truly up the spout.

'How all occasions do inform against me, and spur my dull revenge,' I think to myself moodily, as I start to pace my living room, like some caged beast of prey. I take a brief peek outside my window. The press are still there, doubtless waiting for some sordid comment or other from the arch cad of the century himself. I'm feeling pretty low, and know I need support. Suddenly, I have a fabulous idea. I pick up the phone and call one of my business associates, a brilliant, crazy man I implicitly trust. He picks up.

'Hi, mate. I've got a bit of a problem.'

'Yeah. So I've heard. Get your arse on over here. Let's have ourselves a swift pint.'

We meet at my associate's office in the West End and adjourn for some nectar at the local watering hole. He's an avuncular, charming fellow with a thick set of muttonchop sideburns, like a character out of a Dickens novel.

'How did you meet Griffiths?' he asks me. 'Tell me everything about him. Right from the start.'

So I tell him.

Easter, 1999

I'm in Vancouver. I've come here to work on *Amazon*, one of the flagship films of my fledgling production company, with a very talented man I believe could be a great first-time director. My son's on vacation from school, and I've brought him with me, having picked him up in Boston en route. It's only the second time I've been with him when I've not had a lot of free time on my hands and have had to work like a maniac, so I've asked an English girl along to look after him. I've been told by what I consider to be a very reliable source that she will be an absolutely perfect choice to work for me as a PA once we finally get into production. I've booked us all into The Sutton Place Hotel, a well-known show business haunt in the heart of the city. A lot of the major US TV series shoot here, such as *The X-Files*, and it's a very humming, happening place.

By day I work in my hotel room with Mike, my potential director, on the basic story structure of the piece, while I leave the girl I've come to name 'Sophie the Sorceress' to take my son out, either to ski, or to trek around the kid-oriented sights of the place.

Mike has kindly found me a voluble young man named Richard Griffiths to assist me while I'm here, helping to orient me re. the entertainment side of the city, suggesting things for my

son to do when the weather's not so good, etc. He seems like a
very nice chap when I meet him for the first time downstairs in
the bar of the hotel. A little bit odd-looking with his earrings,
staring bug-eyes and decidedly effeminate manner, but I consider
myself to be a pretty good judge of character and, by and large, it
seems like he's basically a pretty grounded soul with intelligence,
know-how and a good heart. At night, while Sophie the Sorceress
is looking after Connor, he and I hit the bars around town and get
better acquainted. His adopted father's a man called Ken Gord, an
extremely well-respected writer and producer in the city, with an
impeccable professional pedigree having made the *Highlander* TV
series function for five years during shooting in Paris. So it
eventually strikes me that young Richard's quite a clever, well-
connected young chap from a great background who, if he plays
his cards right, could well wind up possibly going places in this
funny old business of ours.

However, Griffiths, it later turns out, is a sly devil, very
much operating from his own agenda.

Sophie the Sorceress, meanwhile, is performing beautifully
with Connor. He's one hell of a kid — funny, sweet, and
incredibly bright. So it's kind of hard to imagine any nanny *not*
having a ball with him. At four years of age, while on a Virgin
Airlines flight to London, he asked me what 'mediocrity' was! I
was so astonished, I couldn't think what the hell to tell him! So I
just gestured vaguely around the cabin.

'Look around you, honey. It's pretty much everywhere.
Everything that's boring and not special in the world is what you
call "mediocrity".' Right! So now whenever you ask Connor
what mediocrity is, he replies: 'Virgin Airlines'! I should get him
doing ads for BA! He'd make a bloody fortune!

But, as fate would have it, Griffiths is apparently not the only
one operating with his own agenda. Sophie the Sorceress was
introduced to me by a helpful old gal who was working on the

budget of *Amazon*. She was the one who thought the Sorceress would make such a potentially very efficient PA for yours truly. When we first met, ol' Sophie struck me as indeed a very nice, well-mannered, well-educated, intelligent and attractive girl. She managed to give the air of being a stable, sincere, hard-working lass who had a great boyfriend in Africa she was devoted to and loved very much. Moreover, she was very keen to get into the film biz. Semi-sexy in a very blue blood, English county way, she actually appeared to be quite a catch. 'Lucky old Doctor Livingstone,' I used to think to myself every time Sophie the Sorceress strolled through my door. (Boy! Was I ever wrong about that one!)

By this point in my life I was frankly very much beginning to tire of my endless rounds of 'boffing for nothing', and was definitely getting interested again in the prospect of maybe finding a 'real woman' with a little something special to her. So one day I asked Sophie the Sorceress if she had any friends as nice as her she might want to introduce me to.

'Oh, no. No, I'm sorry,' she answered. 'They're all taken, I'm afraid.'

Now, pay attention, chaps, *and learn*. Learn about the super-devious ways of certain women. It's a piece of advice you ignore at your absolute peril! The female gender is, by and large, much smarter than we are when it comes to getting what they want with the least amount of effort possible. Why? Because in my very considered opinion it's been pretty much hard-wired by force into their evolutionary systems by us, that's why! For hundreds of years they've had to put up with us sorry, penile-obsessed, macho twits screwing up the world, going endlessly to war over tracts of land not worth a pot to piss in, fucking with the environment big time, and generally causing chaos and ruin wherever we possibly can!

Now, if *you* had to contend with a bunch of us wankers bullying you around for the last couple of millennia or so, isn't it more than highly likely *you* would have been forced, of necessity, to mutate genetically into something maybe slightly devious? I'm telling you, beware! There are literally huge battalions of chicks out there who will lie to you through their teeth simply in order to get what they want! It's not their fault. In my opinion it's just the way they've been taught to function.

Don't get me wrong. I'm a million miles away from being a misogynist. In fact, as I'm sure you're now more than well aware, I adore the little darlings! The truth be told, I bloody well admire them! And, believe me, there *are* rich pickings to be had out there. Women like gold dust, who will nurture you, protect you, shag you into stunned oblivion and, moreover, truly love you till all their teeth fall out! But, take it from me, they're one in a million. And girls like ol' Sophie the Sorceress sure as hell ain't from the same tribe!

You see, Sophie the Sorceress secretly wanted bugger-lugs all for herself. But at the time this was not to be divulged to yours truly until much later on.

Griffiths actually proves to be one hell of a help in Vancouver. He seems to know all the ins and outs of the city, and it looks like he's the kind of guy who can pretty much get anything done. We're out on the town one night when the thought occurs to me he might make a pretty good development person for my new film company if he wanted to move to London. It's a night when I've decided to give Sophie the Sorceress a free evening, and we're out with Griffiths and his mum at a fancy restaurant, when Sophie suddenly decides to have one too many, and starts a heated argument with Griffiths' old lady about the blacks in Africa. It's weird.

We move on to a club where the music's way too loud, the booze flows way too freely, and before I know it, Sophie the Sorceress has plonked herself brazenly down onto my lap, and is trying to deep-throat me big time. It's very awkward.

OK, so I suppose I could physically enjoy her for the odd night or two. But after the weird onslaught of comments at dinner, the character-tally on Sophie the Sorceress's score card has definitely taken a major downturn for yours truly. Eventually we wend our way homewards. By now I've had more than a few drinks too many myself, and suddenly Sophie the Sorceress is all over me again, like a famished piranha, this time in the hotel elevator. I maintain control, tell her it's maybe not so cool, given she's here to work as my son's nanny, and quickly vanish into my room on the valid pretext of sending the hotel nanny home to beddy-byes.

But Sophie the Sorceress turns out to be yet another of those classic female predators in the thinly veiled disguise of the Virgin Mary and, as I'm rapidly to learn over the course of the next few days, there ain't no way in hell she's gonna give up her latest victim without some kind of a fight. When push does eventually come down to shove just a few weeks after the Vancouver trip, and I decide Sophie the Sorceress is maybe not only an inappropriate young lady to be working for me, but also that she's definitely a great deal less than the catch I originally thought she might be, she pulls a classic turn on yours truly, and metaphorically attempts to plant her 'come-fuck-me' pumps right into my testicles.

February 1, 1985

The character of Marco Santorelli proves to be a real hit, particularly with the female members of the world's TV audiences. It was a heady experience. I recall walking down 57th Street in Manhattan one afternoon and a beautiful woman stopping me, saying: 'Aren't you Greg Martin? *Where have you been!*'

I did a story at the time for one of the first *Hello!* editions, back in the days when it was still a strictly Spanish gig called

¡Hola!. The journalist and I took a trip up to the top of the twin towers of The World Trade Centre, where I found myself suddenly accosted by an massive bunch of Israeli tourists from Jerusalem. Apparently Marco, the Italian peasant immigrant son who made good in the land of the free and managed to snag the hearts of all the best-looking chicks along the way, struck a resonant chord within the hearts of both the male and female Kibbutzim!

After the mini-series played a slew of extremely tasty opportunities are sent my way. Odd though it may seem, given my innate dislike of television, the one that happens to appeal to me the most is an offer from MCA/Universal to create and star in my own series. The appeal for me is largely based upon (a) the creative freedom they are prepared to give me, and (b) the ludicrous amounts of dosh they seem so willing to hurl my way. (It was still the breezy salad days of shows like *Magnum P.I.*, *Miami Vice*, and *Airwolf*, when money in Hollywood film and television circles was pretty much being thrown around around like water.)

I fly out to LA to take a series of meetings with the MCA top brass and finalise the deal. The initial approach has been made by someone big in casting (naturally, in my case, a female!) and as I board the plane at JFK, I get the best piece of solid career advice from my Runyon-esque manager, Marty, that he ever gives me.

'Whatever you do,' he intones gravely, 'don't fuck the bitch.' I don't. But I *do* make sure my noble tool gets itself a thoroughly good West Coast workout all the same!

There are a lot of phrases that tend to ring true regarding the immense folly of mixing business with pleasure. One of my favourites is: 'Don't stick your pen in the company inkwell.' It's a lot more accurate, witty, and far less offensive than the old, standard classic: 'Don't shit in your own backyard.' The message, however, is always the same. If you screw around with any broad who's got the power to somehow fuck up your professional life, you're playing with fire. Big time!

Don't do it!

Having said that, of course, I now have to confess that *I* have! Which is one of the reasons why (a) life is such a great teacher, and (b) I am now able to write such a work of such profound wisdom on the vital all-time do's and don'ts of male/female encounters!

It happened to me like this...

Part of my trip out to California this time is to meet with a whole new bunch of people who were apparently smitten with my performance as the 'Italian Stallion'. Some are agents, some were casting directors, some are what they call independent producers, some are studio executives. But ninety-nine point nine per cent of them turn out to be either women or homosexuals. And the ratio goes something like ten to one in the favour of the women. Which means one thing: potentially I could very easily wind up getting myself into a *lot* of trouble.

Now most of the female agents, casting directors, producers and executives in LA are as a general rule ugly as sin! I don't mean to sound cruel. This is simply a plain, straightforward fact and it explains why the majority of them never became actresses. One of the golden rules of the film business is that everyone, to some degree or other, is in their heart a frustrated star. Those damsels in the business in LA without the essential 'glam factor' built into their DNA typically wind up, if they have the necessary chops, as 'power players' of one kind or another *behind* the camera.

This can mean a whole host of things to the up-and-coming young male actor. The best at the game learn to play it as if they are somehow 'available', while in reality at all times maintaining a discreet wall around them, an essential distance. In a lot of ways it's a bit like a flirtation dance, like when a man's trying to seduce a girl, or vice-versa. You know as well as I do there's nothing more boring or predictable, ladies, than some guy calling you endlessly, as if there's nothing else in his sorry life except his next prospect of shagging you again. It's one great big turn-off. So what does a clever actor do in the movie business? Exactly the same! He 'plays the game'. And usually, if he's at all smart, it works like a charm. The problems always begin, precisely as they do in the arena of sex in 'civilian' life, when an ambitious young actor runs into one of the nought point one per cent of execs who happen to be as gorgeous as Elle Macpherson lying prostrate on a Hawaiian beach with nothing else on but a black silk G-string! The trick lies in at all times remembering that *they* want to seduce you, courtesy of their own agenda, just as much as you want to seduce *them*, courtesy of *yours*. And, take it from me, the kind of strength of mind required to resist the charms of this fatal nought point one per cent is enough to make the kind of psychological feats performed by certain sects of ascetic Tibetan Buddhist monks look like child's play.

I know. Because I just happen to have been born with a hide like a Sherman Tank, and the willpower of Friedrich Nietzche. And, yes, this silly bastard ultimately relented!

The are two LA ladies of power in question in my own instance. One is a very prominent casting director, and the other is, at the time, virtually head of her own mini-studio. It's a nasty trap that guys like me are typically prone to. Having a fair modicum of charisma and power, one naturally finds oneself easily getting bored if the 'challenge' isn't there with a bird. To put it succinctly, we always need a chick who's a match for us. Just as every girl needs a man who keeps them on *their* toes. Yet, sadly, in virtually every Hollywood case, the women with the chops and the equality of power seem always to be the very ones in most desperate need of serious psychotherapy. And as a result they are the ones who are potentially the most dangerous to a young actor's future.

Take the first gal I came a cropper with. When I initially met her I knew exactly who she was. I had a very good idea of her track record, the full extent of her power in LA and the kind of very prestigious projects she would be typically asked to cast. What I wasn't ready for, as I walked into the room for my taping session that fateful, sunny LA morning, was just how overwhelmingly attractive I was going to find her. As I mentioned earlier, I have a fatal weakness for Latin women. Generally, I find them infinitely sweeter, sexier, funnier, more nurturing and more loyal than examples of the female species from most other parts of the globe. (Having said that, of course, there's always the other side of the coin — i.e. their tempers, which typically bubble away like huge vats of molten lava, barely a fraction beneath the surface of their soft, adorable skins!)

This particular woman turns out to be the quintessential Mediterranean by way of New Jersey sexual time bomb. With a mass of thick, long black hair, a killer figure, and eyes truly to die for, she could very easily have had herself a major career on the other side of the camera, if she'd had the talent. So, immediately smelling danger I do my very level best to hang on to every ounce of my 'mystical actor's allure'. And I am pretty much doing a damn good job until she suddenly springs a truly fast one on me, asking me point-blank with a very provocative grin, if I'd mind maybe doing something 'a little different' from the usual boring interview and audition speech, once she had the tape rolling.

I raise my eyebrows. 'Different?'

'Yes. You know, hon,' says Carmen Miranda, sultrily. 'Like a kinda change of pace. I'm gonna ask you some very simple personal questions. Don't worry. Nothing *too* personal. It'll be fun. Treat it like a game. OK? Whatd'ya say?'

What the hell *could* I say? *She* was in charge, and *this* was the business. Besides, it did sound as if the experience might make quite a refreshing change. She angled the video camera towards me and started to roll.

'OK. Hi, Greg! I'm *really* glad to have you with us, sweetheart. Now tell me, darlin', what's your favourite colour?'

I've never come across this now very clichéd sexual psychological quiz before. So I think nothing more about it, and go ahead with my set of answers, which turn out to be sexually super-charged.

'Red.'

'Excellent! And, erm, if you were an animal, what kind of a beast would you be?'

'A beast of prey. A puma. A fast, jet-black jungle puma.'

Carmen Miranda shifts ever so slightly in her chair and takes a heavy pull on her Marlboro. I can hear the sound of her stockings rubbing together as she crosses her legs.

'Fabulous! What's your favourite kind of body of water?'

'Hello,' I think. 'I'm starting to get the picture'. I lean back in my chair, stick a ciggy in my mouth and flip open my zippo with serious attitude. Just like Steve McQueen in *The Great Escape*.

'How do you mean exactly?'

'I mean, would it be a lake, a pond, a river, the sea? Set your imagination free. Describe to me as best you can exactly what your favourite body of water would ideally look like.'

I decide to be brutally honest, but by now I can pretty much guess what kind of effect my answer's going to have. So I also choose to embellish it a little, and have myself a bit of a laugh.

'Ooh, I dunno. I suppose steep, dark, craggy cliffs. Rough, raging, foamy seas. Powerful, pounding waves hurling themselves relentlessly, like sex-mad jungle pumas, across the jutting, razor-sharp, jagged, cold rocks below.'

I grin cheekily at Carmen Miranda. Then I turn away to stare lazily out at the frantic buzz of traffic on Hollywood Boulevard below. Out of the corner of my eye I just catch the sexy Latina seductress squeezing her thighs together tightly.

'Shit,' I think. 'Better play my cards right with this one. I've maybe gone and pushed it too far. She's definitely in heat.' But it was too late. I truly had played it way too close to the edge. Bloody fool!

'I'm in town for only a couple of nights, Greg,' Carmen Miranda says, as she dismantles her tripod. 'Like you I'm essentially a New Yorker. (Heavy hint. The babe's sure done her research. Read: 'I live there too, by the way, you luscious big hunk.') I'd love to bring you in for all kinds of things back on the east coast, but why don't we hang together out here for a little while, and get to know each other better first?'

Carmen's hanging her lingerie at The Chateau Marmont, the hip, ultra-trendy hangout on Sunset Boulevard where John Belushi famously kicked the bucket. While I, wouldn't you just know it, happen to be right across the street, at Le Mondrian. This was in the days before The Sky Bar became such a fervent hot spot and pick-up joint, but still Le Mondrian was known, as was The Chateau Marmont, for its in-vogue, easy-going style. The sight of high-class hookers traipsing through the lobby of either joint at 3 a.m. was largely *de rigeur*.

'Where do you wanna meet? Your place, or mine?' Carmen asks me, as she runs her fingers through her magnificent dark tresses. I'm very tempted to reply: 'Does it matter? We both know what we're going to be doing anyway.' But I resist.

'I'll pick you up. Say at about 8.45?'

Now of course, the reason it's so fatal to literally 'fuck' with virtually any denizen of your own line of work is basically the same reason caution is generally to be advised before entering any sexual arena. The difference is that for any young chap in the movie actor's game, an encounter with some bird who's, let's say, a vet, an ornithologist, a cop, or a marine biologist, means that the chances of her having the necessary ammo to do any nasty damage to your work, after things have gone decidedly pear-shaped, are at best minimal. Whereas with some babe who registers on the Richter power scale of Hollywood, you're potentially setting yourself up for some major fireworks later on if things do go up the spout.

Carmen Miranda eventually wound up causing ol' Casanova reincarnated a *lot* of harm. Not half as much as the loathsome group of blue-blood trolls behind the recent T-P-T scandal in any way, shape or form. But still enough major career trouble to warrant a case for her definite inclusion in the pages of these randy memoirs. Some women can really be incredible! I repeat again, the vast majority of them have the capacity to get up to the kind of tricks most of us sorry lads would never dream of even contemplating. And this one really broke the mould! But more of that later.

When I get to Carmen's room that night and she opens the door, it's clear as daylight what I'm immediately *supposed* to do. But I very shrewdly don't. She's wearing an outfit that would turn just about any normal, red-blooded male without his own agenda to into a blithering idiot within ten brief seconds. An ultra-clingy, black silk mini-dress, killer 'come-fuck-me' pumps, and a pair of sheer black stockings with the naughty line of her garter belt showing provocatively underneath. I mentally congratulate myself on my extraordinary self-restraint, decline the proffered large vodka martini, and instead usher her rapidly out of the door and downstairs to my awaiting car.

But as fate would have it, that evening there was no way in hell I was going to get away with it that easily.

We dine at Wolfgang Puck's new happening hub of action, 'Spago's', on one of the hills above Sunset Boulevard. It's an interesting evening. A lot of prominent celebs pop by our table to say 'Hi' to Ms. Casting Powerhouse, ranging from the currently 'hot' actors like Richard Gere and Deborah Winger, to the likes of Billy Crystal and Jeff Goldblum, and beyond. I'm impressed.

The lady holds court like she's Louis XIV. But do I really want to make a trip to Versailles?

My curse is that women seem somehow always to get addicted to me. I've really got no idea why. It might just be the way in which I tend to treat them. This brings us right back to the reference I made at the very beginning of this magnum opus to the original 'bad lad' of the bedroom, the original Casanova himself. My mother always told me: 'Greg, my lad, you're just too damn kind to most of these women.' Maybe the truth *is* that our great Renaissance lover simply treated women so well that when a given situation was winding down and the lady in question was none too happy with the way things had turned out, she turned on him. Hence the theory of 'the united group female nobbling' of his reputation at the end of his life. And hence, perhaps, the very origins of that hackneyed phrase that, like all truly great clichés, is born from truth: 'Hell hath no fury like a woman scorned.'

This may sound like an attempt to whitewash the black-coated face of a die-hard womanising pig. But if you stop me in the street once this book is out, and ask me to join you for a beer or three, you'll get to know me better. Don't believe everything you read in the papers! But I digress. Back to curvaceous Carmen.

To make a long story short, after a vain attempt on my behalf to deflect Carmen's assault, we eventually wind up in the sack back in my room at Le Mondrian, and the night passes very rapidly in a torrid delirium of wild, passionate sex. It's a veritable blitzkrieg! In fact, ol' Carmen's dexterity in the erotic arena is so accomplished that I'm taught quite a tidy stash of stunning new tricks of the trade in the process! We bid each other a fond farewell over breakfast, and arrange to touch base at the end of the day to make arrangements for our next bout of frolics.

Less than an hour later, as I'm busy in my room scheduling my hectic day ahead, the first raging crimson flag is hoisted way high above the smoggy LA skyline. I've just put the phone down, and am about to pick it up again to make my next call, when it gives a frantic ring. (Odd how telephones sometimes seem to take on the very persona of the person who's calling. I always know when I've got myself an incipient 'bunny boiler' on the other end of my line, for example. The ring typically sounds like this: 'Greg-Greg! Greg-Greg! I'm com-coming! to ge-get you!') I answer, and sure enough it's Carmen. Her voice sounds suddenly very strange; tight, wound-up, *somehow desperately needy*! Nothing like the self-confident, cool 'pussy galore' type I took to the sheets with last night at all. Immediately I've got a full-on red alert, as the early-warning antennae in my groin activate, and the sirens start to wail their Protocol Three alarm.

'Oh, my God! You stupid, bloody twat! What the fuck have you done?' The thought echoes through my brain, leaping across my synapses as easily as a razor-sharp, red-hot knife slicing its way through half a pound of butter.

'Hi, sweetie!' she says, uncharacteristically nervously. 'Last night was just *incredible*! My God, you were just *so fucking charming*! And what an *awesome* lover! I just wanna make sure I didn't dream the whole fucking thing! I mean, you're real, aren't you? I mean, you're not just some fantastic figment of my depraved imagination?!'

'Ha, ha!' I chuckle gamely, trying desperately to make as much light as I can of what is, beyond a shadow of a doubt, already developing into a potentially *very* bad situation. 'I'm real, baby. Oh, yes! Am I ever real!' There's a long pause, as I've run out of things to say.

'You still there, sweetie?' Carmen's voice comes crackling frantically down the line in a tone of voice that makes her first comment sound positively blissed-out and relaxed by comparison.

My nerves are seriously rattled. Sweat is spotting my brow. My hands are suddenly so clammy, I almost fumble the phone to the floor. I've been here before, and I didn't like it then either. I know this potential scenario way too well. And it's fucking 'orrible! I can feel that we're maybe headed in the direction of emotional blackmail, something that, without fail, always inevitably goes hand-in-hand with deep-rooted insecurity on the part of the one trying to inflict the guilt. It's about all I can do to stop myself hanging up, leaving the room, and calling her later, pretending we were somehow cut off. I snap out of it.

'Look, love. I'm running late for a meeting. Can I maybe call you later on this afternoon? I had a really great time, too. And we'll make tonight even more special, I promise.' ('Liar!' I'm saying to myself inside my head. 'You're already scared shitless of this one!')

'OK, sweetie! But you make sure you think about my hot, wet, little pussy *all day long*!'

'Don't worry. I will!'

She hangs up. And I breathe again. But, man, inside am I worried! This story is being told principally to illustrate two vital points. (1) As I mentioned above, *never, but never* 'stick your pen in the company inkwell.' (2) As a rule it's sometimes far better to actually *be* the cold, ruthless bastard you may ultimately wind up being accused of right from the start, than simply to be yourself. That is, if you happen to be good-natured chap! Because, take it from me, if you happen to be a 'nice, regular kinda guy', being your simple, straightforward charming self can oftentimes get you into deeper and far more treacherous hot water than you could ever possibly imagine!

This is what happened to me roughly six weeks after this incident, when all the shit finally hit the fan with the nutty sex fiend, Carmen Miranda. Firstly, a bunch of black, very dead roses arrived at my door one afternoon with a macabre note of mock commiseration which read: 'Greg Martin, R.I.P. We mourn your death at the hands of a sweet, honourable woman whose heart and body you so mercilessly toyed with in the name of your highly overrated male member.'

Secondly, Carmen sent a quaint little memo out to every prominent female studio executive and producer in the biz she could possibly think of, telling them that in her opinion I was (a) a classic manipulative actor and a man definitely not to be trusted, (b) heartless, ruthless, cunning and cruel, and (c) dangerous. Moreover, my facility for using a woman for my 'own ends' was, apparently, second to none. It seems I made the pathetic shenanigins of scoundrels like Jack Nicholson and Warren Beatty look like the harmless little connivings of a pair of aging Peter Pans.

'Hell hath no fury'? You bet your sweet arse!

August 24, 1999

My life has somehow been transformed into a mind-blowing episode of *The Twilight Zone*. Last night, as I returned to my flat, I was assailed by yet another hoard of paparazzi wanting quotes and photos of the newly annointed 'Love Rat Par Excellence'. I muttered 'No comment, fellas,' and walked inside my building to find a hastily scribbled note pinned to my front door. It read as follows: 'Greg, you don't know me. But I know you. I live in the area, am very much aware of what has been going on with you — what tirannee (sic) and oppression you are being subjected to, etc., & and I believe I can help you. Please call me as soon as you can on the mobile number below. *At all cost* say *nothing* in your message, except that you have received this note and want to meet me at whatever time and at whatever location chosen by you, and I'll be there!'

The note is signed quite simply 'Reg', and the handwriting resembles that of a retarded seven-year-old. Call it folly if you like, but some sick part of me is actually rather intrigued. I'm both a writer and an actor, remember, and human psychology is a subject

I find fascinating. Who is this nut-case who's been following my story so religiously, and is so utterly convinced he can assist my cause?

I decide to give him a ring.

'Hello.' The voice that picks up on the other end of the line is tense, high-energy; male, but very high-pitched, almost feminine.

'Hi, Reg. I got your note. Can you meet me at Café Rouge opposite Harrods in half an hour?'

'I'll be there.'

Mystery man Reg hangs up. There's a whole slew of messages on my voice mail. Some are from buddies offering solace and/or assistance of one sort or another.

'If nothing else,' one chum says, 'at least call me and let's get seriously wasted together. I can't begin to imagine how the fuck you must be feeling. This is bloody outrageous!'

Some of the other messages are from various television chat shows and newspapers asking me if I'd like to write an article or come on their programme to deliver a response to the character assassination. I'm sitting flipping through my latest copy of *Men Only*, pondering my next move, when the phone rings. It's Tara.

'Hi! Are you alright?' For a brief moment there she actually sounds normal, with a slight tone of compassion in her voice.

'I've been better,' I answer dryly.

The voice at the other end of the line suddenly tightens. 'Have you seen the *Daily Express* today? Why are they doing this to you?'

'You tell me, Tara! I haven't a fucking clue! It feels bloody sinister, though, from my point of view.'

The pitch of Tara's voice suddenly escalates a full octave. She starts to wail down the phone, like a tortured moggy.

'Christ, Greg! Why the hell did you lie to me? Mummy and Santa both say the people who've been calling them are all saying the same thing! Some horrible story about a girl in France you were engaged to! They say that you wanted her because she was rich and well-connected! They say you met her parents, bought her a ring and everything! Mummy says an older man who's close to you and your family wants to meet her in London next week to explain who you are and to tell her I must stay away from you!'

'What? What bloody girl in France, Tara? I've never even come close to getting engaged to any bird since my divorce! Who the hell are all these bloody people?'

'She won't tell me! So she certainly won't tell you!'

'Great! Tell her thanks from me! It's like being tried in public without a fucking jury! What does this weirdo who's supposedly so close to my family have to say for himself?'

She gives me a short outline of the kind of nasty character sketch of yours truly this malevolent, unknown arsehole has already delivered by phone to Patty, and as I'm listening, I feel the blood slowly drain from my face. I drop the phone.

I know who he is.

CHAPTER SIX

L.A., SEXUAL INSANE ASYLUM (PART THREE)

'Every country gets the circus it deserves. Spain gets bullfights. Italy gets
the Catholic Church. America gets Hollywood.'
Erica Jong, *How To Save Your Own Life* (1977)
'A lot of people complain about sex on the television, but as long as you
can avoid the aerial, it's okay by me.'
Tara Schwartz

November 8, 1987

Noon. I'm sitting quietly by myself on the terrace of Le Petit
Four, an ultra-trendy show-biz restaurant and watering hole on
the main drag of Sunset Boulevard, sipping my fifth cappuccino
while going over the script of a piece of episodic television I've

been asked to guest star in. Le Petit Four happens to be a great place for people-watching, particularly if you enjoy examining the bizarre lives of wannabe producers, actresses, models, arms dealers and potential scumbag, serialising philanderers. At this hour the place is typically frequented by a mass of seedy-looking men in *de rigeur* LA garb (black suits, Armani shades) talking pointlessly loudly on their mobiles. I take a brief respite from the awful dialogue on the page and take in the crowd. My eye is drawn to one particular gormless sod who I find sitting at the same table here every time I'm around, regular as clockwork, with a big, fat Monte Christo cigar in one hand, and his cellphone in the other.

He has big, buggy eyes, just like the late, great Marty Feldman — but on bennies — a very obvious toupee, and the kind of vicious glare in his eye that will hopefully keep any of the gorgeous, super-fit, silicone-enhanced babes prowling the sunny sidewalk well away from his Svengali-like spider's web.

One of the waitresses, a mate of mine, stops by for a chat. 'You see that really weird-looking guy over there?' she says, nodding towards ol' Marty F. with the hairpiece. 'You wanna hear somethin' *really strange*?' She leans in closer, her voice dropping to a hushed whisper. '*He's not talking to anybody!*'

I grin up at her. 'You're having me on!'

Her hand immediately covers her heart. 'Swear to God! Cross my heart and hope to die. And may I wind up a lap dancer in Vegas, if I lie. He's here every day *pretending* to be doing deals, setting up pictures, trading stocks, whatever. But he's actually talking to *the fucking wind*!'

I stare again at the pathetic, cream-faced loon. 'So what's his game, then?'

'What d'ya think?'

'Sex. He's trying to impress people, pick people up.'

'Top marks, Einstein.' She turns. And I watch her perfectly formed arse sashay its way off into the proverbial sunset.

It turns out that people playing what I call 'phoney-phone' has recently become a serious problem out here in La-La Land. Tens of thousands of people are plugging up the air waves on a daily basis, as they sit in their leased Porsches, Ferraris and Mercs faking an endless stream of fiery but phony negotiations over some dreamt-up, 'crucial' celluloid deal or other. I return to my piece of 'great classical drama'. The role I've been asked to play is that of a totally fiendish husband who decides one day to knock off his dull millionairess wife and run off to Bermuda with all her money, his foxy little plaything in tow (type-casting once again, it seems!)

It's one of those shows they've just begun experimenting with that has a vaguely risky amount of semi-adult, borderline sexual content. Innocent and innocuous enough, I suppose, but in terms of a serious acting challenge, roughly the equivalent of carrying a lightweight spear in a C-class touring production of *A Winter's Tale*. 'Ah! What the hell?' I think to myself. 'If they want to throw more of that kind of ludicrous money at me for nothing, what do I have to lose?' I pick up my mobile, call my agent and accept the gig.

That's when *she* walks into the restaurant.

Remember I mentioned earlier there were two women of power I made the mistake of getting way too close to in the course of my early Hollywood days? Well this is number two. I'll call her Eve, since she reminded me so completely of the kind of predatory characters Bette Davis played so memorably in her prime. Eve is a major studio exec with the kind of naturally powerful sexual allure that could cause major pile-ups on the freeway, along with a stiff dose of the absolutely one hundred per cent killer personality to go along with it as a side-dressing.

As she stalks her way on inside Le Petit Four that day, I see at least half a dozen grown men ruin their crisply fresh-pressed Armani suits by dropping forkfuls of Spaghetti Carbonnara into their laps, or nervously spilling mouthfuls of Cabernet Sauvignon down their fronts.

Eve sits herself down at the table next to mine for her power lunch opposite a balding, charismatic man with a charming smile and the natural aura of a major power player. I suddenly realise his name which in this town can mean only one thing. The woman either has what is termed in the industry 'serious chops', or she's an extremely high-class hooker. From her looks she could be either one, although as the minutes pass by and I catch the odd snippet of their conversation here and there, it becomes crystal clear to me that she's very much the former.

She seems to be paying zero attention to me until I ask the waitress for the check and start gathering up my script, pen and note pad. At that moment, the man happens to leave to pay a trip to the little boy's room, and Eve suddenly turns my way, proffering her business card, as she flashes me her practised, killer smile.

'Hi. I'm Eve Adams,' she says sultrily. 'I know you. You're Greg Martin. I saw the mini-series you shot with Burton. You're a gifted, extremely sexy man. And you're sitting on a shit-load of talent. I believe you could easily rock this town like no other matinée idol since John Barrymore. Why don't you give me a call?'

Like a true sucker, I'm not averse to such flattery, and I stare at the card, as the guy wends his way back to her table, and the superbly polished 'there's no way in hell any of you men can touch me!' veneer suddenly rears up again on Eve's perfect face, like a beautiful, solid marble drawbridge.

The card tells me that Eve is indeed quite an accomplished lady. For one thing, she's the president of her own production company on the Warner Brothers lot, the name of her outfit does more than just ring a few bells in my head. This woman's been involved with some really heavy-hitting box-office smashes. I glance back at her, and her eyes give me the briefest of come-hither glances, as she sips discreetly on her glass of iced Perrier. She's certainly got my attention. There's nothing more attractive to a man than a beautiful, self-contained woman with power. I'm excited. Who knows? She might just be that really special someone.

Wrong!

Over the next few days I check out Eve's pedigree. She's been married, but is now divorced and has no children. She's roughly forty (although, God knows, with the kind of 'work' done on most of the women in this town, she could easily be well into her mid-fifties!). She has an excellent, solid rep of being more than able to tough it out in what is still very much a man's world (i.e. chances are she's a bit of a ball-buster!). She's got great taste in film projects, and a lovely, sprawling mansion. And, there's a *lot* of very nasty gossip surrounding not only her notoriously ravenous sexual appetite, but also the copious amounts of 'Charlie' she's rumoured to like shoving up her nose.

Tom's fifty. He's been Head of Corporate Finance at one of the largest studios in town for over fifteen years. A close mate of mine since I first hit major pay dirt with the mini-series a few years ago, he's a smart, funny, male chauvinist-pig with the kind of mouth on him that would make Lenny Bruce turn crimson. He also happens to know *everyone* in town, has all of the dirt on the major women, and if he hasn't been in the sack with them himself, it's not a problem. He's got a set of secret sexual dossiers stashed away in the basement of his home in the foothills of Coldwater Canyon that makes the CIA's massive undercover UFO operation look like a highly abridged version of Beatrix Potter's *The Tale Of Mrs. Tiggywinkle*. It's a highly impressive collection of bizarre sexual trivia, and as he takes me through Eve's 'file' one night over a couple of stiff vodka martinis, I force myself to resist the overwhelming temptation to ask him exactly why he does it. 'Each to his own,' I think, as I pore over her file of decadence and debauchery. Still, it strikes me as a bit weird. Why would a mature, highly successful businessman spend the bulk of his free time building up a secret dossier on the alleged sexual preferences and practices of virtually every prominent single female in the film industry?

Why? Because it's Hollyweird! That's why! They call it 'the land of quakes and flakes'. But by now, having truly understood the sheer volume of men and women who've willingly gone under the knife out here solely in the name of prolonging their capacity for sexual attraction and fulfilment, I think it should be renamed 'the land of fucks, nips and tucks'!

'So, when exactly are ya figurin' on doin' the dirty deed with the nasty ol' Black Widow?' says Tom, getting straight to the point, as he loosens his tie and chugs back his sixth martini.

'Do I detect a note of caution and healthy scepticism in your voice, Tom?' I ask, as I take his glass and move over to the bar for refills.

'Correct. Eve is — how shall I put it? — Eve is a law unto herself. C'mon, Greg! You read the dossier! She's a fuckin' A-list barracuda! She makes a woman like Cleopatra or Catherine De Medici look like Julie Andrews singing 'Supercalifradgilisticexpialadocious' on the set of *Mary* fuckin' *Poppins*! Get your fuckin' head outta your ass!!'

'So I take it you think I'm an idiot to get anywhere near her, right?' I hand him his seventh martini. He takes a big hit and shoots me a sly grin, just like Humphrey Bogart in *The Maltese Falcon*.

'Nah! I admire you! You said it! Heck!'

I shrug, just like the cocky, naive prat that I am. 'Exactly, Tom. Just my feeling.'

August 24, 1999 (contd)

Recovering from the shock of realising that someone I had always considered a deeply loyal friend — a man so close to me that I could never conceive in a million years the possibility of our relationship ever changing — has somehow mutated overnight into one of the enemy takes me a little more than just a good few minutes. But eventually I manage to get it together and stroll on over to Café Rouge outside Harrods to meet Reg, the Mystery Man.

Reg has told me that he 'knows' me, so I sit alone for a quiet few minutes over a steaming cup of coffee, and await his promised clandestine appearance. The minutes tick on by and the enigmatic Reg shows no sign of showing. Eventually I down my cappuccino, pay my bill, get to my feet, and am just about to head on homeward when I hear an urgent, sibilant hiss from my right.

'Sit down! Say *nothing*! Don't even look at me! Pretend you've decided to stay and order yourself another cup of coffee!'

I suddenly feel like I'm starring in some bizarre remake of *Three Days Of The Condor* meets *All The President's Men* meets *The Fugitive*. I sit back down, catch the waiter's eye, order my additional cup of cappuccino, then slowly turn. Reg is sitting right there beside me, like the character Deep Throat, quietly pretending to read his copy of the midday edition of the *Evening Standard*. His piggy blue eyes dart frantically from right to left, then back again, before he finally decides the coast is all clear and it's safe for him to speak. He turns to face me, his weird face lighting up in the phoniest, cheesiest of psuedo-smiles I've seen since my days working as the most popular gigolo in the Polo Lounge' of the Beverly Hills Hotel.

'How are you?'

I nod cautiously — *very* cautiously. 'I'm... fine. How are you?'

'Great! Never been better!'

'Good. Good.'

We nod at one another, grinning like a pair of gormless idiots for a few more seconds, then he slowly slides across to the empty seat opposite me.

'Mind if I join you?'

'Be my guest. Like a coffee?'

Reg shakes his head almost angrily in response. He pulls out a large plastic bottle from a Harrods bag. Inside is the most disgusting looking lime-green liquid imaginable. 'Never touch the stuff! I juice!' says Reg proudly, as he pops the cap and takes a hefty pull of the horrible concoction.

Reg is a slim, well-dressed man of about forty with short, fair hair. He's got an extremely elegant briefcase with him, and all in all looks pretty normal, except for his perpetual air of almost manic glee. He starts frantically to jabber away at me in dramatically hushed tones, punctuated by the odd, occasional deeply disturbing snigger, his little eyes shooting across from one side of his face to the other at lightning speed. My first thought is that he may be on drugs, but I've been around enough of that palaver in my time to know the classic symptoms, and ol' Reg doesn't have 'em. So I'm forced to conclude he's quite simply out of his tree. He leans forward, conspiratorially and begins his pitch.

'Before I say anything, we never met, OK? This conversation, none of it, ever happened. The information I'm about to give you, the organisation I work with, what I'm about to divulge, all of it is just way too precious to be tampered with.'

He takes another hit of the awful-looking puke-chartreuse health drink in the plastic bottle, wipes his mouth with the back of his hand, and goes on.

'I just happen to be connected with one of the most powerful sources of energy on the planet. And you, Mr. Martin, are sitting on what my friends and I like to term a "power line of communication". He pauses for effect. 'You look like shit, by the way, you really should start to juice.'

I almost choke on my coffee. The last time I glanced in the mirror, I thought I looked pretty good, considering all the garbage that has been suddenly and so vehemently hurled into my life.

'It's hardly surprising that your physical vehicle is exhibiting these signs of severe depletion. You probably *feel* like shit. But in fact, you're in a *potentially very rewarding position*. You just have to realise it.'

'Really?'

The general goobledygook tone of his conversation I find fascinating. 'This is going to provide some truly great stuff for a movie script one day!' I think to myself, as I quickly light up a fag. A self-taught master of neuro-linguistic programming, I quickly decide on dovetailing my own verbal style and body language to his in order to put him more at ease.

'I understand what you're communicating to me here, Reg. But I think you know as well as I do that my "power line" has somehow been temporarily severely tampered with. How do you suggest I restore it?'

Reg eyeballs me sceptically. For a brief moment the possibility that I may just possibly be 'extracting the urine' big-time clearly flits through his grey matter. Then the thought vanishes, and he's right back on line with his own unique brand of 'gibbldeygobble-speak'.

'You're suffering from what I term a classic line of oppression,' he tells me. 'And my sincere advice to you is don't look for this line of oppression in *this* lifetime.' He leans right in close, his voice falling to a mysterious hiss. 'It comes from elsewhere!'

It's exactly as if all my molecules have been dissolved, à la *Star Trek* and I've somehow just been teleported right back to La-La Land at the speed of light. But this guy, Reg, is so fucking

English! And we're sitting at the Café Rouge in Knightsbridge! Right down the block from the new church conversion on Walton Street by Damien Aspinell! What the hell is going on? I must find out. A vague suspicion borne from my brief fling with Ms. W. way back when filters into my mind, and I decide to dangle the bait. I eyeball him sharply, forcing an icy glaze into my pupils that would make Darth Vader turn pale as a pint of milk. Then I deftly mix it with a 'brotherly love' smile.

'I know you from another lifetime, don't I Reg?'

Reg leans back in his chair, a look on his little face like he's just made a dear friend for life. An air of immense satisfaction settles over him.

'I *knew* you were a receptor! Now, what I counsel you to do, Greg, is to meet with a very special man I know from LA. This man is *the most omnipotent power line surgeon in existence*! He's invincible!'

Reg leans forward again, a magnificent smile suffusing his face, like he's just hit the mother lode. 'It was in the great lost continent of Atlantis that we knew one another, my ancient, much-hallowed pupil.'

'I recall, great master,' I hiss back at him in a deeply reverential tone. 'But back to this lifetime, we must make haste, Reg. How do I meet this power line surgeon? What do I do with him?'

'Let's just call him the Master for now, for convenience sake. I'll call him tonight. He can probably fly over sometime during the next month. He'll need to spend one week with you: *twenty-four hours a day, every day*. For now on you must simply do a 'Fabian'. Go invisible. Under no circumstances whatsoever are you to have any more contact with the outside world. You're keeping all your energy for the Master. He'll need to know everything about you. And I mean *everything*.'

He breaks off, lost somewhere in the shadowy hinterlands of

his cookie consciousness, searching once more for his 'mysterious' look.

'At the end of the week, the Master will know whether he can work with you or not. My guess is that your power line will be restored immediately.'

'Uh-huh,' I nod sagely. 'Sounds very interesting. And, um, by the way, how much does all this cost me?'

Reg doesn't so much as bat an eye. 'Fifteen thousand pounds. You pay half up-front, half at the end.'

'And if it doesn't work out?'

'Then the Master keeps the seven thousand, five hundred.'

'Right. And what about you?'

'What do you mean?'

'What do you get out of it, Reg?'

Reg's face turns suddenly indignant. 'Nothing! Absolute zero! Zip! I want nothing but to assist my fellow travellers in their unique chosen quests for ultimate personal power!'

'Good. I'm glad.' I smile, nod again politely, and then quickly down the rest of my cappuccino. 'You want me to call you on your mobile later with my decision?'

'Yes. You can always get me on the mobile number I gave you. But remember, never say *anything* on that line, bar precisely when and where you want to meet. It's absolutely *imperative*!'

'Gotcha.' I stand. 'Well, I'll take my leave of you then, Reg. Many thanks. It's been truly fascinating.' I extend my hand. 'We'll talk.'

Reg eyeballs me intensely one last time. 'We will.' His grip tightens. 'Get back on line, Mr. Martin! Get your circuits plugged back in!'

'Don't you worry, Reg. I will.'

I leave Café Rouge, cross the street and walk into Harrods. Inside I make a beeline for the book department, pick up a copy of *Bedlam: An Illustrated World History Of Lunatics, Crackpots and*

Madmen, and head on back to my apartment.

November 18, 1987

It's been ten days since my initial encounter with Eve at Le Petit Four, and the two of us have arranged to go out for the night to a celeb party at the Brentwood home of Mike Ovitz, head of CAA, arguably the most powerful agent in the world at the time. I pick up Eve at her hideaway, parking my Mazda MX5 in the driveway, and as I walk towards the obscenely ornate front door (Los Angelenos have this weird thing about doors. They can be as ugly as sin, just so long as they're BIG!), an enormous great German shepherd suddenly bounds out of the shadows, barking like the proverbial Hound of The Baskervilles, making a perfect face-plant, razor-sharp fangs bared, right in my precious crotch. Eve opens the decidedly Sixties motel drawbridge in her skin-tight black leather pants and red bodice, courtesy of Fredericks Of Hollywood

'Ha, ha! You've got him well trained!' I say gamely, as I yank the horrible hound from my balls and she beckons me on inside her lair.

Eve's home is a trip. Just about every spare inch of wall space is lined with a series of intensely erotic paintings done in oils, showing vastly oversized men's genitalia in various stages of arousal. I do my best to act casually as she leads me on through to the living room, but it's not that easy. I feel like I've just entered the den of some kind of female Dracula on heat. And there's evidently still more to come. As she asks me what I'd like by way of an alcoholic lubrication, and gestures for me to sit myself down in front of the fire, I notice the extraordinary piece of 'sculpture' adorning the massive glass-topped coffee table. It's a fully extended penis the size of my tibia, made out of solid silver, and complete with a mass of what are very clearly intended to be crudely pulsating veins ribbing its sides.

Eve smiles naughtily, glancing at the 'sculpture', as she hands me what must be a quadruple Johnny Walker Black on the rocks.

'Do you like it?'

I down most of the Scotch in one rapid gulp. 'It's... it's quite something, isn't it? Yes. Very... Very life like!'

'Recognise him?'

I crunch down nervously on a thick chunk of ice. 'Should I?'

I know they sell what they claim to be replicas of various celebrities' penises in dildo form at sex shops in places like Amsterdam and Hamburg. But finding one done in solid silver masquerading as 'a work of art' in the living room of one of the most high-powered female Hollywood executives is a little different. Eve just sniggers, and plops herself down lasciviously on the black leather sofa beside me.

'I knew you were a man of taste from the first moment I saw you. Oof! God! It's so hot in here!' She undoes a few buttons on her bodice and tosses back her thick mane of hair. 'You don't really wanna go to Ovitz's boring old party, do you, hon?'

Now, I'm actually quite looking forward to this celeb bash. It's going to be a 'power party' par excellence with a chance to meet and greet and generally have a fun time with what are bound to be some majorly serious industry players. I'm caught. I like the business I'm in, relish the social side of things, and am ambitious enough to have learnt, as our own Bonnie Prince Charlie once said to my dear old man: 'It's not *what* you know that counts, Sir George, but *who* you know.'

Surely there'll be time enough for some heavy-duty sexual shenanigins between me and Vampirella later on in the evening. But Eve clearly regards the Ovitz party as a ploy, a simple excuse to get this hot little new English stud Gregoire over here to her 'fuck 'em an' suck 'em pad', and nail him straight away in the sack. I chug back the rest of my Scotch and turn to face her. If I'm going to be treated like a high-class male hooker, then I'm damn well going to act like one.

'Eve, my gorgeous little lovely. You're quite simply one of the sexiest women I've ever laid my eyes on.' I reach over to her, brushing the fingers of my right hand ever so gently across her bodice. 'Believe me, there's nothing I want more than to rip off all your clothes and ravish you right here on the rug in front of ol' Long Dong Silver... ' I break off and delicately remove my hand from her breasts. 'But I know if there's anyone in this godforsaken town who can understand this, it's you. I'm really looking forward to us putting in just a brief little appearance at this Ovitz do. Did I tell you I'm up for the lead in this incredible new pic Universal's trying to get off the ground called *Shakespeare In Love*? They want an unknown. I understand all the Uni execs are going to be in attendance.' (Yes! This was twelve years ago! *Shakespeare In Love* was around way back then! That's how long it sometimes takes to get a movie off the ground!)

Eve stares at me for a long moment. It's almost as if you can see the thoughts hurtling through her brain at the speed of light. On the one hand she clearly loves the fact that she hasn't made a mistake. I'm exactly what she thought I was: a deeply ambitious young actor determinedly set out on his high road to fame and fortune. On the other hand this is clearly a very painful scenario she's doubtless been through many times before (i.e. 'Why is it I'm always so attracted to hunky young men who basically want the same things I do?').

Eventually we reach a healthy compromise, and I do a searing little quickie with her in front of the roaring fire pre-party with ol' 'Long Dong' looking on solemnly for good measure. But as we get up and pull ourselves together for the evening ahead, I already have a pretty clear idea I've again most probably made a boo-boo par excellence, and once more blindly rushed in a mite too quickly where angels fear to tread.

It's not Eve's exalted sense of personal power. That doesn't bother me in the slightest. In fact, I find it quite a turn-on. Nor is it her overtly assertive personality. Nor her weird taste in 'art'. It's the way she tried so desperately to 'talk seriously dirty' to me as I was just starting to do the deed with her that caused the proverbial question mark to appear in such stark relief above my prefrontal lobes that night. Eve was simply one of those ladies who, sadly, couldn't manage to pull it off.

Now don't get me wrong. I love talking smutty when I'm in the sack. We're going to get into that specific aspect of sex in a lot more detail a little later on. Let's just say that a little sordid whispering delivered at the right point in the course of the proceedings can definitely send any erotic encounter way up into the stratospheric heights of ecstasy, as long as it's pulled off with tact and skill. But it has to be done with some degree of delicacy and finesse, or it simply gets way too *funny*!

This is what happened with Eve...

What hadn't been in Tom's voluminous sex file on the beautiful female barracuda, but what I later found out, was that Eve had apparently been raised in what was more or less a glorified Manhattan whorehouse. Her dad, whom she described as 'a simple entrepreneur' was actually an out-and-out thug masquerading as a businessman, and one of his entrepreneurial ventures was a highly successful and extremely lucrative string of high-class knocking shops. So Eve had in fact experienced a far more vivid and colourful upbringing than even yours truly! What this meant for Eve the young girl was that she was tossed unceremoniously into the deep, dark vagaries of sexual reality long before any normal lass would have had the slightest inkling what any of it was all about.

Consequently the sheer volume and variety of her accumulated erotic experience made my massive mental carnal filing system look like a miniature version of The Lilliputian

Public Library. And one of the first things she'd evidently learnt at the feet of her many mistresses inside the chain of whore houses was how to 'talk smutty'. Except that Eve did it to this day exactly like a Madison Avenue floozy.

I'll maintain until I'm finally six feet under that no matter how filthy and lewd you want to make your personal sexual chit-chat, it must always be delivered with a piquant little sauce of seduction. And in Eve's case, in plain simple English, that meant not bellowing aloud right into my eardrums, like a Brooklyn bloody fog horn.

'Do you want me to spread for you, huh, peaches? C'mon! Tell me how much you want me to spread for you, baby!' I can tell you, when I first heard those words, it gave my poor old Peter the shock of his bloody life!

I hurriedly bury the memory deep at the back of my brain as we sally forth together into the smoggy LA night, winding up half an hour later at the Ovitz bash. This turns out to be your typical 'respectable', high-end type of LA show-biz affair, where the only drugs mentioned are Prozac, Xanax and Zoloft, and the only hint of any sexual naughtiness is strictly confined to the plunging neck-lines and arse-clinging gossamer silk belonging to the various Hollywood wives and assorted bimbettes' on show. I make sure I do the rounds, chatting here and there with various power players and glam queens, and at 2 a.m. on the dot, just as I'm on the point of getting into some seriously deep and potentially dangerous conversation with a true 'thinking man's pin-up' I've got the major hots for — Sigourney Weaver — Eve's unfailing feminine radar kicks into action and Vampirella suddenly appears out of nowhere, collaring me, hauling me off well out of any potential harm's way, and back to her spider's web off Coldwater Canyon.

I've just barely managed to shut the door of her Porsche when she grabs me by the throat and forces her tongue down my larynx with the ferocity of a ravenous prehistoric raptor.

'I know I've got a reputation in this town for being a bit of a bitch and a real wild woman, Greg,' she says, as I eventually manage to prize myself free from her paws and fire up the ignition. 'But really, nobody in their right mind in LA — at least nobody I respect — would ever call me a nymphomaniac. I only sleep with good-looking men!'

She giggles sultrily, just like Marilyn Monroe in *The Seven Year Itch*, as I hastily transform Pirellis into rubber and pull the car back out onto Sunset.

I know I'm in for quite a ride when we get back to her place, but nothing could have possibly prepared me for what ol' Eve actually had in store. It's a classic case of 'strip one another naked as we stumble towards the bedroom', and in fifteen seconds flat we're rolling around under the covers, like a couple of crazed wild boars in rutting season. Eve gets on top of me and starts to ride me, panting and groaning, like a donkey running the LA marathon. She keeps this up for a good twenty minutes before she suddenly stops, rolls off me and stands up, a wicked glint suffusing her eyes.

'Be back in a minute, gorgeous.'

Eve vanishes back out into the living room, returning thirty seconds later with ol' 'Long Dong' Silver clutched tightly in her sweaty little palms. She giggles lasciviously again, sticks the enormous celeb phallus on the bedside table and leaps into bed, hauling me to her, her phenomenal tongue rolling out like the proverbial red carpet at a Hollywood premiere, as she plants yet another ferocious kiss inside my mouth.

'Um, what's he here for, sweetheart?', I ask, nodding nervously towards 'Conundrum Cock' glinting eerily in the stark moonlight. It's literally the size of a Kalshnikov rifle, and right now looks pretty much equally as dangerous.

Eve breaks from me, rolling her eyes provocatively. 'Him?

Oh, he's here to share in our exquisite night of pleasure, baby.'

I clear my throat edgily. There's a deeply disturbing feeling slowly welling up way down in the pit of my stomach. And it ain't nothin' to do with the large number of Oysters Rockerfeller I slipped down my throat back at the Brentwood Ovitz bash.

'Really? And how's he gonna do that?'

'Pick him up,' Eve orders, as she rolls over onto her front, head buried deep in the pillows.

'O.K...' I oblige edgily. Long Dong's a *heavy bastard*! And about as cold as Christmas Eve in Lapland. 'What now?'

'Now shove him up my ass!'

The crisp, firmly delivered instruction definitely meets my ears, but it barely registers. I'm in a state of absolute shock.

'What?'

'You heard me. Shove the sexy little motherfucker up my ass!'

I pause. The weirdness of all this has made my own real-life pecker shrivel up into sorry oblivion. The poor, wizened little lad looks like an exhausted midget lying in the massive shadow of what has to be the mother of all dildos. Tentatively I bring 'Long Dong' towards Eve's posterior. Then it all gets too much. I shove the foul metallic member back onto the bedside table.

Eve rolls back over. 'What are you doing?'

I shake my head. ' Sorry, love. I... I can't do it.'

'Why not? It's my ass!'

'Exactly!'

Eve stares at me like I'm just about the biggest wimp in Christendom. Then she reaches over for 'Long Dong'.

'Turn over, then. I'll stick him in yours.'

I'm out of that bed and through the door back into the living room quicker than greased lightning. In under a minute I've got my glad rags back on and am heading out the door. As I get into my MX5, I see the naked Eve with 'Long Dong' in her arms, her horny Hound of The Baskervilles beside her, silhouetted in the gargantuan doorway. She raises her hands to the Heavens. 'Long Dong' glints again eerily in the moonlight.

'You neurotic actor bastard! Don't you realise who this man was? He was a fucking God!'

'I don't care!'

Is it my imagination, perhaps some bizarre trick of light, or is the German shepherd staring at her feminine equipment in the most lewd, disturbing fashion, as I peel off down the driveway like a madman?

I never saw Eve again under those circumstances. I thought it best to nip that particular scenario very quickly in the bud. I still run into her occasionally at this or that business function. She was at the Cannes Film Festival last year, and I regularly catch a glimpse of her face on the live Oscar telecast.

A few days after the 'Long Dong' incident I get a card from her in the mail. It reads:

'You ran out on a magical erotic experience offered only to the rare and privileged few. A close encounter with Rudolph Valentino's penis.'

August 25, 1999

I'm awoken by a frantic phone call from a girl I knew briefly in Cannes. She's phoning from Switzerland.

'Tell me it's not true!' is all she says in her dramatic Slavic accent, exactly like Greta Garbo protesting so desperately that she 'vants to be alohhne!' I try my best to explain to her what I know about all the madness that's gone down, but before I'm halfway through my sentence she hangs up. More trouble on its way, I think to myself as I slowly roll my way back into heavy-duty REM-mode.

All I really know about the lady is that roughly two weeks after we had become 'better acquainted' in the South of France, I had what I felt at the time were legitimate reasons for suspecting her of being some kind of girl on the make. I still don't know the truth. But it wasn't a pleasant experience. I had to ask her to leave my suite in an extremely prestigious Sixth arrondisement Parisian hotel managed by a friend of mine when I felt she was trying to filch some money out of me.

Here's how it all happened.

I had taken Griffiths with me on my trip to the Cannes Film Festival that year. It was the official launch of my new film and television production company, and by and large it was a great success. I had a few red flags thrown up for me while there with regard to Mr. Griffiths' suitability as an employee, but I tried my best to let these slide by, chalking them up to his inexperience.

Cannes is a funny place. For ten days all the surreal madness and insane hoopla of Hollywood descends on one of the sunniest, sexiest and most decadent resort towns on the Mediterranean coast, in a frantic whirlwind of media hype and mayhem. It's a lot of fun. But if you're any kind of a serious industry player, it's also majorly hard work. A lot of what might be more nicely termed 'groupies' and industry hangers-on regularly put in an appearance, amongst them always a veritable hoard of your regular old 'good time girls'. These are your basic play chicks with the kind of manipulative agendas that make the notorious connivings of Prince Machiavelli look like a rudimentary game of snakes and ladders played by a chimp. Most of the smarter ones typically wind up most nights in the wee, small hours at the rather 'shi-shi' locale of Le Terrace Bar, out at The Hotel Du Cap.

The Du Cap is where all the bigger stars, such as Connery, Gibson, Cruise and Costner go, and by 2 a.m., when most of the other hotel bars have shut up shop for the night, Le Terrace is humming like a beehive. One night I was chatting away with Julie Taymor, the talented director of both the smash-hit Broadway version of *The Lion King* and the much-heralded production of

Titus Andronicus, starring Anthony Hopkins and Jessica Lange, when a voluptuous blonde swung by my chair and decided to introduce herself. She was an attractive, slightly chubby girl from Russia. The vixen told me she was in town on business, adding that she worked for a big media figure. I was a lot more than 'merry' that particular night, and can recall asking her if she maybe wanted to meet up with me later on in the week.

To cut a long story short, she came over to my lovely little apartment on the Croisette one night, looking hot enough to turn St. Francis of Assisi back into a fully paid-up, card-carrying member of the 'Lascivious, Lustful Latin Lotharios and Lovers League'. We had a brief, torrid affair as the Festival wound down to a close, finishing with me being stupid enough to ask her if she'd maybe like to drive back to the UK with me in my BMW.

The journey through France was a lot of fun. I love driving, and I made sure we stayed at a couple of lovely, very swanky Relais Et Chateaux hotels en route. We pretty much lived like kings, wining and dining away to our heart's content, and at night I had more than my fill of the lady. Contrary to what she later told the tabloids, I recall 'Greta Garbo' and I having quite a bit of fun together in the sack.

The truth is it was her extra-high-maintenance attitude *outside* the bedroom that by the time we finally reached the City of Lights had begun to eat into me to the point where my pecker was in a state of serious rebellion. Within the space of three short days she was exhibiting sure-fire symptoms of being yet another die-hard wallet-piranha, so by the time we finally got to the fabulous Hotel Lutetia on The Boulevard Raspail, and she asked to borrow some money from me to go shopping because neither her Switch Card, Barclaycard nor Amex Card seemed to be working, I had become a mite dubious. The girl was supposed to have a killer job! I uncomfortably gave her the only cash I had on me that afternoon, about FFr 500, and sent her out with my Girl

Friday to take a tour of the sights. Sixty seconds flat after the door had shut behind them, Griffiths was at my side, her handbag open in his hands. He clapped his hands together, like a camp little kid in a candy store.

'Ooh! This is so much fun! I *love* it! Maybe she's a spy!'

Before I could stop him, he was rifling his way through the bag's contents. He suddenly squealed with delight, holding up an open wallet full of credit cards and her passport. According to her cards, Ms. 'I vant to be alohhne' apparently had three different identities, and more than FFr 3,000 stashed away in cash for good measure. I shook my head and immediately told Griffiths to replace the bag where he'd found it.

'Call the concierge. It's clear as daylight she's got something going on, Richard. So let me teach you a lesson about being a man. I don't care what the girl is. A gentleman never rifles his way through a lady's handbag.'

I was very displeased with his behaviour. Griffiths stared at me in abject disappointment, like a naughty puppy dog. He didn't get it.

'Ah, forget it. Just tell Jean-Marc I'd like the lady in question removed from my suite. Now!'

Now it might sound as if I was taking an excessively severe course of action under the circumstances, but don't forget ol' bugger-lugs has been around the track a few times and, believe me, there's a lot of strange bods out there, particularly around the funny old film business. What attracts all the weirdos to this game is the superficial glamour. If you're a natural-born risk-taker, like yours truly, you hopefully learn to start bringing a modicum of caution into your world as time passes. And I have. But I never allow myself to forget that Murphy's Law is forever in operation. If something or someone manages to slip past your nose, and all those proverbial vermilion banners start flapping in your face, like a crazed bunch of Chinese dragons in the sunset every time a girl or so-called 'business associate' opens their mouth, then you'd better sit up, pay serious attention, and take action. Or you might not only wind up with an empty bank account; you might also have a 'one-way ticket to Palookaville' in your pocket or, worse still, a knife stuck in your back! Life has gotten pretty scary. Fortunately, the French are well used to dramatic interludes between men and women. It's the very stuff of life for these people. The number of women Jean-Marc had had to throw out of his hotel probably rivals the number of pints of Haagen-Dazs 'cookies and cream' ice cream Marlon Brando has shoved down his gullet in his lifetime! And when the coast is all clear and the deed has been done, I wend my way downstairs to apologise to the staff for the incident. Jean-Marc just chuckles to himself and offers me a glass of Kir Royal in the bar.

'Forget eeet, Gregoire,' he tells me. 'Zeess eess notheen. My boys 'eere, for zem you are — 'ow you say — ay eero. My God! Last week I 'ad to call za gendarmerie at fayeeve o'clock een za morneeng! Zere were feefteen femmes de la nuit we 'ad to deespose ovve!'

Jean-Marc is a good man. He's a great hotelier, has a wife, six kids, and he works like a Trojan (in the non-prophylactic sense of the word). 'Why are we Brits always so bloody moralistic and anal,' I wonder (in the non-erotic sense of the word). I smile as we clink our glasses together, and Jean-Marc offers me a few final words of well-tempered Gallic consolation and advice.

'Never forget, my dear friend, Gregoire, zoze magnifique words of za great poet, Goethe. "Women are seelver deeshes into wheech wee put za golden apples".'

December 1, 1987

The gig with the late night episodic television show is to be shot way out in a place called Calabassas — an ugly, sprawling suburban 'village' in the depths of the San Fernando Valley. A lot of the filming is at night, and as I roll up in my Mazda MX5 that first evening, the First AD assists me in parking my car, then walks me on over right away to meet the gal playing the role of my mistress.

'Do you know Heather?' he grins at me hornily, as we stroll across to my waiting trailer.

'No. No, I don't think so.'

'Well, she's a real trip! A true California babe! Get this! Her real name's "Sky, Delicious, Shadow". Cute, huh? Man, do I ever envy you getting to do that scene where you get to deep-throat her in front of the fire! She's one super-hot, ballistic chick! And she's here inside your cabana right now, waiting to meet you! She's *very* excited! She's heard all about you from Dan, our director!'

He opens the door, and there stands the lovely Heather. At first glance she's a perfect caricature of an archetypal blonde Hollywood bombshell. Like a real-life version of the sultry female vamp cartoon character in *Who Framed Roger Rabbit?* She slinks across, takes my hand in hers and kisses me wetly on the cheek. She's got a good, strong grip.

'Hi, Greg. I'm Heather. I've heard *so* much about you! I can't *wait* for us to do our scene together!'

Her voice is husky, low. And she's sexier than some genetically-manipulated super-combo-version of Jennifer Lopez, Marilyn Monroe, Rita Hayworth, Madonna and Cameron Diaz all strung together. She's wearing a virtually see-through mini-dress that clings to her incredible body like gossamer. And her gorgeous eyes are alight, like a pair of hazel, turbo-charged searchlights in the darkness.

She leaves to slip into her costume, which according to the script is basically a G-string, scantily covered by a silk mini-robe, and I'm left to ponder the potential of our upcoming semi-nude scene together in front of a roaring fire. Most untypically for Randy Andy, I haven't been laid in weeks. In fact, it turns out to have been just about the driest period of my life in that arena. So much so that I'm frankly left feeling a bit like Rodney Dangerfield when he quipped: 'If it weren't for pickpockets, I'd have no sex life at all!'

Now sweet little ol' Heather has had quite an effect, and just happens to have left me with an erection the size of Big Ben before I've even so much as laid a predatory paw on her. Frankly, for some strange reason, I'm a wee bit leery of this one. Sex scenes are typically not a major problem for most actors. Maybe occasionally you worry about getting a massive hard-on while the camera's rolling, but usually the knowledge that thirty-odd strangers are staring at you as you attempt to fake your lustful pleasure is enough to kill any 'real' feelings of arousal. But tonight it could be different. Witness the current posture of my eager male weapon! And I must confess, I'm more than a mite disturbed at the prospect.

There's a knock at my trailer door. I open it up. It's the wardrobe gal with a selection of undies for me. 'Do you think you're gonna want the jockeys or the boxers?' she asks me, a barely concealed smirk on her face, as her eyes drop down to the very obvious bulge at my crotch. 'I suggest the boxers. I've got them a size larger than I'd guess you normally take. *Deliberately.*' I grab the boxers from her, and she turns away. As she opens the trailer door, she throws a glance back over her shoulder in the general direction of my pelvic region. 'I see you've already met Heather, by the way.'

Three crushingly tedious hours later we finally get around to doing the big scene. I'm already in a minor panic as we slowly walk it through with the director. Heather has really got my gander well and truly up, and I can feel the blood pumping its way furiously towards my groin from even the remotest outposts of my body, as we lock into our first passionate embrace. Luckily, at this point I've not yet had to fully disrobe. But I know that the entire crew standing around like a bunch of seedy old men inside a porno cinema, waiting for the first take.

We break for a final spot of make-up, the wardrobe gal swanning over to help me remove my robe. So far the boxers are doing the trick, and my Johnson's over-zealous desire to leap into instant, front-line action is being kept well out of sight. But I still have to stand up...

As I cautiously get to my feet, I'm aware of all eyes being very much upon me. I cleverly find a way to skirt around the edges of the set, masking my body with the odd chair or two. Then I face the monumental task of entering the arena. I glance down, a huge sense of relief rapidly sweeping over me, as I see the extra-large size of the boxer shorts still doing its excellent job of keeping my bad lad at bay.

But we still have to shoot the scene...

As the AD asks for quiet on the set, and the camera's about to roll, Heather suddenly grabs me and pulls me to her, like a bitch in heavy-duty heat. 'Wanna hear a secret, big boy?' she whispers huskily, as she giggles coyly. 'Underneath these panties I am *sopping* wet!'

Christ! Perfect! And I was doing *so* bloody well! Her timing's fucking impeccable. As I hear the magic words 'Speed!', and then 'Action!', Heather grabs me by the hair and shoves her crotch right into mine, forcing her powerful tongue down my throat, like a nymphomaniac on heat. I follow my cue, pull her down onto the fur rug in front of the fire, roll her firmly beneath me and utter my scintillating line of dialogue.

'Hang on tight, Carla. I'm gonna take you on a trip around the world tonight, baby. A trip you're never gonna forget!'

Down under I can feel my bloody pecker transforming itself into a mighty dagger with the strength of reinforced concrete. As she deep-throats me again, out of the corner of my eye I catch a couple of grips standing next to my wardrobe gal, absolutely boggle-eyed. The director lets the 'kiss' go on for what seems a veritable eternity. And still once he yells the magical word 'Cut!' Lovely Sky Delicious Nympho-Fruitcake apparently refuses point-blank to pull her tongue out of my mouth.

When I finally manage to prize myself free from the embrace, an enormous ripple of laughter rocks the sound stage, as I stumble to my feet and stare down at the incredible sight at my mid-section. Heather has somehow managed to summon an erection out of my poor, overwrought, weiner, the size of the Empire State Building. My over-sized boxers are literally bulging with the force of my noble tool's now rocketing extension. My shorts look exactly like Brighton Pavilion!

I'm a serious 'on camera pro', and by this stage in my career, there can be absolutely no question in my mind that we 'got it' in the first take. But Herr Director apparently decides there was a proverbial hair in the lens. So we have to do another take. Then another... Then another...

Nothing changes. The towering edifice at my groin refuses to vanish, and for over an hour I'm forced again and again to deliver that dreadful, hackneyed line probably written by some sorry, sex-starved wannabe writer in his sad little Hollywood Hills bed sit while *Deep Throat Three* played interminably on his VCR. At last, Herr Director has the compassion and good grace to say 'Enough', and it's a wrap.

As the wardrobe gal attempts in vain to suppress her laughter and helps me into my robe, Herr Director, Dan, sidles over for a chat. 'So, Greg, what d'ya think of "Sky Delicious"? She's quite a piece of work, huh? Hell, she obviously got your furnace ignited, pal!'

My pecker has by now, thankfully, decided that it needs a well-earned time-out, and I smile gamely. 'Lovely. Yes, you certainly did cast her well. She sure as hell got me going! Good choice, Dan.'

Herr Director just nods, grinning, like a fat Cheshire cat. For a moment he says nothing. Then the words slip out of his mouth. 'She's a guy...' Dan's smug grin widens. 'I'm not kidding you, Greg. Trust me. I've worked in Vegas with these people. Look at her hands.'

He turns and walks away, and I'm left there with the entire thirty-man crew staring at me, a horrible sensation welling up slowly in the pit of my stomach. My faithful wardrobe gal appears at my side, still desperately fighting back her laughter.

'What's up, sweetie? You don't look so good.'

'I don't feel so good. Do you have any idea what Dan just told me?'

She nods. 'I think I gotta pretty good idea. And I'm sorry, but I gotta tell ya, Greg, I think he's right. I checked her out when I was fitting her. He/she/it's certainly had one hell of a job done on her, let me tell ya!' She reaches up, patting me gently on the face. 'Relax, honey. It's time to go home.' She shoots me a sweet, generous smile. 'What the hell! Guess that's show business, fella!'

August 25, 1999 (contd)

The conclusion of yesterday's dramas was another breathy, desperate call from Tara telling me that she can't stand what's happening — that she feels exhausted and badly needs to get away for a few days. She's decided to fly down to Spain for the weekend to hang out with Tang, Lucy and some other rich bods on Anoushka Hempel's private yacht. Then they're all off to Venice together for the Film Festival. For a girl so desperately in love just two weeks before this seems a little odd.

'What a perfect thumbnail sketch of the sweet young lady's character this is,' I can't help thinking. She can't take the heat, so she runs out of the kitchen. Just as she did, quite literally, when she saw I'd gouged my hand open down at her mum and dad's place just a few days ago, because she evidently couldn't stand the sight of blood.

On the other hand, I suppose it's entirely appropriate that I'm left to handle this mess on my own. As I said earlier, it was already virtually over for T-P-T and yours truly anyway. And although Tara is clearly deluded to the point where she fails to see there are hoards of her 'girlfriends' out there secretly relishing that the poor little sweetheart's love life has once again taken a nasty turn and nose dived into a farce of epic proportions, that's essentially none of my business. It's my game now. I have to get to the bottom of this for my own sake. Someone's truly out to fuck royally with my life. And the intensity and virulence of the slander campaign mounted against me is increasing exponentially on an almost daily basis. I've invested a great deal of time and money into my businesses, taken a huge amount of risks, and it's all just about to pay-off. But I'm vulnerable. No way, José, am I in a position either emotionally or financially to fight a major public battle! Not right now. I have to choose my tactics carefully.

I pick up my tattered old copy of Sun Tzu's great military classic, *The Art Of War*, re-examine the passage on the importance of deception, and determine to force myself to wear a mask of good-humoured nonchalance at all times in the future, no matter how sick and upset I might be feeling inside. First off I have to somehow find out who these people are that have been slandering me privately to the Palmer-Tomkinsons. I'm already well aware of the identity of the man apparently so 'close' to my family. But the other mysterious smear-merchants are completely out of my ken. If they turn out to be the types who typically fly in certain power circles close to the heart of the entertainment world, the implications for me professionally could be very serious indeed. I might just as well pay myself a little visit to that well-known kinky Soho gay club, The Mine Shaft, bend over a barrel and drop my trousers for the shared pleasure of all and sundry! And the situation is made doubly confusing, and sinister, by the fact that I can't for the life of me figure out what in God's good name I've done to warrant the attack.

I pick up the phone. Call Sebag-Montefiore. He answers and does his best to be polite. But he refuses, point-blank, to reveal the various identities of any of the wicked people apparently calling the family.

'If I were you, I'd *torture* me until I told you who these people are, Greg,' he pleads lamely. 'But I just can't do it. I sympathise with you. I really do. But you have to understand, a kind of "Faustian bargain", if you like, was struck between these people and the P–T family.'

' "Faustian bargain"? What are you talking about? What "Faustian bargain"?' It all sounds so fucking bizarre and pretentious!

'Look. These people all agreed to tell us precisely what they know about you in return for us keeping their identities secret.'

By now I'm getting more than a little well and truly pissed off. Sebag-Montefiore is no doubt a gentleman. Hell, all the P-Ts and the rest of their tribe obviously believe they're some kind of lily-white spotless archangels entirely justified in taking the moral high ground in order to protect the ultra-confused, frantic Tara. Fine. But where has all the intensely professed moral courage and loyalty suddenly evaporated to that was expressed in the highly emotional and deeply grateful letter I received from Patty just two days after I first met her?

Sebag's still ragging on about how sorry he is. I decide I've simply had enough and hang up. I walk out of my living room. As I pass by the front door, the day's mail plops through the letterbox. An expensive-looking, cream-coloured envelope lies on top with my address written on the front in large, dark blue, florid lettering. I pick it up. Turn it over. Nicky Haslam's London address is embossed in gold on the back.

'This should be interesting,' I think to myself, as I tear the letter open.

A day or two ago I had called Nicky to ask him if he had heard any of these rumours about a number of people having contacted the Palmer-Tomkinsons to warn them I was 'bad news' and to keep Tara P-T away from me. And did he have any idea who they were? Feigning shock, he had told me that he had heard nothing, but promised he would call me the second he found anything out.

'Dear Greg,' the letter begins. 'Earlier today you telephoned me to ask me about the people warning the Palmer-Tomkinsons to keep Tara away from you. I must now confess I am indeed one of those people. Having witnessed the cavalier way in which you so easily dumped Sabrina when a much "better" opportunity was presented to you, I was disappointed.

'Now that events have proved me right, I feel that our friendship should be "put on hold" — at least for the time being.

'I know you will understand. Nicky.'

CHAPTER SEVEN

L.A., SEXUAL INSANE ASYLUM (PART FOUR)

'Who do I have to sleep with to get out of this picture?'
Anon
'I haven't spoken to my wife in years. I didn't want to interrupt her.'
Rodney Dangerfield

October 31, 1999

Witches' night. How very apt, I muse to myself as I leave the portal of a lovely Notting Hill Gate pub and head off into the darkness. I've just finished a meeting with a business associate who raises money for me on the film side, and he's revealed some very interesting information, reminding me of the unpleasant triumvirate of nasty, old Shakespearian hags I've by now found out are the driving force behind this whole sordid affair. 'Hubble, bubble, toil and trouble' — I can almost hear their words echoing out of the shadows of the alleyway across the street, as I cross through the pouring rain towards my Beamer.

People love to talk. And nothing, it seems, gets the good old fires of gossip better stoked than a juicy spot of rich celebrity slander and scandal. It seems my mate attended some kind of celeb party last night where the T-P-T/GM affair was the big topic of conversation. What he claims to be 'a very reliable source' confided in him that they had first-hand, absolutely rock-solid knowledge that I had been well and truly set up.

'Tara's family and close friends needed her whitewashed in some way when she came out of The Meadows. You came along and provided the perfect vehicle. You were a scapegoat, mate. Her reputation was pretty much shot in this country after her shocking appearance on *The Frank Skinner Show* and she went into rehab. It was the perfect way to help get her back into the good graces of the public. Paint the first innocent guy who comes along into her life as a conniving bastard, and she comes out smelling like a rose. I'm afraid it looks very much like it was something they had planned all along, old chum.' I turn the colour of a ski slope and take a big hit of my pint as he goes on.

'Cheer up, old son. Hell, you're a kind of folk hero for Joe Public in this country right now! Enjoy it! At least have a good laugh with this book you're writing! If you've got an image, flaunt it! What do you care? Your friends all know who you really are.'

I know he's right. I also know that the people who really matter to my life in the business arena — what I'd term the nuts-and-bolts personalities behind the real nitty-gritty of the film and television trade — frankly couldn't give a monkey's fart about a crock of libelous garbage some spoilt bunch of female toffee-nosed fruitcakes have decided to cook up in their rancid old cauldron regarding the allegedly sordid personality of yours truly.

Nevertheless, the sinister side of the event hasn't left me. And I wonder if it ever will.

May 1, 1990

Somewhere in between my brief, unnerving erotic encounter with Sky Delicious Shadow the transsexual and today, I have finally taken the plunge and gotten myself hitched. I believe in marriage. I think that if a lad's got both the chops and the chutzpah, is truly in love with a girl, the two of them have really got their shit together, the sex is phenomenal pretty much on a day-to-day basis, and he's *at least* over thirty-five years of age, then he's probably got a fairly good chance of somehow staying the course and winding up his life a still very happily married old man. The problems, in my opinion, generally tend to occur if any of the above don't hold true.

My ex-wife is a very private person. I have a great deal of respect for her and I'd be doing a deep injustice to both her and my lovely little son (a) if I dwelt unnecessarily on our four-and-a-half years together, and (b) if I said there weren't plenty of good times between us. Of course there were. We got married and had a son. Nevertheless, the fact remains I believe I was psychologically too young back then, and probably got married the first time for all the wrong reasons.

It was a strange period in my life. The writing was, sadly, on the wall pretty early on in our marriage but I'd made the commitment and believed I somehow had to make it work. We tried everything: marriage guidance counselling, the lot. In the end, nothing could save it. However, my gorgeous son appeared on the planet and if only for that reason I know the relationship was meant to be.

One of the interests we had in common was the environment. I believe our problems with the ecology of our planet are deeply serious, of far more import, frankly, than all the raunchy escapades of the so-called creepy Casanova. Natasha shared my concern and at the time Connor was born she was partnered with Chevy Chase's missus, Jayni, in an environmental foundation for children. Chevy and Jayni became his godparents, a highly enviable appointment for anyone, in my opinion, as any bod who's met the lovely little lad would surely agree! For a few years there we were all very close, and yours truly attended a lot of LA celeb dos with the Chase pair, particularly around the time I shot a movie with Chevy and the lovely Daryl Hannah, called *Memoirs Of An Invisible Man*.

Chevy always harboured a secret desire to be a leading man and a serious actor. His favourite pastime back when we were very close seemed to be hanging out on the tennis court with the likes of Dustin Hoffman. Chevy absolutely revered what he regarded as 'real actors'. At one time pretty much all you heard out of his mouth was: 'Dusty said this', or 'Dusty thinks that'.

We had a funny relationship. He's a great comedian and truly does have the potential to be a serious contender as a straight-ahead leading man. He was very generous to me. So I wasn't at all surprised when he very sweetly offered me the role of (wouldn't you just know it, typecasting again!) a Terry Thomas scoundrel lookalike who desperately tries to get into Daryl Hannah's pants in *Memoirs*.

I did my best to carry the role off successfully, right down to the seedy ascot, blazer and phony smile. One night during the shoot Chevy asked me to attend a celebratory dinner at Spago's above Sunset Boulevard for Mark Canton, who was at that time in charge of Warner Brothers, the studio producing *Memoirs*, and as of that day, the newly appointed Head of Sony Studios in Culver City.

Mark, then something of a rapidly rising star in the Hollywood executive world, had another half called Wendy Finerman, producer of *Forrest Gump*, so a lot of people wanted to be there. And the majority of those, particularly any still vaguely borderline stars who knew him on his way up, were determined to cash in their chips regarding his recent promotion, and had their talons and fangs out that night in a big way. In fact, as it turned out, the celeb vultures were pretty much prepared to do just about anything necessary to secure their power seat somewhere around the 'A-list table'.

A well-known young actress, who had recently starred in an hilarious and sensationally successful comedy, showed up late with her hubby in tow. Most of the folks were by now already seated and my ex and I happened to have been placed at the 'top table' itself. More to the point, yours truly just happened to have wound up sitting directly to ol' Mr. Canton's right! The diva in question, whom we'll call Kate, walked into the restaurant that night clearly cursing her misfortune at having been stuck in a traffic jam for over half an hour, and immediately scoped out the politics of the seating arrangements with the barely masked ferocity of a puma in heat.

Now guess who her eyes lighted on? Correct! Ol' muggins! Kate made an immediate beeline for Mark and Wendy, drooled over the pair of them for a good full minute, then flipped her eyes in my direction.

'Hi, Greg. I'm Kate. Good to meet you.' She bent down to buss my cheek, discreetly lowering her voice to a frustrated whisper as her lips made contact. 'Can you please move! My next picture's at Sony! I *need* to sit next to him!'

People asked me, when I first made the decision finally to uproot myself and return to 'the old sod' why I left LA. I told them there were basically four reasons. (1) My parents were both getting on in years, and neither one of them had been particularly healthy. (2) The economy was booming in the UK at the time, and the film biz was finally buzzing again. (3) I missed soccer, the wilder parts of the countryside of Scotland, England and Wales, and the pubs. (4) I was fed up to the back bloody teeth of spending my days and nights living in some vast cultural wasteland, largely populated by screwed-up, neurotic, selfish people like Kate! LA is an essentially an extremely dull one-horse town, of which one very famous writer once said: 'It's the only place in the world where you wake up to the sound of birds coughing!'

August 26, 1999

Today my mood perks up, as I start to get what I call some real signs of support from my close friends and associates. I wake up to over a dozen messages on my answerphone, all telling me to 'hang tough'. A lovely lady business pal and her man send me round a smashing bouquet of flowers. My movie legal eagle shows up most unexpectedly on my doorstep with her hubby, and the two of them join me for a cup of cappuccino to commiserate. The pair of them have a small yacht moored down in Torquay harbour. I tell them about Tara fleeing town under all 'the pressure' to hob nob with Tang, Lucy, et al on Annouska Hempel's boat in the Med. By way of consolation, they offer me a spot for the weekend on board their own little vessel moored very conveniently opposite what is apparently the best chippie in Devon!

My PR queen arrives home from Venice to tell me that her own chap, an extremely talented exec-producer in his own right, has very sweetly offered to help me out by lending the weight of his name to all my film projects. Then a highly gifted young film director pal of mine called Luke, whom I've recently commissioned to write a script with me, calls to say he wants to meet up with me for a pint. We grip and grin in my local and settle down for a good, old-fashioned chauvinistic chinwag about those two ever-perplexing subjects for sorry macho shits like us — women and life.

'Do you have any idea exactly who Tara is, Greg?' he asks me, as he sups on his mug of bitter. 'I mean, I'm kind of getting the impression here, from the way you talk about her, that you simply walked slap-bang into a kind of hornet's nest with this one!'

'Dead right, doctor!' I tell him, as I chug back my Guinness. (Why the hell does that drink seem to follow me so doggedly now everywhere I go?) 'Pray do enlighten me, squire.'

'OK. There's a peculiar thing in this country I'm sure you know about, that really hasn't gone away that much since you were in the States. It's called the class barrier. Tara, as far as I know, is one of those girls who generally does her best to cross the line. I was in a restaurant once with a bunch of my mates and she was sitting at a table across from us with some of her nob pals. They were being a little loud, rude and obnoxious in a typically 'Hooray Henry' way, so we decided to heckle them a bit. Tara got fed up with her crowd and came over to join us. She said we seemed to be a far more interesting group than most of her blue-blood pals.'

'Yeah, well that was sort of the impression I got when I first met her. For about a week it was actually quite refreshing. She seemed different. She didn't seem to be the type to be particularly concerned with all that class claptrap. Neither did her mum and dad, either, for that matter.'

'That's right. But you don't know what kind of people her *friends* are.'

'Excuse me for disagreeing with you there, mate. Believe me, by now I've well and truly started to get myself a pretty good idea!'

'Right! You've *started* to get the picture. But there's still a hell of a lot you simply don't know about, nor understand. And it's all to do with the little people.'

I eyeball Luke cheekily. He's half-Irish, and I can't resist the temptation to get a bit of a rise out of him. 'Ah! Da little people! Now would we be talkin' about all dem leprechauns and other such tiny, sweet darlin' folk, now, young Lucas?! Dem cute little fellas who always remind me so much of Ken Dodd's Diddy Men?'

Luke just smiles. 'You know exactly who I mean by the little people, Greg. I mean ordinary working-class folk like me, who grew up hard and tough on the streets without any of the privileges of birth that came to girls like Tara, Tamara Beckwith and Normandie Keith. You've got a chance here to come out of all this beautifully. So far all you've done is given a very elegant interview in the *Daily Telegraph*, while Tara — as usual — is everywhere you bloody well look. It looks to me like she's doing her best to exploit this to the max.'

'So get back to the little people.'

'Everyday folk aren't stupid, Greg. OK, so it's a bit of flashy news right now. But what you're going through will be lining the bottom of my dear old mum's parrot cage tomorrow. Believe me, I've heard a lot of talk about you over the past few weeks from all sorts of quarters, and the verdict's the same. You got away by the skin of your teeth. It was all a set up, and so far you've come off pretty much as the perfect gentleman. Basically the little people think Tara and most of the set she hangs out with are a bloody joke. Most of them have been handed life on a plate and blown it. You're in a potentially very powerful position. The man in the street knows who you are, and he respects you so far for your silence. But he wants to hear what you have to say. And there are obviously a lot of jealous people out there gunning for you. When the time comes for you to open your mouth, please just don't get angry and wind up shooting yourself in the foot.'

'No worries. I am writing a book. But it won't be bitter. It'll be bloody funny.' I polish off my pint. A curious thought suddenly streaks across my mind, prompted by Luke's words about me being 'in a powerful position'.

'Do you by any chance happen to know a bloke from around this neck of the woods called Reg, Luke?'

'You what?'

'Never mind.'

I slink on back to my castle and confront the slew of photographers still dogging my doorstep. Pop! Pop! Pop! As the flashbulbs explode, one of the guys presses me with a question.

'Where have you been, Greg? Have you seen Tara today?'

'No, mate. I've moved on. Just been scouting the immediate area for my next vulnerable, well-connected heiress.' He laughs. Humour is such a bloody godsend.

Upstairs I find yet another message from Ms. T-P-T. This one's asking me, in the now familiar, frantic tone, if it's true what she's now heard — that I'm a man who 'has no friends'.

I heave a weary sigh, pause a brief moment for effect, then decide a thoroughly silly riposte may well be precisely what's in order. I pick up my mobile. Dial her number on Anouska Hempel's yacht in Spain.

'Hi, Tara.'

'Oh, Hi...'

'I know that all the pressure has really gotten to you over the last few days. Are you at least having fun on the yacht?'

'Yes. Yes I am, thank you.'

'Good. Good... So I got your message...'

'Yes.'

'I thought you'd probably like to know that I've got *lots* of friends, chica. But guess what?'

'What?'

'They're all women!'

Click! Whirr! The line goes dead.

August 11, 1993

A few months after my very painful divorce I had a rather interesting fling with a very famous actress in Hollywood. And she was actually famous on more than one count. Firstly, for her undeniable acting ability across the board, from comedy to drama and action material. Secondly, for her notoriously potent sexuality. Her name is Sharon Stone.

Sharon, in my opinion, is truly one of the sexiest women on the planet. She has an edge, a strength on screen — almost a sense of virility in her character — that makes grown men go weak at the knees. But when I first met with the opportunity of making out with her I had an odd reoccurrence of that unique, perplexing and potentially damaging problem known to the male gender. To put it very bluntly, on the particular night in question, though I felt hornier than a hound dog on a double dose of Viagra at first I simply couldn't get it up!

Now the 'flaccid penis syndrome' is one I happen to be an expert on. The first time it occurred to me, way back in the changing rooms of my old school First Fifteen, it was such a total shock that I chose to conduct my own in-depth study of the strange phenomenon. Having come to fully understand every possible reason for a 'limp dick', I had forced myself to learn to master the symptoms to such degree that all my fellow aspiring philandering cads at school had come to term me the 'Zen master of the penis'. The devastating condition now happens to me so rarely that when it does I know, beyond the faintest shadow of a doubt, there's something very much sexually wrong with any given erotic situation. But with Sharon it was extremely hard to fathom the reasons. I found her so goddamn sexy!

I took Sharon out of LA and up to Big Sur for the weekend. A gorgeous, deeply romantic spot on the beautiful, truly rugged section of the Pacific Coast Highway that runs between LA and San Francisco, Big Sur is sort of like a forgotten Sixties hippy haven. Henry Miller, the great American author, rebel and eroticist, lived out the bulk of the latter part of his life here. In fact, it was here that he wrote his extraordinary sexual trilogy — *Sexus*, *Nexus* and *Plexus*. The poet Robinson Jeffers also spent most of his time in Big Sur. The Beat poets Jack Kerouac and Allen Ginsberg were great lovers of the place. And Esalen, the famous experimental campus for alternative lifestyles so favoured by the likes of George Harrison, Paul Simon, the Maharishi Yogi and the great US mythologist Joseph Campbell, is still there to this day, and going from strength to strength.

I awoke that splendid morning in our fabulous luxury hotel room above the Pacific, and lay listening to the waves pounding across the dark cliffs below, going over carefully in my mind the events of last night following our arrival. I recalled Sharon's incredibly provocative request to 'Come over here and fuck me rotten', as soon as the concierge had closed the door softly behind us.

Now such a comment delivered by an ultra-sexy bird like Sharon would normally cause me to rip my jeans off like greased lightning, immediately throw the bodacious babe down onto the bed, and ravish her from top to bottom for hours on end with the relentless fervour of the great bullfighter, El Cordobes, in his prime. But for some bizarre reason this just didn't happen.

What caused this completely unwished for delay in my libido's mounting excitement? Quite honestly, I was overawed. Call it first-night nerves, call it what you will. I was, quite simply, out of my depth. For once, yours truly was downright intimidated by the extraordinary red-hot sexual aura of a woman...

'What?' I hear all you lusty lads out there ask. 'It was Sharon you were in the bloody sack with! The sultry beauty from all those amazingly hot pictures! One of the most erotic women on the face of the earth!! The very woman who had managed to so stun the world into silence just a couple of years before merely by the act of crossing her legs on a cinema screen!

So what? If I had a fiver for every bloke who's come up to me since this weird recent debacle came down, and made some envious comment on both my awesome success rate with women of all shapes, sizes, colours and creeds, *plus* the fact that I'd somehow managed to snag ol' Ms. Tara P–T herself, I'd be rich enough to purchase a whole goddamn harem of It girls, and keep 'em perfectly kitted out in Agent Provocateur, Prada, Joseph and Gucci for the rest of their days, to boot!

But you perhaps forget, chaps, this man's essentially a pro. I'm older, wiser, and more sexually sophisticated now than I've ever been. And something about Sharon's persona in the flesh, now that I'd finally had my chance to examine her up close and personal at close quarters, had definitely caused some kind of initial total power failure somewhere crucial in my central erotic nervous system!

I've said it before, and I'll say it again. Sex is a very mysterious matter. You can be designed and manufactured by the Good Lord precisely like yours truly , and be in every possible, conceivable sense of the word 'hard–wired' for the maximum amount of carnal bliss in any given possible lifetime. And yet, when the chips are down, and the writing's on the proverbial wall, if it ain't happening, then it ain't happening! And in this case, at least initially, the raging furnaces within ol' bugger-lugs' typically rampant testicles was simply not there. My old Johnson was like a sodden Roman candle, refusing point-blank to light up the skies on bonfire night!

August 26, 1995

I'm really starting to tire of the sexual scene out here. Maybe I'm just getting old, but I find myself having a distinct hankering for something good and old-fashioned. A beautiful, honest, intelligent and fun woman who's truly sexy and warm.

In LA she evidently doesn't exist. But the eternal bunch of

fruitcakes certainly do! There's the Oriental plastic surgeon. I spend most of my time with her playing frisbee with the implant samples lying around the bedroom. There's the past-life regressionist. She eventually ruins it for me when she tells me she's had a dream. We were Adam and Eve together in Eden many moons ago! There are the sexy Tex-Mex twins — Conchita and Rita — two girls who I have a lot of fun with as a threesome. But I ultimately get turned off by their endless cheesy cowboy greetings such as: '*How* the *hell* are y'all doin?' And then there's Divine, a stunning black lady for whom I have very high hopes until I suffer the most embarrassing evening of my life when one night I take her out for some sushi at a very swanky joint. The oyster dish arrives on our table, and she promptly very loudly delivers the gobsmacking comment:

'Shit! These things both *look and taste* just like a woman's pussy!!!'

Time to go home. Time to go home. Andy is waving goodbye....

CHAPTER EIGHT

LONDON, RETURN OF THE PRODIGAL

'Contrary to popular belief, English women do not wear tweed
nightgowns.'
Hermione Gingold
'It is true from early habit, one must make love mechanically as one
swims. I was once very fond of both, but now as I never swim unless I
tumble into the water, I don't make love till almost obliged.'
Lord Byron

November 9, 1999

There's some very interesting stuff in the papers today. Gary
Glitter's making a bit of a scandal again. This time he's apparently
been accused of seducing some fourteen-year-old fan. In the

Daily Telegraph there's an extremely revealing insight into the notorious womanising habits of the great old Hollywood matinée idol, Gary Cooper, courtesy of the director of *Some Like It Hot*, Billy Wilder, who details Cooper's 'seduction techniques'. And in the *Daily Mail* there's a splashy column about Jerry Hall publicly fessing up how glad she is to be finally rid of old Mick — something more or less to the effect that he'd done *too* many horrible things *too* many times during their many years together. And, all in all, this gives me much food for thought, mainly by way of scurrilous comparisons.

To begin with there's the sorry case of 'Mr. Rock 'n' Roll Part 1'. The habit of preying on his teenage fans, added to an allegedly major penchant for some serious dabbling in child pornography, seems to me to be the kind of sick behaviour that for any sane member of society would warrant an appropriately nasty label. He made the front page. I made page three. What merited the two-page difference?

It appears to be the simple fact that all I could be found guilty of was having a sexual history that involved a somewhat over-large number of female partners. So how come the assault lasted so long? And why is it I'm now evidently regarded as something of an 'icon' amongst regular working chaps? Two answers, short and sweet. (1) I was the subject of a carefully calculated, premeditated character assasination. (2) All I was guilty of was acting out an impulse that over ninety-nine per cent of the healthy male population feel on a regular basis while single!

We now move on to Cooper. Part of the *Telegraph* article, an interview with Cameron Crowe, director of *Jerry Maguire* and *Singles*, reads like this: Crowe: 'The first time we met, we discussed *Love In The Afternoon*. You said you were looking for a man who could play "a real f---er, a lover of women." Wilder: 'Oh yes, Gary Cooper, he was one of those guys... he was a goer, and he had that wonderful trick, you know, about how he operated with women.'

Here's my point about this article. Both men and women truly adored him. The men because they all secretly wanted to be like him, and the women because they all wanted to have him. In real life he was, as on screen, a born womaniser. Yet he was a happily married man for most of his life, and also apparently faithful.

As for the third item on our agenda, all I have to say is this. Mick has recently been through his own 'ritual slaughtering' in the English press, and this news item is clearly the *coup de grâce*. Far be it from me to adopt the judgmental posture of my esteemed detractors, but surely there's a slight difference between a man screwing around on his wife left, right and centre, and a healthy bachelor merely having a little bit of harmless fun and sowing his wild oats? I repeat, I remained faithful to my first wife for the entire time I was with her. Will someone please be so kind as to explain to me just what the hell all the bloody fuss was about?

March 21, 1999

My return to London has been truly fascinating. Finding a flat I'm happy with in the part of the city I love the most, Knightsbridge, has been particularly illuminating. Here, it seems, for a man who so loves women from all nations, creeds and colours, it is a virtual paradise. I have only to take a step outside my front door to encounter members of the female gender from all around the world! In the course of the past nine months, for example, I have found myself dating girls from Russia, Poland, Iran, Venezuela, the Seychelles, France, Spain and Malaysia!!

England has quite definitely taken a change for the better, from a man's point of view. Apart from my getting used to the entirely alien concept of girls talking very freely and openly left, right and centre about the joys of 'shagging', there's the massive explosion in the market of 'lad's mags', such as *Maxim*, *Loaded*,

FHM.

I'm a very happy camper once again!

November 17, 1999

The lunacy still hasn't completely gone away. Last week an old girlfriend of mine met up with Sophie the Sorceress, the vicious, vindictive pal from her school days whom I made the mistake of hiring back in April and took to Vancouver with me as Connor's nanny. She apparently spent over an hour slagging me off, told my pal that both she and Tara agreed my dear old mum lived in a 'positively awful little dump' in Hertfordshire (my mother lives in the house I was born in — a sweet, beautifully kept little semi in Hatfield), then read her the famous *Mail On Sunday* Griffiths article in full, finishing up in a searing finale with the chilling assertion: 'I'll do everything I can to sabotage your relationship with that man.' There is no 'relationship' of the kind she's referring to between me and this girl. But that apparently doesn't stop her quest for nutty vindictiveness.

'My guess is you'll be hearing a lot more from Sophie,' I tell my friend later. 'She's clearly one of the witches who wants to destroy my happiness. I gather she went to Sherbourne with Tara. I wouldn't be in the least bit surprised if you get a letter or phone call from the lovely T-P-T herself.'

So tonight I'm sitting on my tod in my apartment, writing away feverishly, when — hey presto, the phone rings! It's T-P-T! I haven't heard from her for more than three weeks.

'Hi, it's Tara. Have you spoken to David Tang recently?' She's referring to a fax I'd received from Tang regarding some gifts for her and her family I'd purchased at his Hong Kong store. Given what has subsequently transpired, I'd assumed the gifts had been graciously returned.

'Yes. I faxed him yesterday. It's all cleared up. He says he finds the whole thing too boring for words. And, frankly, I don't blame him. Have you spoken to Sophie the Sorceress recently?'

'Of course I've spoken to her, you bastard! Sophie and I were at school together, you moron! And guess what?! We're having lunch with one of your girlfriends next week, and we're going to make sure we tell her *everything* about you, love rat!'

Click. Whirr...

A couple of hours later I get a sweet call from the young lady friend in question. She's off in Oxford visiting an old chum.

'I got an extremely smug call from Sophie the Sorceress during dinner about Tara apparently phoning you. I just want you to know it's nothing to do with me. Pay no attention to those fucking witches.'

God bless the sane, the loyal, the grounded, and the true of heart.

May 18, 1999

The official launch of my film and television production company, Rebel With A Cause Films, at the Cannes Film Festival. I'm happy as a pig wallowing in a trough full of shit (1) because I'm one of those boring types who basically just plain loves to work, (2) because I adore the film business, (3) because I have a big soft spot in my heart for the people of the Mediterranean, and (4) because my fabulous publicist, Claire, has managed to rent me an absolutely killer two-bedroom bachelor apartment right on the Croisette.

I rapidly become bosom buddies with a very lovely, elegant French-Vietnamese woman from Paris called Mei-Chen Chalais. Mei-Chen's a sweet, classy lady who runs a charity in honour of her dead husband, a man who had been one of the most famous and revered film critics in France. And the patron of this charity is now Sophia Loren.

One night I'm sitting alone on my magnificent terrace overlooking the splendid cobalt-blue waters of the

Mediterranean, sipping a glass of fabulous vintage Pomerol and thinking how life can sometimes be so bloody funny. One of the flagship films of my production company is the romantic-comedy *Amazon*. The film has an awesome role specifically written for 'the sexiest older woman on the planet' (read: Sophia Loren). It's the part of 'The Amazon Queen', the all-powerful, elder and shamaness of the mystical, ancient tribe of Amazons who for thousands of years have been lost somewhere in the depths of the Colombian jungle, guarding the famous, mythical lost city of gold, El Dorado. (Another rebuttal for my monstrous regiment of slanderous critics. If I 'm such a classic cad who makes a career out of preying on weak, vulnerable women, then why does every film I create always revolve around a strong female who makes all the men around her look like a bunch of blithering, penile-obsessed idiots?)

When I was five years old, just a couple of weeks before my dad vanished, he landed a great gig recording a very funny song with Peter Sellers and Sophia Loren for the film *The Millionairess*. It was called: 'Goodness, Gracious Me!' At the time both Sophia and her husband, producer Carlo Ponti, both desperately wanted kids. In particular they wanted a boy. My mum brought my sister and I up to the studio for an hour or two, and Carlo immediately grabbed hold of me and started kidding around. I was an extremely exuberant, very male child, and loved a bit of the old rough-and-tumble. At first Mr. Ponti tweaked my cheek. So, me being me, I tweaked his back. Next he gave me a playful pat. I returned the gesture in kind. And this went on with slowly, ever-increasing intensity of playfulness, until ol' Carlo and I were bashing away at one another, nineteen to the dozen.

My dad, being a deeply ambitious, somewhat old-fashioned and politically correct sort (in the early days he used to make the Beatles go into the men's toilet if they wanted to smoke a joint at Abbey Road), was apparently none too pleased and asked my mum to remove me. But Carlo and Sophia, I'm told, evidently found my boisterous, quasi-Latino behaviour quite charming. Sophia swept me up in her arms, held me tight, and kissed me. And, wouldn't you just know it, the junior Casanova reincarnated delivered one hell of a lip-smacking smoocher by way of a reply.

I pick up my cellphone. Dial Mei-Chen's number. I've asked her to arrange a meeting for the lovely Sophia and myself the following week. 'Hi, Mei-Chen,' I begin. 'C'est Gregoire. I forgot to tell you, when you speak to Ms. Loren please tell her that she and I have met each other before some years ago under some very amusing circumstances. In fact, we've been quite intimate! I'll tell her the rest when I see her... '

People's schedules change. Time flies. I'm still waiting for that meeting. One more kiss for the gorgeous Sophia, please dear God, before I die!

CHAPTER NINE

THE SUBTLE ART OF SEDUCTION

'Brisk confidence still best with woman copes/ pique her and soothe in
turn — soon passion crowns thy hopes.'
Lord Byron, 'Childe Harold's Pilgrimage' (1812–18)
'Every man is to be had one way or another, and almost every woman
any way.'
Lord Chesterton, *Letters To His Son* (June 5, 1750)

December 15, 1999

I'm about a week away from the end of the initial draft of
this great work of art, and today I drive up to Oxford at the
behest of my publisher, John Blake, to talk to a group of buyers.
John and his gorgeous associate, Rosie, have both been incredibly

helpful and supportive, offering good, solid advice, guidance and support wherever it's been needed, and by and large the book's been a hell of a lot of fun to write. More than anything it's been a pleasant, therapeutic little jaunt for Casanova reincarnated, going a long way to help me put what started out as a bit of a nightmare experience into some kind of perspective.

When I arrive at The Belfry Hotel I find one other of John's authors there — the magician Paul Daniels. I love magic, and as the pair of us sit there over coffee, talking about Tommy Cooper, Orson Welles, Harry Houdini and others, it occurs to me what a first-class seduction tool a little stash of sleight-of-hand tricks would make! It seems to me that what most people want, both men and women, when they encounter someone new, is to feel something different, something fresh and vital from the other person they've somehow never felt before. True romance should ideally make a person feel like they've somehow suddenly come alive again in what is otherwise, let's face it, sadly a very grey, mundane world.

By far the most attractive women I've ever met were a hell of a lot of sheer fun just to be around. And, most crucially, they've all had the gift of making me laugh. Oddly enough, in my considerable experience, this frequently has absolutely nothing to do with looks. Sexual charisma is very different from beauty. You can be the most drop-dead gorgeous creature on this godforsaken planet, but if you're essentially as dull as ditch water you're never going to turn anyone on!

Tara, for example, is arguably one hell of a foxy chick. But she also knows better than anyone that having a fun personality is a truly awesome seduction tool. OK, so it's maybe partly just a simple, straightforward gift of her zany nature. But she's also very cleverly managed to develop a unique little line of party tricks and crazy stories all of her own over the years, that will forever stand her in very good stead around male company. A beautiful girl is nice to look at. A beautiful girl with style, grace, wit, humour and a great sense of fun is typically a total knock-out.

Over dinner one night some years ago, a girl showed me this absolutely brilliant lateral thinking gag with a couple of wine glasses and some water. Not only was the trick truly awesome, when she finally pulled it off it was one of the sexiest things I've ever seen. She had me and just about every other man in the restaurant eating out of the palm of her hand for the rest of the evening. I learnt to do the trick myself, but it somehow never has quite the same impact as when a woman does it. There's something about a girl showing her naughty, playful side that is always so bloody damn appealing!

This sense of the unusual and different is part of the reason that taking the time to learn about something a little off-the-wall, like astrology, can be so effective with a woman. Especially when you actually start to be really good at it. This particular hobby of mine was the cause of a lot of trouble for me back there during my Black August days. Tara, in particular, got deeply upset when Griffiths claimed in his article I frequently used my skill in the subject as a devious tool to get my women into bed. As I often do with people I like, male or female, I had offered to do Tara's chart for her. And the natural assumption, once all the hysteria broke out, was that it was simply another of the 'lines' I was shooting in order to have my wicked, wicked way with her.

The objection I have to all of this is quite simple. A man or woman's gifts, talents and abilities are all a part of their unique, overall charm. I also sing, write poetry and songs, can dance a mean bossa nova and salsa, and tend to tell a lot of very bad, sometimes absolutely filthy jokes. So what? Does that make me some kind of scumball, or merely a little more interesting than your average Joe?

The odd and actually truly naughty thing about astrology, if you really get to know your stuff, is that you can actually learn to see from the positions of the planets when a given person is likely to be at their horniest! I know this sounds like a total crock of rot, but it's the absolute God's truth. Ask me about your girlfriend next time I see you, and I'll fill you in! Better not introduce me to her, though. My little box of party tricks might just leave you in the dust!

Enough men have stopped me in the street since all of this bizarre caper began expressing their admiration for what they apparently consider to be my unique success rate with women to convince me that a chapter or two on 'essential everyday seduction techniques' may well be in order. Even the CEO of one of the companies I'm currently in business with now habitually pounds away at me in the course of our daily phone conversations to 'Please come down soon and give my boys a little seminar'!

Personally I believe there are six fundamental tools to the art of successful seduction for any man or woman: confidence, humour, chivalry, generosity, passion, and smarts. And while it's true you're either born with these or you're not, there are many additional lessons to be learned that can ultimately make or break you in the successful seduction stakes. I've narrowed my list down to a nice round number for the sake of convenience.

So here they are! 'The Arch-Serialising Scumbag Pig's All-Time Top Ten Tips Of Seduction'!

1. LEARN THE ART OF WOOING WITH WORDS.

'All really great lovers are articulate, and verbal seduction is the surest route to actual seduction.'
Marya Mannes 'More In Anger' (1958)

Love poetry has, without question, been just about the most effective and powerful romantic tool in the world since time began. If you can somehow manage to pluck up the courage to

string a few choice words together in praise of your heart's desire,
I can guarantee you'll nail him or her every time. Now naturally
that means putting in a little bit of work. But as we all know,
nothing good comes without a bit of solid, hard graft. Particularly
a fabulous lover! Now, I admit ol' bugger-lugs may have gotten off
to a head start in this particular arena. For some reason a deep love
of language has always been a part of me, and I've been writing
poetry and stories literally since I was nine years old. But it's really
not that hard once you dive in and start. So here are a couple of
brief pointers. Firstly, writing powerful, effective love poetry
doesn't mean churning out awful, turgid, crude, silly stuff like
this:

> Your eyes are hot,
> Your bod's real awesome.
> Come back to mine,
> Let's do a foursome.

Or this:

> You're sex on legs,
> You're a bitch in heat.
> Come lick my love-pump,
> Come suck my meat.

No way! Come on! Get real! Put yourself in her shoes! If
you were her and some gormless, horny twit came up to you
spouting a piece of garbage like the above, you'd more than likely
give him a bloody good smack around the kisser and tell him in
no uncertain terms to kindly piss off! No, the verbal art that will
stand a good chance of making her truly swoon is something
completely different. Ideally it should go something like this:

Sonnet For My Love

If I could write in burning gold
My passion's love across the sky,
If I could all the stars enfold,
Or drink the seven oceans dry.
If I could heavenly moonbeams ride,
Or swim ten leagues within one breath,
Or leap the continent's divide.
If I could vanquish, conquer death.
If I could halt the phantom, Time,
Or heal the blind. Give men their sight,
Or swallow all the blood and tears,
That men have shed in the name of right.
Know this, my love, all this I'd do,
To win the very heart of you.

Eternity

Your eyes, my darling, sweet lady, hold the secrets of eternity,
How you and I have loved, and danced, and laughed, and cried
together
Down the hallways of time forever.
Your beauty, the gorgeous wonder of your heart, is like a brilliant
crystal flame burning in the hollow darkness of the night.
It bursts forth, like radiant sunshine splitting pitch, sombre cloud
cover over the black, dun moors.

Your silky laughter ripples tenderly through my soul,
tinkling so softly,
Like the gentle peal of ancient, mystical church bells over
hill and dale,
And I smile.

Sometimes when I look at you, my angel, the strangest, deepest
warmth floods the depths of my soul,
And inside I just have to laugh.
For how can these feelings, so tender, so lovely, so contented, and
soft,
Breathe the kind of rapturous new life into every tingling fibre of
my body,
Every muscle and sinew of this hollow frame,
When you and I have slept at each other's side such a short
while?

I know the answer. And so do you.
Yet every time I try to voice it, the words simply fade and die,
Like delicate, fragile water drops trickling slowly through my
fingers.
There is a reason.
It is because these words cannot, nor will not be spoken.

We know. That is enough. And so...
We sleep.

A-hah! Gotcha! Didn't think ol' bugger-lugs had a single
sensitive bone in his lascivious body, did you? But there's much
more to it all than just this. Using the art of powerful language
effectively in any given sexual situation isn't only about mastering
the technique of writing smooth love poetry. Language was
invented as a tool of communication, remember, and what are
love and sexual passion all about if not developing a unique and
powerful rapport with a given human being of the desired gender?
So if, like me, you enjoy encounters with members of the
opposite sex from different cultures, be smart and take the time to
learn their language. Take it from me, you can only go so far with
Si, *Non* and an Oxford mini-phrase book clutched in your hands.

Even if you happen to be a veritable master of 'the international language of love'! And there's nothing more flattering for a girl from a foreign locale if she finds out you're actually making the effort to learn to speak her lingo. She'll find it absolutely adorable! Entrancing!

The price you pay for not bothering with the above can also be considerable. Take my own case, for example. I'm currently enjoying what I truly feel to be potentially the most special relationship of my life with a sweet, tender young Italian girl. I've already purchased my requisite BBC 'Italiananisimo' book and tapes, and am thoroughly committed to mastering the lingo in three months flat. Last night the *bella donna* showed up on my doorstep extremely tired, and quite pissed. She'd been to a Christmas party after work and had knocked back one or two cocktails too many. Though she was delighted to see me, it very quickly became crystal-clear she'd heard some talk of my newfound dastardly reputation. Being a Latina, and very emotional, after initially plopping herself down in my lap and smothering me with kisses, she then promptly proceeded to pull a swift, total U-turn, and burst into floods of tears.

'You joke with me!' she wailed. 'I hear all about you in newspaper! You marry Tara! You tell everybody you use her! You no good man!!'

You could've knocked me down with a bloody feather! I was completely stumped! I've found my complicated personal truth behind all this nasty business has been hard enough to explain in straightforward English, let alone to a gorgeous young lady besotted with me, via my feeble grasp of the lingua Italia!

I eventually managed to calm her down with a few *no capices* and the odd irate, passionate *Io sonno un huomo con corazon bene!*, etc., and coax her into bed where, as always, a healthy peace was very soon restored. But let me tell you it was touch and go there for a good few minutes!

The moral of the story? For Christ's sake, master her bloody language!

2. MAKE HER LAUGH

'I wasn't kissing the lady. I was just whispering in her mouth.'
Chico Marx

A profound and incontrovertible truth is that the ugliest of men will forever be able to bed the most stunning and desirable of women, merely by making her chuckle. As the esteemed author Eva Hoffman once said: 'Laughter is the lightning rod of play, the eroticism of conversation'.

Simply get a woman into perpetual fits of giggles, and not only will her heart open up to you, so too, more than likely, will another rather lovely part of her anatomy! But there's a crucial footnote to this second, vital tip. Don't be too crude. At least at first. On the other hand, it all depends on how you gauge the situation, and on your delivery style. Personally I always get a bit of a naughty kick out of seeing just how bad I can be with my jokes. And I've got quite a stash of them locked away in my grey matter! It's always interesting to see just how sexual you can make your japes. It gives you some indication of where the land lies and of just how far you'll ultimately be able to take the situation.

Never forget, as a rule when women club together for a 'girl's night out' they're typically far cruder than men. But there's a kind of unwritten law that says a lady cannot admit you into the more intimate areas of her mental fantasies until she's given you her permission. So, to begin with, be gentle, sweet and subtle. Then, later on, when you're sure the water's safe, launch in with perhaps something along the lines of the following:

Hymie and Rebecca Goldstein, residents of Hampstead Garden Suburb, have a lovely eighteen-year-old daughter called

Jessica. One day Jessica gives her mum and dad the shock of their lives when she announces she's in love with Mohammed, an Egyptian prince.

Distraught, Hymie and Rebecca throw the poor young lass out of their house. Jessica vanishes to Egypt, and does not speak to her parents for five years.

Then, one day, a letter arrives at the Goldsteins' house, postmarked Alexandria. It's from Jessica. She's written begging them to please come and get her. She's miserable and wants to come home.

Hymie and Rebecca immediately fly out on one of Mohammed's private Lear jets, and are deeply impressed by the incredible grandeur of the experience. No expense has been spared. Vintage Dom Perignon, a chauffer-driven Rolls-Royce out to Heathrow, a red carpet on the runway when they arrive at Alexandria. Then Hymie and Rebecca are driven in a silver-plated Mercedes to an incredible palace. The place is massive and there are peacocks and fountains in the garden. They're overwhelmed.

They get inside, and see their lovely, long-lost Jessica standing at the top of a vast marble sprial staircase, dressed in a stunning black Versace gown. She looks gorgeous. Rebbeca rushes up the stairs to greet her, kisses and hugs her, then begins:

'Darling! You look so fabulous! This place is wonderful! We're so happy for you! Why do you want to come home?'

Jessica starts to sob.

'Mummy, when I first came here five years ago my arsehole was the size of a five-pence-piece. *Now it's the size of a fifty-pence-piece!*'

Rebecca just stares at her daughter, stunned. Then...

'*For forty-five pence you want to give this up?*'

3. *LEARN HOW TO DANCE.*

'Every dance is a kind of fever chart, a graph of the heart.'
Martha Graham

The other night I was hanging out in one of my favourite local salsa bars with a chum, watching the talent. There was a Spanish guy out on the dance floor with the kind of spectacular dance moves down pat that make women go weak at the knees. It was extraordinary to watch. The man was tiny — about five foot four — and about as attractive as Quasimodo. But his incredible talent had most of the chicks in the place completely eating out of his hand. All of them wanted to take their turn with the lucky little sod. They were literally queuing up, begging for him to take them in his arms for a quick, sexy spin around the room!

What's the moral of this story? It's obvious! Learn to bloody well dance! It's a well-known medical fact that music gets the heart beating faster, and apart from the obvious advantages that dancing provides in the potential sexual arena — i.e. you'll naturally find it much easier to get physically closer to your bird — it's also a sure-fire way to make any lady with an ounce of life in her and red blood in her veins begin to smile. That is, unless you happen to be an absolutely hopeless bloody chump who finds it impossible to put one foot in front of another! With Latina women in particular, becoming a master of the dance floor is an absolute must! Moving sultrily and sexily to a beat is in their very blood. So if you want to have more than a passing flirtation with this fantastic part of the female world, you'd better sign up for your next salsa class double-quick! Take it from me and take a hefty leaf out of my book in the process. Trust me! You'll be missing out big-time if you don't!

4. LEARN HOW TO COOK

'Cooking has become an art, a noble science; cooks are gentlemen.'
Robert Burton, 'The Anatomy Of Melancholy' (1621)

There's a handy little assortment of unique tricks of the seducer's trade absolutely cast-iron guaranteed to catch any sophisticated, truly worthwhile woman's attention. And one of the best I know is when a man knows how to cook her a damn good meal.

Make it stunning. Pull out all the stops. Be so romantic, you knock her off her feet. Candles, soft music, fine wine — the works. But do it all yourself, in the quiet intimacy of your own home. It'll absolutely stun her! Particularly if you set her up first by telling you've ordered a pizza and want to watch *Blind Date*!

A close friend recently asked me when I typically choose to trot out this particular area of my expertise, and my answer was this. I take my time. You have to understand that when you're seducing a woman, it's like you're doing your own male of version of 'The Dance of The Seven Veils'. You don't show her all your aces at once. That's not only boring, it can also be downright stupid.

If you overwhelm her with all your brilliant talents at once, you could not only wind up intimidating her, you'll also have nothing left to show her when, as it inevitably one day will, the going gets a little rough. There'll be no rabbit left for you to either pull out of the hat, or yank out of the pot! But this is also an indisputable fact of life and love: the man who pampers his woman, nurtures and caresses her intestines, as well as the other parts of her body, will conquer and rule!

When I was a boy, there was a show on television called *The Galloping Gourmet*. The host, Graham Kerr, was TV's first culinary sex symbol. Convinced that the art of cooking was the key to stardom, I was hooked. Every Wednesday night, at the age of ten, I would persuade my dear old mum to pop out to Tesco and buy me the ingredients for, say, a Brisbane Prawn Soufflé. Needless to say, I couldn't even fry an egg, and the soufflé never rose, but the budding seducer in my heart sensed where mastering the skill would ultimately lead him. Look at British television today — over two dozen cooking programmes a week, and the latest incarnation of Graham Kerr is a hot young stud brazenly entitled *The Naked Chef.*

5. LEARN HOW TO KISS

'When you kiss me, / jaguars lope through my knees; / when you kiss me, my lips quiver like bronze / violets; oh when you kiss me.'
Diane Ackerman, 'Beija-Flor', Jaguar of Sweet Laughter (1991)

The best and only teacher for this subject for a heterosexual man is, naturally, a woman. And if you're suffering from a lack of experience, I suggest you get your arse out there right now and get some serious practice in!

Women absolutely love a fabulous kiss. And that means a whole lot more than frantically sucking at her tongue, like it's some kind of sexual ice lolly!

In this arena, practice truly does make perfect. Listen to what they tell you. Learn from all the feedback. Eventually you'll reach that stunning place where both of you will be exchanging the kind of kisses that reduce your bones to rubber, and your brains to gruel!

6. THEY WANT IT JUST AS MUCH AS YOU DO.

' "Shame," he said softly. "See you Monday," and gave me a look so dirty I felt like throwing myself after him shouting, "Shag me! Shag me!" '
Helen Fielding, Bridget Jones's Diary (1996)

One of the greatest revelations of my life was the moment when I finally realised that a lot of women I was encountering truly loved sex as much as yours truly. Now this may sound a little naive to a lot of you folks out there, but I was raised in a household where you were taught that the female gender were very much from a world apart. My mother's Scottish, from a conservative, working-class family, and sex was considered a strictly off-limits subject of discussion. The concept of a female having a prodigious sex drive was simply unheard of. Any girl with a habit of aggressively pursuing men was a big, bad no-no. Women simply didn't behave that way. Any young lady who did was an out-and-out slut, pure and simple.

As I mentioned earlier, things have changed quite dramatically since I was a boy. Nowadays in any pub in England it's considered quite normal to hear girls chatting together about going out and having themselves a 'damn good shag'. It's refreshing. But don't kid yourself. The game still has to be played!

One of the things that intrigues women more than anything is when they meet a bloke they think they can't have quite so easily. It's really no different than it is for guys. Think about it. Don't you hate it when a girl's all over you constantly, day in, day out. I mean, if you're a horny bastard, you might enjoy all the attention at first. But it very soon wears thin. A little bit of intrigue from a girl is by and large far more exciting.

I remember having a chat with Bill Wyman, the Stones' ex-bass guitarist a few years back. Wyman was always one of the two quieter, less flashy members of the band, along with drummer Charlie Watts. But curiously enough he had a far higher success rate with the fairer sex than either Jagger or Richards. He was a legend! His technique was very simple, but always powerfully effective. This is what ol' Bill would do.

At a party, he'd quickly clock the girl he wanted and eyeball her rather winningly a few times in between snatches of conversation with whoever he happened to be talking to at the time, until he was absolutely dead certain he'd got her attention.

Then he'd completely ignore her for the rest of the evening!

It's an absolutely infallible technique. Women just can't take it. As a girlfriend said to me only just today at lunch, 'I love a challenge. Someone I know I can't get right away just invariably turns me on so much!'

Of course, Bill made absolutely sure the girl would always have a way to find out his number, and if you're clever, there are plenty of easy, subtle ways to ensure that the strategy doesn't somehow backfire on you. But the point is this. Women are often naturally just as maniacally driven in the sexual arena as men are — in fact, sometimes they're even more so — but though they generally tend to *talk* about having sex much more openly today, they still can't allow themselves to be openly *seen* as thinking that way. It's not nice. So we have to pretend. Being cool when you want something or someone so bad it makes your teeth itch is an art in itself. And a searingly crucial one to the budding master lover.

When a gal pal first split up with her live-in boyfriend a couple of years ago, she had a brief fling with a very talented young man who, at first, seemed to turn her on quite intensely. Then things suddenly went sour. Why? Simple. The silly twat became way too bloody eager way too bloody quickly! He became a man obsessed. And obsession is always a huge no-no, as far as I'm concerned. Push came to shove for her one Sunday morning, when she returned from a quick visit to the local shop to find the bod had not only dusted and cleaned all over the house, but had also pinned up endless notes in obscure places around the house proclaiming his undying love and devotion for her. An argument ensued, and when the silly idiot finally suggested that maybe he should cover her in melted chocolate and make wild, passionate love to her by way of compensation, it was sadly all over. At all cost, whatever you do, *never, ever* be too keen! Or at the very least, if you are, *don't* show it!!

As I mentioned earlier, women amongst their own kind tend to be far cruder than men. If you've ever had the opportunity of being a fly on the wall during a hen night — one of those amazing evenings when girls get the opportunity to be alone with their own kind and let loose — you'll know this.

I've listened in on more than one occasion. And let me tell you, the first time you're privy to an evening like this, it's a shock. They're incredible! As a rule, women are far more crude than us blokes when they get the chance to have a little natter about matters erotic! And they'll admit it if they're honest. Ask any bird you know the next chance you get. And this means only one thing. Essentially they want it just as much as men do!

7. BE UNPREDICTABLE. CHOOSE THE UNUSUAL.

'During sexual intercourse the heartbeat quickens to a frenzied tempo.
Therefore there are certain fast-paced activities that will typically help a
man pave the way for consumption of the event. Like taking a sexy girl
fifty times around on a ferris wheel, for example.'
Groucho Marx

The message here is short, snappy and simple. Don't be boring! This not only refers to the way you choose to approach her, (i.e. don't call her every day, regular as clockwork, at exactly the same time, shooting her exactly the same schmaltzy line), but also to the way you entertain her. Never forget, sadly for most of us most of life is frequently dull, grey and just plain bloody boring! So bring a little fizzle, dazzle and glamour into her life! This can be accomplished in literally hundreds of different ways. And it does take a little careful thought, energy, commitment and planning. But, by God, can the pay off ever be worth it!

Groucho was a master. Fairgrounds and theme parks are not

only a hell of a lot of fun for most adventurous women. Roller coasters typically induce an internal state almost identical to that of the orgasm!

8. LEARN TO TONE DOWN YOUR AGGRESSION. BE GENTLE.

'Venus yields to caresses, not to compulsion.'
Publilius Syrus, *Moral Sayings* (1st B.C.)

One of the most attractive things on God's green earth is a man or woman who exudes massive amounts of personal power, but is fundamentally also a gentle soul. It's absolutely winning when you encounter a strong human being of the opposite gender who somehow has the ability to make you feel safe and warm.

Banish the Neanderthal in you! Forget your sorry mates who tell you it's all about getting the ball between the goalposts. It isn't. It's about making her feel one hundred per cent special.

Overwhelm her in the sack, by all means. She'll more than likely adore a bit of healthy aggression in the bedroom. But woo her gently, softly, sweetly first. She'll want you all the more for it. And, above all, remember those great words of counsel from the poet Goethe, quoted to me back in Paris by my dear old pal, Jean-Marc:

'Women are silver dishes into which we put golden apples.'

9. ALWAYS BE A GENTLEMAN.

*'A gentleman is a man who climbs Everest, never mentions it to a soul,
and listens politely to Pochet's account of how in 1937, in spite of his
sciatica, he conquered the Puy de Dome.'*
Pierrre Daninos, *The Secret Of Major Thompson* (1957)

Mastering the art of simple, old-fashioned courtesy is a winner every time. It's true that grace and good manners can oddly sometimes work against you. Sadly, today some women are innately suspicious of guys opening doors for them, etc. They automatically assume that you must be a recent graduate of my 'International Academy For Seducers, Cads and Philanderers'! A man who shows a woman abundant gentility will, by and large, still manage to convince her of his ultimate sincerity a lot faster than some slob who treats her like she's a cheap slapper from Brixton.

Be a gentleman. As the classic old saying goes: 'Manners maketh man.'

10. LIVE DANGEROUSLY. BECOME A FIREMAN.

'I live for the danger. I love the thrill of being on the edge of life and death.'

Kurt Russell in *Backdraft*

The other night I was in a pub with a mate of mine, a smashing chap called Chris Mcevoy who works for the best travel agency in the West End, City Bond Travel in Maddox Street. We were discussing the profundities of this magnificent tome, and I was making him chuckle as I regaled him with various anecdotes from my 'life of crime', when he was suddenly seized with a thought he simply *had*, at all cost, to communicate to me.

'Hey, Greg. Know what the sexiest profession in the world is for women?'

My vanity got the better of me. 'Actor-writer-producer-entrepreneur-serial-scumbag philanderer?'

'No way! Sorry, mate! It's a fucking fireman!'

And this fascinating fact he then promptly proved to me, on the spot. He walked over to a very sexy girl sitting with her chums, whispered in her ear, then quietly strolled back to join me. Within thirty seconds, she was at his side. My pal was telling the truth. Assuming some kind of cunning deceit (i.e. that he'd actually told her he was a multi-millionaire internet-king), I checked it out with the young lady while my mate was in the loo.

'Oh, no,' she told me, 'he told me was a real-life Kurt Russell from *Backdraft*. I love firemen! They're so bloody sexy!'

CHAPTER TEN

HOW TO HANDLE A WOMAN

'Sex without sin is like an egg without salt.'
Luis Bunuel
'If a woman hasn't got a streak of the harlot in her, she's a dry stick as a rule.'
D. H. Lawrence

December 12, 1999

This week's been very interesting, newswise — particularly *vis-à-vis* the crap I went through back in August. Tara's now apparently fallen madly in love with ex-Duran Duran member Nick Rhodes, and Tory MP/London Mayor candidate Steve Norris has gone through his own unpleasant version of public sabotage at what he's termed the hands of 'the monstrous regiment'.

Of necessity, having by now well and truly left behind the bulk of the pain I went through in the summer, I find myself feeling genuinely happy for Ms. T-P-T. I know she's known Rhodes for quite a number of years, and hopefully this time she may be able to find true happiness. I wish her well.

Re. poor ol' Steve, however, I have a lot more to say. A few nights ago on television one of the women responsible for nobbling Mr. Norris gave a brief interview. The deeply sanctimonious, judgmental attitude of the lady I found quite extraordinary. It was as if we were viewing our own version of the Bill Clinton/Monica Lewinsky, scandal played out on a much smaller scale. Perhaps I'm being a little naive here, and forgive me for taking the very obvious stance of making a firm case of siding with Mr. Norris in his current unfortunate predicament — but what has any given man or a woman's particular failings in the personal arena to do with his or her ability to function effectively and responsibly in public office?

Clinton's case was different. Clinton was stupid enough (a) to do the deed he did, and (b) to lie under oath. Still, the intensely 'holier-than-thou' nature of the public witch-hunt *he* endured I found sad, silly and very distasteful; more indicative of the sorry depths to which his enemies will sink to sabotage a man's career than of the innate 'moral corruption' of such a public figure.

I was in France, Italy and Greece at the time of the Clinton scandal. The reaction in those countries was hilarious. Take it from me, all that the sordid business did in the eyes of the saner, less anal countries of the Western world was to confirm their unflinching opinion that the United States was in a condition of major internal breakdown. How can you take any world super-power seriously that spends gobs of time and taxpayers' money publicly crucifying it's own chief executive, while the rest of the globe is in a state of turmoil? Particularly when that chief executive has arguably done more than any other President in recent history to right the considerable internal wrongs of that superpower?

December 18, 1999

To me the actual act of sex has always seemed rather like performing some kind of an extremely delicate high-wire act; mixing tenderness with lust. The most skilled and accomplished women I've found, for example, are always well-versed in the classic concept of being something of a 'whore in the bedroom', while managing somehow to remain remarkably feminine. While, for myself, it's always a matter of being sensitive, gentle and romantic, yet strong and a little forceful at the same time.

The bottom line is that you can be a veritable expert at an infinite variety of tricks, piquant sauces and spices culled from a whole lifetime of passionate romancing, but still, when push comes to shove, you've simply got to be naughty, but nice. Vulnerable, yet deeply assertive. Dominant, yet sweetly generous.

Many years ago I realised that probably the greatest key to becoming a great lover was learning to project yourself into the mind and body of the person you're making love to. At first this sounds very highfalutin' and esoteric. But it isn't at all, really. It's just plain, simple common sense. *I* enjoy the act so much more if the woman with me is clearly experiencing *total pleasure*. It's a massive turn-on. So I always do my best to imagine as precisely as possible what she must be feeling. It's as straightforward as that. And it's really not that hard to do. You just have to learn to use the bit of your grey matter that might conceivably have gone temporarily AWOL called the 'imagination'.

I believe all truly great lovers, both male and female, are fundamentally generous. That means taking pleasure in the pleasure you give another. There's nothing better, in my book, than getting a woman so phenomenally stimulated that she's literally yelling out for you to 'take' her. And to accomplish that state you've got to first be prepared to bring her gently, slowly to that wonderfully intense point of arousal.

And to do this you have, in a sense, to *become* her. (And I'm not talking about some weird form of mental cross-dressing!!) Put very bluntly, you have to try to feel what she's feeling — or at least what you imagine her to be feeling — as you kiss, touch and caress her. She'll not only adore you for it, she'll also more than probably lead you onward into a realm where perhaps, in the hallowed words of *Star Trek*, you're 'to boldly go where no man has gone before'!

CHAPTER ELEVEN

PROBLEMS: WHAT NOT TO DO

'Send two dozen roses to room 503, and write: "I love you, Emily" on the back of the bill.'
Groucho Marx
'Contraceptives should be used on every conceivable occasion.'
Spike Milligan

1. DON'T TALK DIRTY UNLESS THE WEATHER'S RIGHT.

Let's talk about 'talking dirty'. It's always seemed to me to be a bit of an odd one this, because under the right circumstances and conditions it naturally works like a charm. But conversely, if the climate isn't ideal it tends to go dramatically pear-shaped.

Remember old horny Hollywood exec Eve with her die-hard Brooklyn whorehouse twang? Like everything else important in life, there's an art to the matter. And if you don't have your technique down right, or you somehow find yourself misjudging the timeliness of the moment, you can very rapidly wreck the mood of what would otherwise have been a superbly seductive evening and send your potential connubial partner running, screaming for the nearest cab homeward.

Take the instance of a gal pal of mine who was dating a guy who loved her to tell him to 'fuck me like a dog'. Now I can understand a chap getting off on a gal giving his little lad these kind of highly provocative, nasty marching orders. I'm sure it's a real turn-on. The problems for my friend arose when (a) it became crystal clear over the course of time the bod couldn't possibly get his rocks off any other way, and (b) due to a series of strange signals the young lady in question was getting, she began seriously to question whether her boyfriend might not perhaps have some serious tendencies towards more than flirting with the odd team member from 'the other side of the tracks' from time to time, so to speak. The shit finally hit the fan one wild, drunken night when she hadn't seen him for a while and he happened to be in town on business. The fella called my friend up late one night and begged her to come over to his room at a fancy West End hotel to perform the deed with him in the aforementioned canine fashion. She was at a fancy-dress function at the time, but agreed to pay him a visit later on in the evening, and subsequently showed up still dressed in her cossie, which happened to be a highly provocative little number, since she'd decided to go to the bash as a French tart. Feeling uncomfortably like some exotic Parisian high-class hooker, she arrived at his place, was given the quick once-over by the smirking night-porter, and then promptly sent up to the guy's room via the service elevator.

The boyfriend, being a somewhat natively kinky sort, had

left the door ajar and was hiding somewhere inside the room in the darkness. Having caused her a near heart-attack by suddenly springing out on her from the shadows, grabbing her and hauling her off into the bathroom, he then proceeded to bend her over the sink and ask her to tell him to fuck him like the proverbial woof-woof. The only problem was that my friend had definitely had a couple of voddie and Red Bulls too many, and was, to put it mildly, pissed as a fart. In addition, she's a bit of a giggler by nature and hadn't been able to get the thought of her man maybe being a bit of a semi-poofter in disguise out of her mind all night. As she ends the story: 'I was very drunk, and as he unzipped his fly, I just couldn't stop myself from falling about laughing. All these really wild visions of what I imagined might be his gay other self were rollicking through my brain. Then, from some ridiculous part of my imagination I suddenly got this incredibly vivid and overpoweringly hysterical image of him dressed in a bright crimson cassock and surplice. "Go on! Do it! Fuck me like a choirboy!" I blurted out.'

2. DON'T BE OVERAMBITIOUS WITH JET-LAG

I once returned to LA from a trip back home and found myself as hot-wired like I'd chugged back twenty espressos laced with speed. It was pouring with rain, a truly miserable Friday night, and after I unpacked, I knocked about my apartment in my dressing gown for a good few hours, nursing a big glass of Scotch, trying everything in my power to unwind. It was no deal. Nothing worked. For those of you who don't know, LA is hardly all it's cracked up to be. Basically it's a one-horse town where everyone drinks Perrier water at lunch and goes to bed most week nights by 10 p.m. Even on weekend nights it's not exactly an all-night party town.

Now personally, I've always found a nice bout of sexual intercourse to be one of the most effective ways to relax known to humankind. Before I left for London I had been seeing a smashing bird from New York, on and off, who spent half her time out in California. A beautiful, extremely intelligent woman, and a seriously talented and very original painter, she also had a lovely daughter about my own son's age, so we basically had quite a bit in common. The day I flew out of LA she had told me she wanted to do a painting for me of one of the characters from the I Ching. I was on the point of polishing off the last drops from my last bottle of McCallan, when I suddenly realised the lass was probably in town. I quickly picked up the phone and dialled her number.

Susie was in bed reading and was delighted to hear my voice. She told me she'd be over like a shot. She'd finished my painting and was dying to show it to me. I hung up, drained my glass, and did a little joyous jig of sexual anticipation around my living room.

Ten minutes later I was in my bathroom finishing a quick shave and dousing my cheeks liberally with lashings of Susie's favourite aftershave, Egoiste Platinum, when the doorbell rang.

'Hello,' I thought. 'That was quick.' I tightened my robe, grabbed my umbrella and hauled open the sliding glass door that led down the path to the garden gate. By now the rain was literally pounding down to the ground. It must have been one of the wettest, dirtiest nights in LA's history, like the prelude to the proverbial Great Flood. As I opened the garden gate and peered out through the torrential storm, to my utter astonishment I saw not Susie, but Rebecca, a completely wacky absolutely knockout blonde stand-up comedian I had casually bonked one night many moons ago.

'Hi, sweetheart! I was just passing by and saw your lights were on! Mind if I come in?' And before I could so much as open my mouth, she'd swept past me and was marching up the path towards the house.

My reactions were not, I'm afraid, exactly what you might

call razor-sharp that night. Not only did I leave the garden gate wide open, Rebecca was inside my living room, warming her lovely bum in front of my fire inside ten seconds flat. I closed the glass door behind me, grinned, and offered her a quick snifter. There was nothing else I could do.

For some inexplicable reason, Becky chose that night to meekly sip at her Scotch like a timid nun, instead of heartily knocking the whole glass back in one gulp, as was her usual style. With each passing minute I was getting more and more nervous, and things eventually reached a moment of terrible truth when she finally finished the Scotch, turned and made a sudden lunge for me, yanking open my bathrobe in one passionate, brutal gesture.

At precisely that moment, through the glass doors my eyes caught sight of a lonely, bedraggled figure standing outside in the garden, watching. It was Susie. In her right hand was my painting wrapped inside a plastic bag. I felt awful, primarily for poor Susie. It was like a scene from some kind of Brian Rix farce.

Slowly, Susie slid open the glass door and walked inside. She was absolutely soaking wet from head to toe. A terrible silence ensued. The torrential rain was pounding on the roof like a giant's fist hammering away at the tiles. Susie stared at Becky. Becky stared back at Susie. Then they both turned to face me.

'Becky, this is Susie. Susie, meet Becky.'

What else could I possibly say? Poor old Susie looked utterly devastated. But beautiful, bonkers Becky just grinned, and clapped her hands together with a kind of insane, childlike glee.

'Oohhh! Isn't this fun!

3. PUT A TOE IN THE WATER FIRST BEFORE YOU DIVE IN.

Somewhere way back there during my randy old drama

school days a mate and I had come up with what we thought at the time was a very amusing idea. We called it 'The Great Sexual World Tour'. We got hold of a big map of the globe, tacked it up on the kitchen wall of our flat in Highgate and challenged each other to a long-term duel. He had the blue flags. I had the red. The first man to be able to truthfully (and for this to stick we both had to provide conclusive evidence of each successful erotic encounter) pin his coloured banner up on every major country of the world would be crowned 'Global Sexual Super-King'. One night several months ago we finally got back together after twenty years and compared notes. It was fascinating. We were just about even. Indeed, Kev, my dear old pal, had done very well indeed, and I was deeply impressed with the rate of his progress. There was only one continent left entirely untouched, and it just happened to be my favourite: South America!

I, on the other hand, had almost completed that particular section of my global marathon, the only country left for me to conquer being potentially the most exciting: Brazil. And it was with a great deal of relish that I regaled ol' Kev with a series of stories of my Latin American conquests over several double vodkas and Red Bulls.

It had all begun back in 1994, the year following my divorce, when I had been asked by the former Film Commissioner of the city of Miami to accompany her and a group of fellow film producers down to the Cartagegna Film Festival in Colombia as guests. It was an opportunity I happily leapt at. I had fallen in love with the South American culture many years before when I had first discovered how deeply passionate the women from that part of the world can be following a brief encounter in Manhattan with a magnificent young model from Peru. These females, I was quick to note from the experience, were typically quite exceptional — fiery, hot-blooded, and so refreshingly uninhibited. I was basically hooked for life.

Little was I to know, however, what kind of cunning Colombian karma awaited me in Cartagena! The trip was fantastic! A lot of fun! More like a bloody carnival than a film festival, and on the last night we all wound up at a fabulous, insane nightclub called Mr. Barbetta's. It was a case of dancing the night away on table tops till 5 a.m. And towards the end of the evening, I clocked a truly gorgeous young lady dancing away on a table opposite. She was a classic Colombian beauty: long dark hair, an absolutely killer body, and the kind of deep, brown pools of eyes you could lose yourself in forever. There was only one problem once I had made my initial approach. She couldn't speak a single word of English, and I was totally ignorant in Spanish!

Initially, I was frustrated to hell. Then help arrived in the form of one of the other male members of my party who thankfully spoke fluent Spanish. She was with her mother that night, so that fact combined with the language barrier meant that no serious progress was to be made at the first encounter. But the fire had been ignited, big-time, and I returned to LA and proceeded to conduct a series of very expensive three-way phone conversations with the Miss and my translator pal back in Miami in order to keep the flames fanned. I managed to pick up a basic smattering of Spanish, and eventually a second Colombian foray was planned with me going down to spend a month with the lass in her home city of Bogota. I hopped joyfully onto the plane at Miami and had myself a whale of a time with the flirtatious Colombian hostesses en-route. Arriving in Bogota, I was a man filled with intense sexual anticipation. My sweetheart was there at the gate to meet me with her sisters, and she looked incredible! Even sexier than I remembered!

We grabbed lunch together that first day before she took me to my hotel, and I can clearly recall the highly erotic way that she played with her napkin before we ate — just like it was a very specific, precious part of my own anatomy! She also, I was pleased to note, had a good, healthy appetite and was yet in great physical shape — a cheering contrast to a lot of other girls I'd dated who tended to pick at their food, like fragile birds. I checked into my room, and then she went home to get ready for a special dinner that night at her family home. The dinner was superb. Her family were magnificent. And again I watched the young lady chow down with the fervent passion of a lion devouring its prey on the Serengeti Plain. But when the time came for me to say goodnight, my girl refused to accompany me back to my hotel. I quickly realised that I was a guest in another country and should behave with decorum. Why be so impatient? I was there for a whole month.

The next day we drove to a wonderful resort town in the hills called Villa de Lleba to stay at a fabulous, romantic hotel. But when we checked in, the beautiful babe asked for a separate room for herself! 'She's probably just doing this for appearances,' I told myself. 'She'll be between the sheets with me for sure later.' But she wasn't. We played Colombian Monopoly until 3 a.m., and then she went to bed in her own room! And it turned this was a pattern that was destined to repeat itself again and again, night after night!

By the second week, not only was I noticing the first ominous signs of a distinct change in the layout of my gorgeous girl's physique, I was also beginning to tear my hair out with sexual frustration. Instead of indulging in an endless series of wild, passionate nights locked in each other's arms, we'd sleep apart and spend the days driving around the streets of bloody downtown Bogota with the once sexy, but now distinctly plump little chica pointing constantly out of the window saying things like, 'Greg! Bebe!' and 'Greg! Banco!'

There was absolutely no sex in sight! Not even so much as a harmless good old-fashioned blowjob! Every time I so much as made as if to touch her arm, a metaphorical great bloody wall would come slamming down inside her, totally sealing the gorgeous young woman off sexually from the outside world, like she was suddenly inside some kind of erotic Fort Knox!

By the next week she was making a habit of ritually sucking on the fat of every hefty steak she consumed in my company, and had ballooned to the size of a miniature Michelin Man. When I tactfully confronted her on her dramatic change in shape since my arrival, she cheerily told me, in between downing large spoonfuls of vanilla ice cream, that when we first met she was unhappy, so she was slim. But now I was here, she had become ecstatically happy — so, she was eating well again!

Re. the grand sexual impasse, I eventually got the message, via my minuscule smattering of Espagnol, that my loyal translator back in Miami had somehow managed to give the lovely Miss the distinct impression that I came from a background roughly tantamount to that of a Jesuit priest, and that I had apparently very chivalrously agreed to not lay a single finger on her until the very day we were wed!

The finale came when we took a trip to Cali, a town where, so the saying goes, the women have 'arses from heaven'! I'm afraid it all became just a bit too much for me. Playing Colombian Monopoly at arm's length with one of the most erotically charged women I've ever laid my eyes on, who had by now managed to transform herself into a Colombian version of the Goodyear Blimp, while outside sex was literally running rampant in the streets finished me off!

I bid her *ciao*, and quickly hopped the next flight back to Miami.

CHAPTER TWELVE

THE RULES OF THE GAME

'Women can always be caught; that's the first rule of the game.'
Ovid, *The Art Of Love* (A.D. 8)
'Once you have won a woman's heart, you can never get rid of the rest of her body.'
John Vanbrugh, *The Relapse*

December 23, 1999

Today I hand this manuscript in to my publisher. In a few days' time I leave for Boston to see my son for the New Year. On my way over to John Blake's office, I pick up a copy of the December issue of *Tatler*. The magazine had called me three months ago to ask if I would agree to feature in their Millennium issue as one of 'The 100 Hottest Male Dates Of The 21st Century', giving my 'top-ten all-time seduction tips'. I was flattered, and met with two of their staff members in the New Bar at Claridges together with my publicist, but for my own reasons chose to decline. They apparently got a little irritated and subsequently were thinking of including me and my 'seduction tips' in the edition anyway. So I'm kind of curious to see what's been going on.

They've apparently relented. But have very obviously chosen to refer to the subject via the 'Books' column, written by Sebastian Shakespeare (apparently no relation, I hasten to add). Ol' Seb has written a two-page article entitled: 'Type Writers. The Christmas book guide for particular personalities.' The first item is entitled: 'The Upper-Crust Love-Rat', and under 'Who' we find the names: 'Greg Martin, James Hewitt'. If only these guys at Condé Nast would do their research properly. I don't know about Hewitt, but I'm about as 'upper-crust' as a jelly doughnut bought from a 7-Eleven!

Tatler, I've come to learn, is very much like Tara — a particularly English phenomenon specifically designed around the lives of the rich, titled, well-connected and famous. And Tara, plus her fellow It girls, is the approximate equivalent of the Jewish American Princess. In fact, it's perfectly possible to substitute the word 'It girl' for 'JAP' in any of the classic JAP jokes. For example:

'What's an It girl's favourite position? He's on top. She's at Prada.'

'Why do It girls use gold diaphragms? They want their husbands to come into money.'

'How do you know when an It girl has had an orgasm? She drops her Joseph catalogue.'

'What's an It girl's favourite wine? Piers, I want to go to Klosters!'

What strikes me as particularly odd is that though the mag *Tatler* claims to adore Tara P-T, along with Nicky Haslam and Mick Jagger, a trio to whom the publication typically pays at least perfunctory lip-service as some of their darling favourites, they are similarly lampooned in the article — Tara as 'an inveterate snob' who lives beyond her means — Haslam and Mick as members of 'The Aging Roué Club', 'mellow meatballs well past their display-by-date'.

As you'll have gathered by now, I love using apt quotes. And a pair of them spring to mind now as I bring this bizarre tale to a close: 'Moral indignation is jealousy with a halo', H. G. Wells, and: 'The happiness of others is never bearable for very long', Francoise Sagan.

One of the last calls I received from Tara was also one of the strangest. The focus of the conversation, from her point of view, was to convey to me her 'discovery' that she had indeed been right all along. The only reason she and I had spent any significant time together in her mind was because of who she was, and what I perceived that *she* could do for *me* via her 'connections'.

'Daddy says I should feel sorry for you,' she said.

'Really,' I responded. 'Why's that?'

'He says he's found out that your father raised himself from the gutter, left your mother and then married his way into the aristocracy, leaving you and your sister behind. He says you wanted to marry me only because you're still bitter that he left you, and that in some way you're trying to get your own back and better him.'

There was a long pause. This was probably by far the most insane comment I'd heard throughout the entire ludicrous, heartbreaking affair.

'Tara, I have three things to say to you by way of a response. One: the kind of social paranoia exhibited by you, your friends and family is extraordinary. Two: I never wanted to marry you. I needed time. You wanted to marry me. Three: the word 'aristocracy' will eventually have about as much meaning in the UK 2000 as a gnat on the back of a T. Rex.'

If you recall, earlier on in this book I discussed what I perceived as the origins of the phrase 'love rat'. My brief affair with Kara Noble was mentioned, along with the fact that the occasion was the first time that I found myself appearing in the Nigel Dempster column in the *Daily Mail*. Why did none of the scandalous claptrap about me come out then, I wonder? It's an interesting question if you really stop to think about it.

On July 29, 1999, I met Tara's parents for the first time at her family home in Hampshire. It was a happy day for me. As I mentioned earlier, Patty and I, in particular, hit it off together immediately. The following Tuesday she sent me a letter. It was tender, and deeply affectionate. This is what it said:

> My dear Greg,
>
> Hippocrates said 'Music is the heater of the soul' — in fact I had decided it was treatment at The Meadows — but for the past week I have realised that it is, for Tara, the arrival in her life of someone who suits not only her needs, but her whole personality so perfectly as you do. That you say it is mutual brings me indescribable happiness. That feeling, Greg, is endorsed by the whole family.
>
> We love our prodigal deeply, perhaps because life has been such a battlefield for her, and we have suffered on her behalf. However, we never lost sight of her enormous generosity, sense of the ridiculous, delightful lack of convention and intense loyalty — but during the fog years, these qualities frequently backfired — she gave when she couldn't afford to, was unwise in her lack of convention, made bad choices that hurt her and misplaced her loyalty. The Meadows stripped down the engine, exposed and

explained the reasons and gave her a chance to make amends and direct her life anew. This she has done conscientiously since she returned, earning true admiration and the pride of us all.

Her support of her fellow patients was made clear to Charlie and me on our arrival for Family Week, by the love they had for her and many heartwarming descriptions of her being 'there for them' — we were warmed by their tributes — and all said she had made them laugh when they thought they never would again.

She has volumes of love to give, and she has found the perfect person to whom to give it. Having met you, we can all understand why.

Had you not been you, Greg, I may well have had misgivings about this whirlwind romance. But I am not in the least anxious. I am so very happy that we can welcome you into the family, to make us complete — and if membership of this close and precious unit means half as much to you as it does me, I have no doubts for your future happiness together.

You have both drunk deep from the well of unhappiness, and so are truly able to experience real joy — but the strength you have achieved will act as a fortress against everything life throws at you — and your compassion, Greg, kindness, understanding, sensitivity and capacity for love will achieve for you both, I am sure, great happiness.

With much, much love,
Patty

This was a moving, heartfelt message to me from Tara's mother, and as a writer I deeply appreciated the open warmth with which she expressed her feelings. I so well recall, in the course of that first meeting, warning her quite explicitly about certain individuals I felt might well try to sabotage my relationship with Tara. And although she appeared at the time to listen and absorb what I had said, apparently this was not to last.

The sadness of this story revolves around the fact that for a brief moment in time two people felt they had possibly found true happiness in each other. I'm sure you'll gather from these pages that Tara and I had our share of problems together apart from the slanderous attack. Yet I truly believe these were intensified by the kind of stress we were under. As a result of the intense bitterness and envy of others, any happiness we perhaps might have enjoyed was shattered.

Why did Patty not heed my warning? The answer is that she did. But both her own social paranoia and the overwhelming and brilliantly constructed campaign of personal slander against me clearly, in the end, by far outweighed both her own better judgment, and that of her youngest daughter and the other members of Tara's family.

I was ultimately to learn that the intention and desire behind the campaign of personal malice against me extended much further than merely the total ruin of my relationship with Tara Palmer-Tomkinson. What the principal individual (and there definitely was one main instigator) wanted beyond this — and yes, I am completely aware of how dramatic this sounds — was nothing less than the total destruction of all my hopes and dreams on both a personal and professional basis upon my return to this country.

This person is a woman who, since the first day we met, I have done my utmost to always treat with the greatest respect. Moreover, she has spent significant time with my son, played with him, enjoyed the beauty and innocence of his company, and has a very clear handle on the sweetness and depth of the love between he and I. She also knows, beyond the shadow of a doubt, that I am in my heart a solid, devoted, loving father.

This individual was apparently joined in her campaign by several others. Several are members of my own family. Another, a man I mentioned earlier who met up with Tara's mother to 'warn her' to 'stay away from me'. And for the time being, for me, it is simply enough that they know that I know.

I kid and joke around about my 'image'. It's the only way to deal with what has been the most bizarre experience of my life. As I mentioned in the first sentences of this book, I have indeed always been something of a 'womaniser'. I quite simply adore the female gender. Yet despite my colourful past, I am mature and sensible enough to be able to sense the possibility of real personal happiness presenting itself to me in the future, and indeed hope with all my heart that I can find it before too very long.

Sex is fun — pure, unadulterated physical passion, when it's right is a blissful, mind-blowing experience. But I'm no longer kidding myself. It doesn't beat 'the real thing'.

Maybe, given enough time and the arrival in my life of the right woman, even yours truly will be a leopard who at long last decides the time's finally come to change his spots!

I rest my case.

EPILOGUE

'Love is the white light of emotion.'
Diane Ackerman, *A Natural History Of Love* (1994)
'When the moon hits your eye, like a big pizza pie, it's amore!'
Dean Martin

January 21, 2000

Today is my birthday. I'm forty-three. Yesterday my publicist and I had a meeting with John Blake and Rosie, and I received a wonderful birthday present. They love the book. Some slight suggestions re. additions, deletions and adjustments have been made, but by and large they're very excited by the manuscript. I'm particularly cheered by Rosie's comments. I both trust and respect her, and I'd naturally prefer it if women enjoyed the book as much as men.

I'd been deliberately keeping my expectations low. For me, when the idea of the book was first mooted, it seemed more like an appropriate piece of therapy than anything else, a way to exorcise any demons in my mind following the weird experience of the T-P-T debacle with a degree of humour and comedy. Laughter is, after all, well known to be the best palliative for discomfort. Hopefully now we may have something else on our hands.

February 12, 2000

In November the most magnificent reward for all the unpleasantness and strange circumstances of the months following August 11, 1999 walked into my life: a beautiful young lady from Sardinia called Vittoria. For the past two months we have been living together. To me she is the most perfect and desirable example of femininity I've ever met, and I am now in love with her in a way I could never before have possibly imagined.

I thought very carefully about writing of this wonderful development in my life and discussed the idea in detail with Vittoria before deciding to go ahead. Given what's gone down with me recently, I'm not particularly interested in sharing any more intimate details of my private life. But I feel this could be a case of serendipity.

I've chosen to write about Vittoria, you see, because she embodies all I have ever wished for in a woman. Hence the marked contrast for me between what has gone before in my life, and what now exists, and the fascination for me in the relationship providing a perfect mirror, if you like. The timing is perfect, and the feelings that have developed between us so beautiful that for what is frankly the first time in my life I am truly happy in a relationship without the nasty spectre of any nagging doubts.

As I write, she and I are sitting on the Eurostar travelling to Paris for Valentine's Day weekend. On the morning of February 14 I shall give her an engagement ring.

Who knows what the future holds? I pray to God that we stay together forever. But as Vittoria herself says in her profound Mediterranean way: 'The only thing that is sure in life is death.' One thing is for sure, however. Whether we are lucky, and stay as one, or not, she has changed this leopard's spots. Forever.

Why is Vittoria so different? The answers are legion. But they are all naturally based in Vittoria's character, which is so decidedly different from any other female I have hitherto met. Remember I spoke earlier of those wonderful women that do indeed exist — platinum-coated diamonds that would do anything for you? Well, Vittoria's one of them.

If I was terminally ill, or bankrupt, for example, I know beyond a shadow of a doubt that Vittoria would be there for me. She would support me, go to any lengths to pull me through the difficulties, as I would for her. This is true love. It's based on the kind of male/female friendship that goes way beyond the sexual chemistry necessary to begin any passionate liaison.

The strength of Vittoria's character comes from the hardship of her life to date. She left home at thirteen and has worked to support herself ever since. She has a wisdom way beyond her years, an independence and depth of heart that blows my mind and an innate spirituality that makes her shine like a sparkling jewel in the midst of this tired, grey cynical world.

We spend our nights eating gorgeous Italian food (she's promised me never to go down the route of Ms. Colombia!), and watching classic movies from her homeland, like Vittorio De Sica's *The Bicycle Thief*, *Cinema Paradiso* and *Il Postino*. I am truly happy.

March 6, 2000

The book's being rushed to print. Serialisation rights have been bought by the *News of the World* and the *Daily Mail*. Word of mouth is apparently good. I'm about to embark on the roller-coaster of public exposure again. This time, however, I'm ready.

Last Saturday morning Tara called me again, then showed up on my doorstep demanding to know why I've written a book about her, and warning me that 'my family are very powerful in this country and will stop its publication.' She added that 'you don't know who you're messing with'.

It was a chilling moment. Like a scene out of *Fatal Attraction*. Vittoria and her brother were upstairs, and my mum was about to arrive for lunch. Not for the first time I felt like I was being stalked. I had recently changed my phone number and requested that it be unlisted. Two bods had access to it. Neither of them would have traded it for their lives. Yet somehow Tara got hold of it. How?

Half of me feels sorry for her. I've just learnt that her relationship with Rhodes is over. Pity. The other half of me ain't a too happy camper. Last week in Saturday's *Daily Mail* she did an interview with Lynda Lee-Potter in which she accused me twice in print of being a con man. Interesting...

One final word about class. It's a funny old world we British live in at the Millennium. A place where we still pay lip service to the idea of being a well-integrated, modern society, where the boundaries of the past have ceased to exist. Yet the truth, as I have recently discovered, is something different. Social snobbery still abounds here, in spades. And while we used to despise what was, years ago, very much regarded as the trivial and sordid nature of the American press in terms of slander and gossip, our own newspapers have now, by and large, surpassed those of the US in that particular arena.

Last night Channel Four broadcast a fascinating programme called *Slander*. The show documented, in a highly entertaining fashion, the rise of 'the sleaze factor' in independent journalism in this country during the past thirty years. Following the notorious Profumo Affair, the lid was effectively blown off the notion that the privacy of public figures in the UK was sacred. After 'Profumo', anyone was to be considered fair game for the press.

I'm sure by now Joe Public clearly senses yours truly is by no means a moralist! Indeed, one of the reasons Vittoria and I are so well-matched is that in my heart I am more Mediterranean than English. The French, Italians, Spanish and Greeks have always to me seemed so much more psychologically free and unencumbered than the inhabitants of this green and pleasant land. Yet I do believe in the privacy of the individual. And I can see no reason why a man or woman's personal life should have any bearing on his or her ability to perform their given public duty.

It all seems so sily and hypocritical. Most of us have some skeletons in our closets. None of us is lily-white, crystalline pure. What difference does it make to her ability to perform in office now if Mo Mowlam smoked pot while she was at university back in the Sixties? Didn't most of the British student population do exactly the same thing at the time? Don't they now?!

I'm a staunch defender of Norris not because of his 'philandering' past, nor because I'm a supporter of the Conservative party, nor even because the woman he intends to marry, Emma Courtney, is nineteen years his junior (roughly the age difference between Vittoria and myself). I speak out for him because the man is so clearly an eloquent, intelligent, deeply committed politician who had the balls, when all the mud was being hurled at him, to stand up and say to what he termed 'the monstrous regiment' surrounding him: 'So what?'

Given his notorious 'womanising profile', Norris was naturally interviewed on the programme and came across as smart, savvy and rather charmingly avuncular. A two-page in-depth article on Emma Courtney appeared the day before in the *Evening*

Standard. The article bore the headline: 'So What's A Nice Girl Like You...?' Need I say more. The general tone was patronising, condescending and judgmental. Ms. Courtney was treated like a naive little girl by the author of the article, albeit in a suitably subtle way.

Isn't it about time we took a good, hard look at the way we judge men and women who lead public lives?

Bibliography — Suggested Further Reading

Most of the research material available on the market for budding, would-be serial scumbag philanderers is to be found in the US. On a trip to visit my son for the Millenium I picked up the following splendid tomes worthy of serious consideration for any sexual connoisuer.

Hot Sex: How To Do It by Tracy Cox (Bantam Books, 1998)

How to Suceed With Women by Ron Louis and David Copeland (Reward Books, 1998)

Sex Tips For Straight Women From A Gay Man by Dan Anderson and Maggie Berman (Regan Books, 1997)

The Big Book Of Filth by Jonathon Green (Cassel, 1999)

The Blue Blood's Guide To The Best Bestial Bonking in Britain by Walter Windbag-Furrymountie (Tradimento Books, 1999)